PLANNING
AND MANAGING
ADULT DAY CARE

Pathways to Success

PLANNING AND MANAGING ADULT DAY CARE

Pathways to Success

Edited by Linda Cook Webb, MSG

Published by National Health Publishing
A Division of Williams & Wilkins
in cooperation with
The National Council on Aging, Inc. and
The National Institute on Adult Daycare

Planning and managing adult day care

Published by
National Health Publishing
99 Painters Mill Road
Owings Mills, Maryland 21117
(301) 363–6400

A division of Williams & Wilkins

Printed in the United States of America
First Printing

Acquisitions Editor: Sara Mansure Sides
Developmental Editor: Cindy Konits
Copyeditor: Eileen Power Baylus
Production Coordinator: Karen Babcock
Designer: Sandy Renovetz
Compositor: National Health Publishing
Printer: Edwards Brothers

ISBN: 0–932500–95–1
LC: 88–063454

Dedicated to my teachers, my guides along the path:

Granney and Grampy
Mom
John Ashton
Vern Bengtson
Sharron Collins
Marty Conway
Therese Elias
Kim Flora
Gary Jarvis
Clay Marcusen
Eddy Ray
Betty Ransom
Phyllis Snyder
Madame Spidell
Mamie Thomas
Mrs. Wolf
and all the others
and most of all, to my companion on the journey,
David

Contents

Appendices

Contributors

Marianne Rawack Brannon, B.S.Ed., P.H.N., is Program Manger/P.H.N. at the Elderday Adult Day Health Care Center, Santa Cruz, California. Before working at Elderday, her nursing career centered on operating room, home health, and hospice work. She has also developed and managed a Problem Back Service and an in- and out-patient rehabilitation center.

Linda J. Crossman, R.N., M.S., is Executive Director of Marin Adult Day Health Services, in San Anslemo, California. She has been a strong advocate for adult day care (ADC) funding. During her term as National Institute on Adult Daycare (NIAD) Chair, federal legislation was introduced to allow Medicare coverage of adult day health care. During her term as President of the California Adult Day Health Services Association, the state authorized Medicaid and special start-up funds. Ms. Crossman has also served as NIAD Region IX Representative and as a member of the advisory committee to NCOA's Family Caregivers Program. She holds a master of science degree in Community Health Nursing.

Kathryn S. Katz, A.C.S.W., is Director, South Central Office of Connecticut Community Care, based in New Haven, Connecticut. She is currently serving her third term as NIAD Secretary. For eight years, Ms. Katz was Director of Adult Day Care Services at the Jewish Home for the Elderly of Fairfield, Connecticut, and for four years, she served as president of the Connecticut Association of Adult Day Care. Ms. Katz holds a Master of Social Work degree.

Winnifred Kelly, S.C., M.P.A., is Director of Project L.I.N.C., in Pompton Lakes, New Jersey. She has been Region II Representative to NIAD for the past four years. She has published articles on ADC in the *Home Health Services Quarterly* and *Perspectives on Aging*. She holds a Master of Public Administration degree with a certificate in Gerontology.

Kay Rooney Larmer, B.S.N., M.S., is Coordinator of Adult Day Health Care for the Fairfax County Health Department, Fairfax, Virginia, where she has worked since 1979. She is currently Immediate Past Chair of NIAD and also chaired NIAD's Standards and Guidelines Committee during the formation of *Standards for Adult Daycare*. She has a Bachelor of Science degree in Nursing, a Master of Science degree in Family and Community Development, and a certificate in Gerontology.

Paul D. Maginn, M.S.W., A.C.S.W., has been Director of the McAuley Bergan Center, in Omaha, Nebraska, since 1980. He served as NIAD Region VII Representative from 1981-85, continues to the present as a member of the NIAD Conference and Training Committee, and currently heads the NIAD Tenth Anniversary Task Force. He holds a Master of Social Work degree, and has worked in human services for 17 years.

Kathryn Mesler Mehlferber, R.N., M.A., is the founding Director of Adult Day Care Services for the Queen Anne's County Health Department, Centreville, Maryland. She has worked in the field of aging for 24 years, and served on the planning committee that developed NIAD as a membership unit of the National Council on the Aging. She was a charter member of the NIAD Steering Committee, and has recently completed two terms as Region III Representative. She is a Registered Nurse with a master's degree in Human Services Administration and Planning.

Greg Newton, M.P.A., is Principal of Newton and Associates, a Boston-based training, marketing, and management services firm that helps forward looking nonprofit and public organizations use private sector strategies to find market place and mission success. He has done training and consultation for NIAD, state adult day care associations, and for several adult day care centers. He holds a Bachelor of Science degree in Journalism and earned his Master of Public Administration degree from Harvard.

Ruth Von Behren, Ph.D., is Adult Day Care and Adult Day Health Care Specialist at On Lok Senior Health Services, San Francisco, California. In that capacity, she provides technical assistance and consultation to numerous agencies. She is currently NIAD Chairperson, having been a member of the Steering Committee since 1984. She has also served as cochair of the NIAD Research and Publications Committee. Prior to 1982, Dr. Von Behren served as chief of the state MediCal adult day health care (ADHC) program, which she brought from pilot project to permanent status. Among her various publications is *Adult Day Care in America: Summary of a National Survey.*

David S. Webb is a co-founder of D.L. Webb & Associates, based in Kansas City, Missouri. He is a computer programmer and systems analyst, who consults with a variety of health care providers. He has worked with adult day care since 1981, and has designed and written software to assist in recording and analyzing financial and management information for adult day care centers. His degree is in Business Administration.

Linda Cook Webb, M.S.G., consults with providers and potential providers of adult day care, through her Kansas City-based firm, D.L. Webb & Associates. She has been working in adult day care since 1979 and in long-term care since 1973. Ms. Webb has been elected twice to the position of Region VII Representative to the Steering Committee of the National Institute on Adult Daycare. She is Chair of NIAD's Conference and Training Committee, and sits on a Board Committee of the National Council on the Aging. She was one of the co-founders of adult day care associations in Kansas, Missouri, and Kansas City. While a day care director, she served on the State of Missouri's task forces to write adult day care certification and licensing standards. Ms. Webb holds a Master of Science degree in Gerontology from the University of Southern California (Andrus Gerontology Center).

Foreword

Adult day care is increasing in importance in this country. We are all familiar with the statistics relating to the "graying of America," the phrase coined to demonstrate how rapidly the older population (those age fifty-five and over) is growing. In the early 1900s, fewer than one American in ten was age fifty-five or over and one in twenty-five was age sixty-five or over. Now, less than a century later, one in five Americans is fifty-five years old and one in eight is sixty-five or over. The United States Census Bureau estimates that the number of people who are eighty and over is growing five times faster than the total population and is expected to double in twenty years. The fastest growing age group is now people over eighty-five.

Functional limitations increase with age. Such impairments affect one's quality of life and need for health and social services. Nearly one-quarter of the older persons surveyed by the National Center for Health Statistics had difficulty performing at least one of the seven personal care activities (bathing, dressing, eating, transferring, walking, getting outside, and toileting). As the older population continues to grow rapidly, we need to face the challenge of how to help our older citizens with impairments live their lives with dignity.

Adult day care helps meet the physical and emotional needs of this segment of the older population. Day care provides services and activities while participants remain in the community, fulfilling the wishes of the older persons and their families alike.

Adult day care was just beginning in this country in the early 1970s. The U.S. Department of Health, Education and Welfare estimated that there were fewer than fifteen adult day care centers at that time. The National Institute on Adult Daycare (NIAD), a membership unit of The National Council on the Aging, estimated that there were approximately 1,200 adult day care centers in 1984. There are over 1,500 today. As more individuals and organizations realize the need for adult day care and seek resources for starting and managing centers, they will require concrete information on how to set up and implement programs. *Planning and Managing Adult Day*

Care provides a "soup to nuts" guide for those new to adult day care as well as for those who are experienced.

A number of prominent persons in the adult day care field, including many current and former NIAD Steering Committee members, contributed chapters to this book. They provided their considerable expertise to this very comprehensive volume. NCOA/NIAD cooperated in the publication of this book because it is a valuable contribution to the resources already published by NCOA/NIAD.

The first four chapters provide an overview of the adult day care field. Chapter One defines and explains adult day care. Chapter Two gives the history of adult day care, which has its roots in Europe in geriatric day hospitals. Chapters Three and Four explain how to investigate rules and regulations at the state and local level and the need for adult day care in the community.

Chapters Five through Eighteen explore more specific topics that delve into the various subject areas. Chapter Five on facilities development emphasizes the importance of a well designed facility that can enhance functioning. Sample floor plans are included for those who are able to design their own space. Chapter Six shows how transportation is both "the boon and the bane of adult day care" since its availability is vital to participant use, but putting together a transportation service is often difficult. The chapter offers several alternative ways to provide transportation and describes how to implement them.

Staffing practices are particularly important in adult day care. Quality of care depends to a large degree on the performance and attitude of the workers who provide direct services to the participants. Working effectively with the impaired elderly requires "special people." Such employees need to be able to balance their genuine interest and concern for the participant with their knowledge that older persons retain abilities which they should continue to use to remain as independent as possible. Staff roles are discussed (including support staff as part of the team) and training is explained in chapters Seven and Eight.

The "patchwork quilt" of diverse funding sources and the inability of most adult day care participants to pay the full cost of their care contribute to a difficult financial management situation for the adult day care administrator. Chapter Nine gives basic guidelines for successful financial management, and Chapter Ten provides specific methods of dealing with common fiscal problems in adult day care.

Many providers are optimistic about the potential success of their programs because they are located in a community with many older persons, and they are assured of the need for the service. They are surprised and perplexed when months and even years after opening, their program is still not full. Successful marketing of the program may be needed, and Chapter Eleven provides many "how-to" ideas.

After decisions have been made about the population to be served and the eligibility requirements, the center staff needs to determine intake procedures, how to develop a plan of care for participants, and discharge plans. Chapter Twelve explains how to accomplish those important tasks. Chapter Thirteen provides ideas on methods to develop a therapeutic activities plan so that the participants' time at the center is productive and stimulating. And since there is wide recognition that adult day care benefits both the participant and the family members, Chapter Fourteen discusses ways to meet the needs of the family through counseling, support groups, and other means.

The last three chapters deal with administrative matters. Chapter Fifteen presents the benefits to participants of record-keeping. Such records can chart the progress or decline of participants so that the plan of care can be adjusted, if necessary. Incident and accident reports can identify and correct problems, and financial records can document the fiscal health of the program. What to record and how to do so are essential elements of this chapter. Chapter Sixteen shows that computers are a basic and necessary management tool that will aid the staff in a variety of ways. In order to use computers successfully, it is important that the expectations of computer use are realistic, that the appropriate hardware and software are purchased, and that staff are sufficiently trained. Evaluation is an essential component of any program. Chapter Seventeen provides sample evaluation forms to be used when discussing the program components that should be evaluated. The final chapter provides the adult day care administrator with the information needed for research: What it is, how it's done, its limitations, and its usefulness.

As adult day care continues to grow as part of the community-based long-term care system, it becomes more important that these programs be planned and managed efficiently. The aging of the general population and the desire of older people and their caregivers to see that as individuals age they are able to remain in the community rather than be institutionalized, will increase the need and demand for adult day care services. Administrators will have to demonstrate that their programs are of high quality and cost effective in order to justify increased resources for their programs, such as private insurance coverage and Medicare. The information in this book should provide helpful guidance in getting started and solving some of the problems faced by those who provide the service.

NCOA/NIAD is pleased to cooperate in the publication of this book as a contribution to the fast growing field of adult day care.

Dr. Daniel Thursz, President
The National Council on the Aging, Inc.

Preface

There was a time, not so long ago, that we, as adult day care directors, often felt we were reinventing the wheel. In large measure, it was frustrating. There we were, with tight budgets and pressure to get our programs "up and going" quickly. And no sooner did we find solutions to problems, than we discovered someone else had already been doing the "same" thing for a year.

Now, the field has grown enough that adult day care directors are much better equipped to learn from each other. We have annual conferences and newsletters and state/local associations. There seems to be less of the feeling of duplicating efforts. Best of all, we are now discovering that our early history was not a process of exact duplication. In trying to address local needs, our programs actually developed a great deal of diversity. We may have used similar methods, but because we applied them with sensitivity to the needs of our own communities, the result looks different in each case.

We have found a new metaphor.

In that early time, we were wandering through the forest. We may have been going toward the same destination, but we took different paths to get there. Some took us where we wanted to go, but very slowly. Others led us quickly to the places we wanted to be. The most amazing discovery has been that there could be many paths toward our goal! We could use our creativity, and knowledge borrowed from others, to find a multitude of ways through the forest.

If this book has value, it will be in its ability to set signposts for some of the pathways the authors have walked. We will point the way to well-worn and less-traveled trails that can all lead to success in adult day care. Adult day care directors haven't always agreed about which is the "best" path. Perhaps that is because there are so many that lead to interesting places. We have tried to at least provide directions for the routes that have worked for us.

We hope that you will use this volume in a way that helps you through your own part of the forest. Interpret our suggestions in the light of your own knowledge and your own situation. If you're new to adult day care, you might want to stay on the main roads until you get "the lay of the land." Don't feel that you have to do everything or be everywhere at once. If the main roads are already familiar to you, you might want to strike out in an unexplored direction that is merely suggested by our words. We'll be interested in what you find!

As authors, we can only be thankful that we have been brought to places from which we could see pathways described in this book. We did not create the paths, and may not even know you, who travel them. And still, we feel honored to have had a part in this book. It is a delight to be able to say to fellow travelers, "Look! Over there!"

Let's get going.

Acknowledgements

First, I want to thank the publishers, who had the foresight to seek out a book on adult day care, and who have been an absolute joy to work with, during these many months.

Of course, heartfelt thanks go to each of the contributing authors. Their work on this volume has been a wonderful gift.

Members of the Steering Committee of the National Institute on Adult Daycare (NIAD) have been especially supportive, especially those who volunteered to serve on review committees for the book: Maria Alvarez, Tom Hardin, Larry Henson, Kathy Katz, Winnifred Kelly, Dorothy Ohnsorg, Ruth Von Behren, and Bonnie Walson. Betty Ransom and Dorothy Howe, from the National Council on the Aging have also been helpful as reviewers, as has Paul Maginn, a past member of the NIAD Steering Committee.

I believe that a major strength of this book comes from the wide diversity of expertise and backgrounds among both the authors and the reviewers. Not only has the book been evaluated by professionals in the field, but I also owe thanks to my father, Robert Lee, and to Jane Pickett for reviewing the manuscript with an eye toward readability by the general public.

I also want to thank my sister, Kareen McKenzie Broddle, for helping with last-minute typing.

And, as Helen Padula did in her book, I thank Lionel Cosin, who got the whole thing started.

CHAPTER 1

Where Do We Start?

Linda Cook Webb

Paula,* age 90, was quite depressed when she first came to the adult day care center. She had severe physical limitations, had been in and out of nursing homes, and most recently had been isolated at home while her daughter worked. She felt that her burdens were the biggest in the world. With the help of the staff, Paula soon found someone at the center whom she thought had problems more distressing than her own—someone she might help. Paula quickly developed a special and close relationship with 65-year-old Ruthann, who was quite disoriented much of the time. The two ladies sang together, read magazines, and sometimes worked puzzles. This particular day care center also served younger adults with physical disabilities. Paula developed a special interest in these young people, and the intergenerational relationships that developed were beneficial to both. Paula became not only a patient, but also a caregiver, thus giving her a reason for living. She was no longer severely depressed about her own situation and no longer wondered, "Why does God keep me on this earth?" She knew.

Adult day care centers offer a special place for daytime care of adults who need professional supervision, but who do not need 24-hour institutional care. They offer fun, friendship, and acceptance to frail or disabled persons who might otherwise be isolated with their problems. Most of all, these centers remind out society that to be different is not to be unacceptable—and that in being challenged by catastrophe, each of us may find our greatest strength.

---

* The names used in case studies and stories in this book are fictitious.

1

But what of the families of the people who come to day care centers? Theirs has not been an easy road, either. Too often, we hear the myth that families don't really care about their old and/or disabled relatives, and are ready to "dump" them in nursing homes.

In fact, families often go to great lengths to keep aging and disabled persons at home. For Paula's daughter Marjorie, it meant holding down a full-time job, caring for her own home, husband, and son, and at the same time taking full responsibility for Paula's needs. This schedule resulted in 18-hour days, seven days a week. Even while at work, Marjorie worried constantly. Since Paula could not transfer to the toilet alone, it was not unusual for Marjorie to return home several times during the work day to provide help. The family did hire a sitter for a while, but could only afford one day a week, on a temporary basis. The feeling of constant giving, giving, giving was beginning to become overwhelming. After Paula had been participating in adult day care for a while, Marjorie told the staff, "I used to feel guilty when I came home and Mom was feeling depressed or abandoned. Now, when I get home, she has her own news to tell me—I can hardly get a word in edgewise!"

In the past, as was the case for Paula and Marjorie, families often had little recourse other than the nursing home. Because of this, many persons who did not really need care 24-hours a day, seven days a week found themselves in institutions. This is where adult cay care comes into the picture.

Definition of Adult Day Care

Adult day care occupies a significant position within the network of health and social services for the aged. That network ranges from preventive services and social experiences for the well elderly to almost total care and support for the very impaired (see Appendix A). Within the adult day care field, we see the entire continuum of care in miniature. Some day care centers focus their efforts toward the frail and/or isolated adult who needs minimal supports. Others seek to serve extremely handicapped persons who may need close to total support. Most centers fall somewhere in between. This diversity can make defining adult day care difficult.

The National Institute on Adult Daycare (NIAD), in its *Standards for Adult Day Care* (1984, 20), provides a generic definition of adult day care as being

A community-based group program designed to meet the needs of functionally impaired adults through an individual plan of care. It is a structured, comprehensive program that provides a variety of health, social and related support services in a protective setting during any part of a day but less than 24-hour care.

Individuals who participate in adult day care attend on a planned basis during specified hours. Adult day care assists its participants to remain in the community, enabling families and other caregivers to continue caring for an impaired member at home.

It is important to distinguish adult day care from two related types of services—the senior center and the nursing home. Adult day care is like a senior center, in that they both provide socialization, recreation, meals, and transportation. The senior center, however, does not take a role of establishing treatment goals for its members. In adult day care, in contrast, the individual plan of care is a major focus of the service. The individual plan of care, and the fact that day care centers can serve very impaired persons, may also lead to confusion between adult day care and the nursing home. The difference lies in the amount of time that the individual uses the service. Persons served by nursing homes actually live in the facility. They are there around the clock, seven days a week. Adult day care centers, as the name implies, provide care primarily during daytime hours. (Some centers are open 12 hours per day, but this is rare.) Further, most participants in adult day care attend only two or three days per week. This difference in scheduling grows from the day care center's goal of supporting participant's abilities to live in the community.

Goals

The goals of adult day care grow from the premise that the daytime group setting can provide relief for family caregivers and offer outlets for growth to the disabled participant. The NIAD *Standards* (1984, 21) discuss the following goals for day care centers:

- Promote the individual's maximum level of independence

- Maintain the individual's present level of functioning as long as possible, preventing or delaying further deterioration

- Restore and rehabilitate the individual to his/her highest possible level of functioning

- Provide support, respite and education for families and other caregivers

- Foster socialization and peer interaction

- Serve as an integral part of the community service network and the long-term care continuum.

Clients: Participants and Their Families

While the people who come to adult day care represent a wide spectrum, we can begin to understand their situations by reviewing demographic information from NIAD's national survey of adult day care centers (Von Behren 1986). The average participant is a 73-year old Caucasian woman. She has only $478 in monthly income and lives with relatives or friends. Half of the participants require supervision, and one-fifth require constant supervision. Walkers or canes are needed by one-fifth of participants. One in eight participants cannot transfer from their wheelchairs without the assistance of another person. Close to one in 13 participants needs changing during the day, due to incontinency problems. A similar percentage are behaviorally disruptive.

Adult day care participants are a severely impaired population. It is often difficult to care for them within the day care center. Care at home may be even harder—and that home care is most often provided by family or friends who have no special training to do what they must do. At the same time, if the home situation breaks down, all the work the day care staff has done with the participant may be for naught. For this reason, adult day care centers take on the large task of serving not only the participant, but also attending to the needs of the participant's family. The extent of involvement with families varies among centers, as described in Chapter Fourteen. All adult day care centers, however, must somehow determine that the care provided at home is adequate to support the goals of the center. And that involves caring for families.

Adult day care services, then, have a dual nature—focused both toward the participant and the family. Because of this, the term, "client" when used in this book, will refer to the whole family unit. This terminology is one way of recognizing a basic fact of day care: as providers, we must work in concert with the participants' families, and in attendance to their needs.

Services

Most adult day care centers are open Monday through Friday, and close to half are open eight hours or more on those days. Some centers offer care only two or three days a week, while others are open Saturdays. The average center serves 19 people a day and has a total case load of 37 (Von Behren 1986).

Even though a center may be open 40 to 60 hours a week, many participants attend only part time. By the same token, each participant or family may not require all of the services offered by the center. One of the advantages of adult day care is that it provides only those specific services—and only for the specified amount of time—required by the participant and the family.

Each center will have its own unique package of services, just as it will have its own particular target population, funding, staffing pattern, and access to community resources. Certain basic services are, however, common to all adult day care centers. The following services constitute the basic components of adult day care (taken from NIAD 1984, 34–9).

An Individual Plan of Care which includes an assessment, plan of service, progress notes, reassessment, and discharge plan is necessary. The assessment should include evaluation of the individual's physical, mental, and social status, functional skills, support systems, and financial resources. This evaluation should form the basis for each participant's individual written plan of service. Evaluation should be carried out at repeated points in time, to assist in updating the plan of care, and it should contain elements which facilitate eventual discharge planning.

Supervision or assistance with walking, eating, grooming, toileting, and personal hygiene should be provided to all who need it. Planned activities which include socialization, stimulation, motivation, education, and exercise should be designed around the plans of care for all group members. Health screening, monitoring, and education will be necessary, both for participants and families. Provide nutrition services, including a noon meal and snacks. Simple modified diets, such as those for low-salt and for high or low calories should be available upon physician recommendation. Dietary counseling should be available, as needed, to train participants or caregivers in providing well-balanced meals at home. Transportation to and from the center will be required for some adult day care participants.

Develop written policies and procedures for handling health care emergencies and other types of disasters (fire, flood) and provide training for all staff and volunteers in how to carry out these procedures. Emotional support services should be offered for participants and their families to assist them in better adapting to the stresses of accommodating to impairments and disabilities. The center should also be able to provide information concerning other related programs. Center staff should also provide referral, coordination, and follow up when services are needed outside the day care center. Advocacy on behalf of the day care center, its participants, and their families will be a final, necessary service.

Other services which may be provided at some adult day care centers include:

- Distribution and/or supervision of medications for those participants unable to control their own medications. (This service will prove to be necessary in the large majority of adult day care centers.)

- Skilled nursing

- Physical, occupational, and speech therapy

- Physician services

- Podiatry, audiology, opthalmology, dentistry

- Homemaker, home health, or chore services

- In-home respite care (sitters)

- Art or poetry therapy

- Sheltered workshop

- Specialized services for particular patient populations, such as persons with Alzheimer's disease, head trauma and stroke

- Other services which grow out of the special resources of the sponsoring organization.

Some of the optional services listed here might not be necessary for the particular patient population of every center, and some might be provided through linkages with other agencies. Similarly, the location and physical arrangements of services and the methods of financing will vary from site to site.

Sponsors

Existing adult day care centers are sponsored by a wide variety of organizations. Seventy-four percent are private not-for-profit agencies. Sixteen percent are operated by public agencies or through joint public-private sponsorship. In recent years, we have seen the beginnings of for-profit organizations entering the day care field. Those centers now make up 10% of all adult day care (Von Behren 1986, 7). Sponsoring groups include home health agencies, rehabilitation centers, hospitals, homes for the aged, senior centers, churches, schools, local governments, business and industry, and others.

Location

Day care centers can be located in the sponsoring agency's own facility, but they do not have to be. Many organizations wanting to start a day care center, but lacking an appropriate area, have made arrangements for the use of space elsewhere in the community. For example, the ABC Home Health Agency may start a day care center in a local church building. ADC centers may also be in freestanding or purpose-built facilities.

Most centers are located in space that has been adapted for the service. Some newer facilities, however, have been designed and constructed specifically for the purpose of adult day care. Details of the features of environmental design, which will be important to the successful adult day care program, may be found in Chapter Five.

Financing

Most day care centers use some sort of fees or donations from clients as a major funding base. Typically, however, clients are unable to afford the full cost of care.

Many centers engage in community fund raising activities to supplement client fees. Many also attempt to obtain governmental support through grants or contracts.

Increasingly, reimbursement sources such as Medicaid, Medicare, and private insurers are recognizing the worth of adult day care services. Some centers have improved their financial picture by accessing these additional sources of revenue. Specific funding strategies that have increased the financial viability of many centers will be found in Chapters Nine and Ten.

Seeking Pathways to Success

All true pathways toward success in adult day care lead us toward responding to the community—walking hand in hand with those we serve. This means letting go of any preconceptions about what "they" need and what "they" have to offer. It means letting go of whatever feeling we may have that the future of the day care center is entirely in our hands. Like Paula and Ruthann, we must seek ways that we can all share in caring for each other.

Once we take this approach, we find a great deal of flexibility available in the design of specific adult day care programs. The potential for creativity in meeting people's real needs is high. Using that creativity, planners and managers can find many pathways that lead toward success. This book has been written to point the way toward some of them.

References

National Institute on Adult Daycare. 1984. *Standards for adult day care.* Washington, DC: National Council on the Aging.

Von Behren, R. 1986. *Adult day care in America: Summary of a national survey.* Washington, DC: National Council on the Aging.

Further Reading

O'Brien, C.L. 1982. *Adult day care: A practical guide.* Monterey, CA: Jones Bartlett Publishing Co.

On Lok Senior Health Services. 1987. *Directory of adult day care in America.* Washington, D.C.: National Council on the Aging.

Ransom, B. and B. Dugan. 1987. *Adult day care: An Annotated Bibliography.* Washington, D.C.: National Council on the Aging.

Von Behren, R. 1986. *Adult day care in America: Summary of a national survey.* Washington, D.C.: National Council on the Aging.

Weiler, P.G. and E. Rathbone-McCuan. 1978. *Adult day care: Community work with the elderly.* New York: Springer Publishing Co.

CHAPTER 2

The Development of
Adult Day Care in America

Winnifred Kelly and Linda Cook Webb

The Beginnings of Adult Day Care

Adult day care had its roots in day hospitals for psychiatric patients, first started in the Soviet Union in 1942 (Padula 1983). These psychiatric day hospitals were designed to help patients continue functioning in their own homes while receiving intensive therapy on an outpatient basis. "The reason for the development of...day hospital was to decrease the acute shortage of hospital beds. The goal was to increase hospital-bed turnover by discharging clients earlier" (O'Brien 1982, 146). Practitioners in day hospitals soon found an interesting side effect: Some patients seemed to benefit more from placement in this community-based service than from treatment in a hospital setting. Perhaps the more "normal" environment of day hospital combined with living at home provided stronger encouragement for the use of appropriate behavior patterns.

Day hospitals began to develop in the United States between 1945 and 1949, in locations such as Adams House in Boston (O'Brien 1982), the Menninger Clinic in Topeka, Kansas (Wish 1980), and the Yale Psychiatric Clinic (McCuan and Elliott 1976-7). Today, many community mental health centers operate day hospitals, sometimes calling them day treatment or partial hospitalization programs.

Following development of the psychiatric model, "England began using day hospitals for disabled adults, many of whom were elderly..." (O'Brien 1982, 146). Dr. Lionel Cosin, the "father of adult day care,"

9

initiated the first British geriatric day hospital in 1950. Nurses and occupational therapists provided the backbone of these programs; additional services included physical therapy, social work, geriatricians, transportation, and meals. The English day hospital was designed to reduce inpatient hospital stays. It also provided a place for intensive preadmission assessments which could, at times, entirely prevent placing patients in the hospital.

Adult day care centers, as we know them today, did not begin to appear in the United States until the late 1960s, when Dr. Cosin transplanted his model to the Cherry State Hospital in Goldsboro, North Carolina (Padula 1983, 1-3).

Adult Day Care Comes to the United States

During the 1960s, with the enactment of Medicare (Title XVIII) and Medicaid (Title XIX), the system of care for the aged began to focus on acute care. Nursing homes were the only form of insured long-term care, and reimbursement for their services was provided only in conjunction with hospitalization for an acute problem. In many cases, this led to inappropriate institutionalization of the elderly (Blum and Minkler 1980, 134).

Nursing home services began to account for an increasing proportion of the nation's total health bill. In 1950, nursing home care had represented 1.5% of all personal health expenditures. By 1981, this figure rose to 9.4% (Brewster 1984, 92). Long-term care became equated with institutional care, and this view was reinforced by public policy.

Unfortunately, nursing home care is an expensive item in the national health budget. Further, a variety of studies have shown that there are patients who do not need full-time care, and would not be institutionalized if community-based alternatives were available. Only 41% of nursing home residents get the intensive medical and nursing care offered by the institution, and only 32% receive routine care such as blood pressure readings (O'Brien 1982, 151). Policy makers and health care providers began a search that continues today for less costly alternatives. The widespread belief is that an expansion of community health and social services is one cost-effective strategy (Nusberg 1983-4, 14).

Professionals in the field were also recognizing the human costs of inappropriate institutionalization. Billings pointed out that "consistently it appears that the quality of life for elderly people who remain in the community and receive care is better than for those who enter long-term care facilities" (1982, 2).

In the context of these new approaches to long-term health care, adult day care was a service that seemed to "make sense." In spite of this, day care was slow to develop in the United States. Not many people had heard of the idea, and funds to support new programs were limited. Still, the few existing programs moved forward in developing models for what day care was to become. Between 1966 and 1968, the concept of day care was expanded to include supportive health and social services for marginally impaired and/ or isolated persons residing in the community.

In 1971, Dr. Cosin came to the United States again to describe his program during a hearing of the Senate Special Committee on Aging. This prompted an increasing interest in adult day care as a viable component in the continuum of long-term care services.

By 1973, there were still fewer than 15 programs in this country (Department of Health, Education, and Welfare 1978, 1). At this time, public legislation began to bridge the gap created by the medical approach of the '60s, and to incorporate human service components in the health care system. In 1973, "the passage of [amendments to] Title XX of the Social Security Act and Title III of the Older Americans Act was aimed at assisting persons in achieving or maintaining autonomy, and preventing or reducing inappropriate institutionalization through provisions of community and home-based care alternatives" (Blum and Minkler 1980, 135). Through Title XX and Title III, funding for such services as adult day care, case management, counseling, foster care, nutrition, homemakers, information and referral, recreation, and transportation became available. In 1974, the U.S. Department of Health, Education, and Welfare decided to encourage alternatives to institutionalization, and agreed to make Medicaid funds available to the states for adult day care.

By 1978, 300 adult day care centers had been started and two years later the number had risen to 618 (Department of Health, Education, and Welfare 1980, i). Approximately 1200 adult day care centers were in existence in 1986 (On Lok 1987, vi). With an average enrollment of 37 (Von Behren 1986, 12), these centers may be serving more than 44,000 families at any given point in time.

Expansion in adult day care is expected to continue, based on current trends in the growth of the older population. In 1980, 11% of Americans had passed their 65th birthday. By the year 2030, it is projected that 20% of the

American populace will be age 65 and older (Select Committee on Aging 1987, 7).

There are already approximately five million older people "living in their communities who need assistance to perform one or more personal care activities" (Department of Health and Human Services 1987, 49257). The segment of the aged population that is growing most rapidly is the age 75 and older group. Typically, these are the persons with the most long-term care needs and the least social supports for at-home care (Brody 1977, 64–5). Not only are those 75 and older often frail, ill, or disabled, but their spouses and adult children may also be at risk of health care problems.

Compounding the demographic changes in the older population are several shifts in social structure and public policy. Older people, especially women, will be more likely to live alone or with a person other than the spouse. At the same time, the increasing trend of married women to enter the labor force may limit the availability of family caregivers (Congressional Budget Office 1983, iii). Further, recent revisions in Medicare reimbursement have resulted in many older people being discharged from hospitals "quicker and sicker" and in more need of community alternatives in care.

In addition to demographic changes in the older population, we are now seeing a demand for adult day care among younger handicapped adults. Individuals with head trauma, muscular dystrophy, multiple sclerosis, cerebral palsy, and many other conditions are beginning to benefit from adult day care services.

The definition of "long-term care" currently reflects an array of services including nursing home care as part of the continuum of support services, but also including adult day care and other community-based services as viable levels of care (Brody 1977; Koff 1982, 3).

This new definition of long-term care is being reinforced in public policy, with the recent introduction of several bills allowing Medicare coverage of community-based chronic care services, including adult day care. Two bills (Panetta, et al. 1987; Melcher, Bradley, and Heinz 1987) specifically define the types and extent of adult day care services which NIAD recommends be covered. In April, 1988, the Senate Special Committee on Aging held a hearing on adult day care to review its place in the long-term care continuum. Several speakers, including a participant, a family member, providers, and governmental personnel testified as to the many benefits of adult day care. Later in the year, a bill allowing Medicare coverage of "catastrophic" health insurance costs was passed by both houses of Congress. Although this act included no coverage for chronic care services, it did provide for a study to determine how Medicare might cover adult day care. Ironically, the acute care focus of this act spurred momentum for bills allowing Medicare coverage of long-term care. Experts are now predicting that within the next few years a bill will be passed, allowing Medicare payment for community-based long-term care. It is most likely that adult day care will be a part of this new coverage. Adult day care is making its mark on the American health care scene.

Our History of Trying to Describe What We Do

As the field has grown, researchers, practitioners, and legislators have attempted, with difficulty, to define adult day care. The problem in defining the service lies in its diversity. As previously stated, adult day care can serve a wide range of people. It can provide companionship and a supportive environment to frail and isolated elders. It can help in the long-term rehabilitation of an older individual who has had a stroke. It can also be a resource for younger adults with physical and/or mental impairments.

Because of the multiplicity of populations using adult day care, a wide variety of programs has developed. Some centers include intensive medical and rehabilitation services, some focus on socialization and daily living skills, and most include some degree of both health and social services.

Early researchers in the day care field attempted to describe this variety of centers by using models (Levindale Geriatric Research Center 1974; Weisert 1975; and Robins 1975). Following Weisert's Models I and II, centers are typically presented as a dichotomy between social model and medical model. This terminology is intended to indicate the primary focus of program services in different types of adult day care centers.

When we look at day care centers in action, though, we find that the variety of functioning centers is so great as to defy any such superficial categories as social and medical. Centers that may be primarily social in nature often include nursing services. By the same token, those centers that serve persons with strong medical needs may also offer extensive social services. The staff must be able to respond fully to the needs of the entire person. This is best done when medical and social needs are addressed.

For this reason, Edith Robins developed four models of day care, as illustration in Figure 2-1. Even this greater number of models has failed to fully describe developments in the field. For example, many community-

Figure 2-1 Models of Day Care in the United States. Reprinted by permission from Jones Bartlett Publishing Co.

Model Type	Services	Type of Participant	Facility
I.	Intensive restorative, medical and health services (medical nursing and therapies, activities)	Persons who are in active phase of recovery and otherwise would remain inpatients	Extended care facility or hospital
II.	Time-limited, restorative, medical and health services (nursing and therapies, activities)	Persons with chronic problems who are post extended-care or hospital care	Nursing home
III.	Long-term health-maintenance services (nursing and other support services, activities)	"At risk" persons who would be prematurely institutionalized	Nursing home or freestanding community center
IV.	Preventative health services (psychosocial activities in protected environment)	"Frail" persons needing psychosocial activities	Freestanding community center, multi-purpose senior center, or nursing home

based adult day care centers (located in senior centers and senior housing) have the client base, service profile, and goals identified with Model II. By 1980, Robins had moved away from advocating a models theory. (For more information on the development of models, see Appendix B.)

The definition of adult day care developed by the National Institute on Adult Daycare in 1984 (see Chapter 1) broadened the range of day care services to incorporate both the social and health needs of the individual participant. In providing services to persons at risk of institutionalization, such a definition allows opportunity for creativity of planning.

Unfortunately, just when leaders in the day care field are attempting to encourage flexibility in responding to community needs, funding patterns are tending to force a dichotomy between social model and medical model centers.

Because of persistent funding distinctions between social and medical programs, some providers may continue to think of themselves in one category or the other. This categorization may have some usefulness, if we speak entirely in terms of existing insurance patterns. By separating the more medical level, adult day care seems to fit more easily into the traditional Medicaid, Medicare, and private insurance definitions of "health care." These categories are, indeed, primarily used by the states for reimbursement purposes under Medicaid. An emphasis on nursing and therapy components is also found in pending legislation (Panetta, et al. 1987; Melcher, Bradley, and Heinz 1987). Finally, those day care centers that have found the most success in billing to private insurance companies seem to be the centers that include a medical component. In contrast, in some areas, governmental supportive services funds may be targeted for centers describing themselves as social models.

We urge that center directors use caution in applying the social and medical model division in ways other than simply to work within the existing funding system.

In reality, centers should not focus on service patterns, as the dichotomy of models would suggest, but rather on the needs of their participants.

On paper, the participants appear to be a group of adults whose major characteristics seem to be that they are more or less dependent. This does not describe chairbound participants who work aggressively and painfully with intensely interested [staff] to leave their wheelchairs for walkers, to leave their walkers for canes, to take their first steps...to the patio of the center. It does not describe the willing participation in a set of tedious...exercises applied for simple purposes which may be either ignored in the "social" model or overstressed in the "medical" model (Special Committee on Aging 1976).

Uniqueness in Diversity

The diversity found among adult day care centers may be unique in the long-term care field; and it is precisely this diversity that has brought adult day care to where it is today. Diversity of definitions, models, service components, and funding permits ADC to better fill some of the gaps in long-term care. If we refined its definition, we would diminish its potential!

Variety in models has focused our attention toward developing levels of care that allow for mobility within the adult day care system. These levels can then respond appropriately when individuals' dependencies increase or decrease. Diversity in service components provides opportunity to explore and implement services unique to the profile of a specific community. Funding, fragmented as it is, has afforded many the opportunity to benefit from this unique community support system. As adult day care moves into the twenty-first century, we must continue to build on this heritage of "uniqueness in diversity."

References

Billings, G. 1982. Alternatives to nursing home care: An update. *Aging* 2-11:325-26.

Blum, S.R., and M. Minkler. 1980. Toward a continuum of caring alternatives: Community based care for the elderly. *Journal of Social Issues* 36(2):133-52.

Brewster, L.G. 1984. *The public agenda.* N.Y.: St. Martin's Press.

Brody, E. 1977. *Long-term care of older people.* New York: Human Sciences Press.

Department of Health and Human Services. December 30, 1987. FY 1988 coordinated discretionary funds program. *Federal Register.* Washington, DC: Government Printing Office.

Department of Health, Education, and Welfare. 1978. *Directory of adult day care centers.* Washington, DC: Health Care Financing Administration.

Department of Health, Education, and Welfare. 1980. *Directory of adult day care centers.* Washington, DC: Health Care Financing Administration.

Koff, T.H. 1982. *Long term care: An approach to serving the frail elderly.* Boston: Little, Brown, and Co.

Levindale Geriatric Research Center. 1974. *Preliminary analysis of select geriatric day care programs.* Washington, DC: DHEW.

McCuan, E., and M. Elliot. 1976-77. Geriatric day care in theory and practice. *Social Work and Health Care* 2(2):153-70.

Melcher, J., B. Bradley, and J. Heinz. 1987. *Senate Bill 1839.* Washington, DC: U.S. Government Printing Office.

Nusberg, C. 1983-84. The impact of aging populations on health care budgets: Part II. *Aging International* 10(4):13-16).

O'Brien, C.L. 1982. *Adult day care: A practical guide.* Monterey, CA: Jones-Bartlett Publishing Co.

On Lok Senior Health Services. 1987. *Directory of adult day care in America.* Washington, DC: National Council on the Aging.

Padula, H. 1983. *Developing adult day care: An approach to maintaining independence for impaired older persons.* Washington, DC: National Council on the Aging.

Padula, H. 1981. Toward a useful definition of adult day care. *Hospital Progress* 42-45.

Panetta, L. et al. 1987. *House Resolution 550.* Washington, DC: U.S. Government Printing Office.

Robins, E. 1975. *Operational research in geriatric day care in the United States.* Presented at the 10th International Congress on Gerontology in Israel.

Select Committee on Aging, United States House of Representatives. 1987. *Exploding the myths: Caregiving in America.* Washington, DC: U.S. Government Printing Office. Comm. Pub. No. 99-611.

Select Committee on Aging, United States House of Representatives. 1980. *Hearing before the subcommittee on health and long-term care: Adult day care programs.* Washington, DC: U.S. Government Printing Office.

Special Committee on Aging, United States Senate. 1976. *Adult day facilities for treatment, health care, and related services.* Washington, DC: U.S. Government Printing Office.

Von Behren, R. 1986. *Adult day care in America: Summary of a national survey.* Washington, DC: National Council on the Aging.

Weissert, W. 1975. "Adult Day Care in the United States. A Transcentury Report." Washington, DC: Department of Health, Education, and Welfare.

Wish, F. 1980. Day care: Its value for the older adult and his family. *Journal of Jewish Communal Services* 174-80.

Zaki, G., and S. Zaki. 1984. *Counseling services in adult day care centers.* Rhode Island: Rhode Island College Gerontology Center.

CHAPTER 3

How to Plan for Adult Day Care: Getting Started

Linda Cook Webb

We thought adult day care sounded so "right" that it just *had* to work! We found a site that was in the middle of a concentration of frail elders, we told the community what we were doing, and we opened our doors. So here we are, six months down the road, and we're not filling up very fast. What happened? (Comment from an adult day care director.)

Adult day care *does* sound like a good idea in most communities. We have all heard about the phenomenal increase in the aged population. We have heard about the increase in the "old-old" who can be expected to need supportive community services because of their great risk of institutionalization. Many of us have encountered touching stories of the lengths to which families will go in trying to keep their elderly family members at home.

So, is adult day care really as good an idea as it sounds? The answer is, "Yes...but...." Yes, day care does have a lot to offer many communities...but that does not mean that it is easy to get started.

Day care directors across the country often say that it took from three to five years for centers to go from opening day to a condition of full census. Now, some of that time has been spent in reinventing the wheel. Many centers currently in operation started during the *same* period, so all were learning together. As more solid knowledge is available to help in starting and running adult day care centers, start-up times may be decreasing.

19

The first steps in planning a new adult day care center may either look overly simple or simply overwhelming. In fact, the planning process is somewhere in between. The keys to a smooth start-up involve:

- Identifying goals for the center, and having the courage to continue believing in those goals even during discouraging moments

- Assessing the community's service needs related to adult day care, and providing what people want

- Evaluating alternative methods for accomplishing goals

- Mobilizing resources effectively

- Evaluating program development and operations on a continual basis (Adapted from Lawton, Newcomer, and Byerts 1976, 224–6).

First, start to develop a clear idea of *why* your organization is interested in adult day care and how day care might fit into the agency's mission statement or existing goals. The people involved in planning the center should write brief statements outlining their reasons for wanting to pursue an adult day care center. Reasons for interest in adult day care will vary, depending on the individual and the organization involved. The following examples of interest statements illustrate the range of goals that might be found among different types of agencies.

- "I am losing my home health patients to nursing homes, not because the patient gets sicker, but because the family wears out. Adult day care might help these families to 'hang in there' a little longer."

- "Our senior center's members are getting older and frailer. Some of them just can't join into existing programs very well. They need something special."

- "The hospital board has set a priority of offering more community-based programs. Since our area does not currently have an adult day care center, this may be a good way to extend services to a new population."

Developing Goals

The first round of goal setting will help to establish directions for planning a center. Goals must be refined, however, with information about the specifics of program development and operations. This will help to ensure that objectives set for the adult day care center can be reasonably met. Before proceeding with actual development, spend at least one to three months to learn about adult day care. Review available resources, such as books, films, and workshops. (See Appendix C for special resources. Also, browse through the bibliographies at the end of each chapter in this book.) Speak with other day care providers about their experiences. If there are other day care centers in your area, definitely contact them. If not, you can contact your state adult day care association for technical assistance and/or networking. An especially good resource for new centers is the National Institute on Adult Daycare, a membership unit of the National Council on the Aging. (For more information on these organizations, see Appendix C.)

Contact regulatory agencies that may have authority over adult day care in your area. Find out early what they will be requiring in the way of facilities, staffing, and infection control. (See Figure 3-1 for a listing of potential regulatory agencies.) Also contact other groups that may have developed standards for adult day care. While it is not a regulatory body, the National Institute on Adult Daycare does have voluntary standards for centers (1984). Several state associations have also written standards, and some are currently doing peer review to ensure quality of care.

Having investigated the "nitty gritty" of providing adult day care, go back to review the original goals for developing this new service. Does it still look as though it will be feasible for your organization to attempt starting a center? Can your agency support the financial losses that will be associated with a lengthy start up? (Some preliminary budgeting may be in order at this point. See Chapter Nine.) Will the adult day care service fit well within the existing goals of the organization? If the answers to these questions are all "Yes," then look outward to your community: Is day care desired? If so, what types of services should be included?

Community Assessment

Community assessment can be expected to take a minimum of one to six months. There is currently no widely accepted tool for determining the need for adult day care in any given area, but certain steps will help in developing an approximation.

I.   Adult Day Care (ADC)

    A.   Licensure regulations must be met in many states in order for a day care center to legally open its doors. Contact the state agency in charge of licensing. This will vary from state to state. It may be your state Division of Aging, the department handling Medicaid, or perhaps an alternate agency. (See Appendix D.)

    B.   Certification regulations apply only in those situations in which the state offers Medicaid coverage of ADC. Each center wishing to be a Medicaid provider must obtain certification before billing for covered services. Contact the state agency in charge of Medicaid. (See Appendix D.)

II.   Food Service regulations will affect both the facility design and food handling procedures. Even if food is not prepared on site, these regulations are likely to apply. Contact your local Health Department for more information.

III.   Facilities

    A.   Fire Safety Codes must be met. You may be asked to conform with the Life Safety Code (established for nursing homes). Since this code is the strictest fire code, inquire whether you could use the general fire safety codes or the codes developed for places of public assembly instead. Contact your local Fire Department for more information.

    B.   Handicapped Accessibility is determined by standards established by the American National Standards Institute (ANSI). To be considered handicapped accessible for federal (and often for state) funding, you are required to meet these standards. A copy of the ANSI standards for handicapped accessibility should be available in the public library.

Figure 3-1 Regulations, Codes, and Standards You May Have To Meet...and Who To Contact for Information.

Consult with other day care centers in your community or a similar community. Ask about the capacity each center can serve and the current average daily attendance. Especially try to determine responses to particular service patterns within the centers.

Consult with providers of related services. Do they see a need? What do they think of the adequacy of existing ADCs? Organizations you may wish to survey can include:

- Area agencies on aging
- Hospital social workers or discharge planners
- Home health agencies
- Social service agencies
- Senior nutrition sites and meals-on-wheels providers
- Mental health centers
- Senior housing
- Services to the handicapped
- University extension specialists
- Physicians

Potential referral sources may say, "There's a big need for adult day care. Just tell me when you're opening and I can fill you up with referrals from my agency alone." When people say this, they really do seem to believe it. In reality, though, it rarely happens. Costs, transportation, scheduling, family resistance, and a whole host of other factors can combine to reduce referral levels.

Also consult with providers of related services to identify those community resources that may help you start a day care center. Churches, senior citizen centers, and so forth may offer space. The caterer who contracts for nutrition sites and meals-on-wheels may be a cost-effective option for providing lunch. The special system of transportation for the elderly and handicapped may be able to provide transportation. Your community may be especially oriented to volunteerism or corporate giving. Use your creativity in looking around. The willingness of community organizations to help in this undertaking may tell you a lot about the perceived need for adult day care—and identifying those resources early on will certainly make your job easier down the road.

Gather census figures regarding numbers of aged and handicapped persons in your community (numbers and concentrations). The need for geriatric day care can be estimated somewhere between 1/2% and 2% of the total 65 and older population in the area to be served. These figures do not come from scientific research, but rather from informal observations. Their main usefulness is in reminding planners to be conservative in estimating potential utilization of a new center. Some estimate the need for adult day care at as high as 5% of the aged population (Padula 1983, 20). When determining need, look for concentrations of persons aged 75 and older and concentrations of handicapped persons of all ages. Is there an area that has concentrations of these groups and is generally under served? Also look at the concentrations of low-income persons. How will this affect your location and the population you will be serving? Demographic information of this type can be obtained from a number of sources, including reports from the:

- U.S. Census Bureau

- U.S. Bureau of Vital Statistics

- U.S. Public Health Service and local health departments

- National Center for Health Statistics

- Local planning commissions

- Hospital, nursing home, and home health associations

These reports may be available at your public library. If not, the librarian can help you to locate them.

Some adult day care centers have approached families directly in attempting to measure service needs. This seems to have met with uneven success, but still may be a method you wish to try. There is a constant difficulty in identifying those families who may actually be potential users of the day care center. A mail survey would be the most efficient method of reaching these people, but available mailing lists do not identify households in which there is a frail elder. The closest mailing list that could be used would perhaps be one that identifies the head of the household as being age 35 to 70. This is obviously not a very discriminating list, and postage will therefore be expensive. Another method is to distribute a questionnaire through grocery stores, laundromats, and the local newspaper. This method will yield some results, but depends on people who are already burdened being able to take the time to respond.

Community needs assessment is the first step in a good marketing program. The methods described in Chapter Eleven will help you to determine what people want in the way of services. Compile results and finalize assessments of your market. Does your organization still want to proceed? Chapter Four describes the next steps.

Don't Try To Do the Job Alone

At some point, the wise day care planner will begin to involve "outside" people in the development process. These people may be potential consumers, professionals from future referral agencies, the local media, or others who can offer a unique perspective in planning. Two methods can be used for working with these advisors: the task force and the advisory committee. The task force is a less formal group drawn together for initial planning tasks, or to review and critique staff planning. The advisory committee functions over a longer time period (i.e., indefinitely for the life of the program) to advise in planning, implementation, program evaluation, and so on.

Some planners prefer to begin with the more temporary task force and then develop the permanent advisory committee later. This is particularly appropriate if the task force is developed when the agency is investigating, but has not committed to implementing a day care center. At a later time, if an advisory committee is formed, its members may be drawn from the task force *and* other sources. In a different situation, the planner may opt for proceeding directly to the formation of an advisory committee. Both processes can function well. The choice of whether or not to use a task force should be based on the needs of day care planners and their organization. In any event, an advisory committee will be a necessity for an operational center.

Development and functioning of the task force and the advisory committee will be similar. In further discussion, both groups will be called "the committee."

The committee can be formed at any stage in the planning process, but generally, earlier is better. Developing the committee can be a potent part of your marketing campaign—even if you are not yet totally obligated to starting a day care center. If the group really "buys into" the idea of adult day care, each of them will take a positive attitude back to their coworkers. This is also your chance to let the community "design" a solution to the problems they see or deal with daily; try to create a sense of program ownership among the committee members.

Another major role of the committee will be in adding to the expertise supplied by staff. For this reason, it is wise to include persons with a wide range of experience and community contacts. In some cases, it may also be advisable to include persons from other departments of your own organization. Figure 3-2 illustrates a checklist for analyzing committee composition. You can adapt the categories to suit your center's specific needs.

		AGE						RACE				ORGANIZATIONS													ACCESS TO						SKILLS										POSITION						OTHER			
COMMITTEE MEMBER	YEARS ON COMMITTEE	21-35	36-50	51-65	65+	MALE	FEMALE	CAUCASIAN	BLACK	LATIN	OTHER	HOSPITAL	MHC	SOC. SVSCS.	HOME HEALTH	VOL. AGENCY	SM. BUSINESS	CORPORATE	MEDIA	CHURCHES	POLITICAL	EDUCATION	NEIGHBORHOOD	OTHER	INFO.	PEOPLE	CORPORATIONS	GOVT.	FUNDERS	OTHER	PROGRAMMING	FISCAL MGMT.	VOLUNTEERS	FUND-RAISING	NETWORKING	MARKETING	PERSONNEL	PLANNING	MED. RECORDS	OTHER	SOCIAL WKER.	NURSE	DR.	ADMIN.	REFERRAL SOURCE	OTHER				

Figure 3-2 Committee Composition Analysis.

Let the committee be your eyes and ears and arms and legs in the community; soon, the job of planning will be much too large for one person.

References

Lawton, M.P., R. Newcomer, and T. Byerts. 1976. *Community planning for an aging society.* New York: McGraw-Hill.

National Institute on Adult Daycare. 1984. *Standards for adult day care.* Washington, DC: National Council on the Aging.

Padula, H. 1983. *Developing adult day care.* Washington, DC: National Council on the Aging.

Further Readings

Spiegel, A., and H. Hyman. 1978. *Basic health planning methods.* Germantown, MD: An Aspen Publication.

Weiler, P.G., and E. Rathbone-McCuan. 1978. *Adult day care: Community work with the elderly.* NY: Springer Publishing.

CHAPTER 4

How to Plan for Adult Day Care: Getting Open

Linda Cook Webb

Chapter Three described the initial stages of planning for a new adult day care center: setting goals, gathering information, assessing the community, and developing a task force. It will be important to review goals when these steps are completed. Planners should ask themselves:

- Why do I want to do adult day care? (Be honest!) After initial data-gathering, are you sure you really want to proceed?

- Are my initial goals for the center reasonable, considering the experience of other day care centers and the desires of the community? (Look closely at financial goals, in particular.)

- What is my organization's mission statement or philosophy? How does day care "fit"?

Assuming that goals for the center are still in line with the agency's philosophy and with "real world" experience, proceed to developing the program plan.

Evaluating Alternatives

No two adult day care centers in the country are exactly the same because each center responds to the needs of its individual community. Community needs can vary dramatically from one locale to the next, and

29

therefore the specific operational features of adult day care centers vary as well. Hours per day, days per week, specific service packages, pricing structures, staffing patterns, and many more factors vary widely from one center to the next. The fact that there is no "set" way to do adult day care is an advantage to creative program planners. Diversity in the field allows us to make the best use of those resources available locally, while minimizing the effect of resources that we may lack.

In planning for a new center, look first to those other services you already offer. Outline current staff skills, space, equipment, and so forth. Especially identify any assets that could be shared among programs. Identifying available resources may direct planners' attention toward particular day care service patterns that could be most effective. By the same token, determining eligibility criteria or scheduling can be guided by resources available. For example, suppose a home health agency and a church wish to cosponsor an adult day care center. They have found from community assessment that there is a need for day care with a rehabilitation component. There is also a need for day care that could serve people who are incontinent. The home health agency can provide therapists and nurses on a part-time basis, thereby accommodating both needs. The church is willing to provide space, but can only offer a carpeted area. They worry about severe soiling of the carpet if incontinent people are admitted. The two agencies agree that their first attempts at adult day care should focus toward rehab and away from serving incontinent persons.

The specific service package you offer, your target population, your location, and certain site characteristics should be closely linked. Throughout developing your preliminary plan, frequently double-check to make certain that all of these factors are planned in concert.

A number of factors will come into play for site selection. Accessibility and image considerations may affect the number of people who are willing to use the center. If the center is hard to find, or if it is not adapted to the needs of the handicapped, families may not even complete the admission process. If the center is located in a part of town that seems "foreign" to your target population, families may feel uncomfortable sending their elders to you. Renovation may improve handicapped accessibility, or it may improve the building's image, but it can be costly. Consult with an architect and a contractor to get firm estimates of work needed.

The site may also affect program policies regarding eligibility and capacity. For example, if a number of doors offer easy exit, it will be unwise to admit persons who are likely to wander. The upper limits of the center's capacity will definitely be set by the area of the facility. The National Institute on Adult Daycare recommends a *minimum* of 40 square feet of program space for each participant. (This excludes halls, offices, restrooms, and storage areas.) (NIAD 1984, 47) If possible, it is more desirable to allow 80 to 100 square feet per participant. Several states now have regulations controlling square footage. (For more information on facilities planning, see Chapter Five.)

Develop a service plan, or listing of services you intend to offer. The service plan outlines those specific services you will be providing, along with hours of operation for each. For example, you may provide supervision from 7 am to 5 pm, but only provide therapy from 9 am to noon. Review the list of services in Chapter Three; be certain to include all basic services listed; and determine the means and costs of providing each service. Give special attention to transportation services, as described in Chapter Six.

Evaluate alternative methods of providing staffing and write job descriptions for each position. Some possible means of staffing include:

- Pay full-time staff salaries or wages
- Subsidize staff wages, through older worker programs, Comprehensive Training & Education Act (CETA), or similar projects
- Contract for specific services from an outside provider (i.e., pay a home health agency to do therapies)
- Share services with another agency (i.e., two day centers share one music therapist)

Staff qualifications should be closely linked to eligibility criteria for participants. For example, if no staff have a mental health background it would be unwise to admit persons who have a history of abusive behavior. For more information on specific staff responsibilities, hiring, and management, see Chapters Seven and Eight.

Develop marketing plans based on the principles outlined in Chapter Eleven. Especially focus on community education to raise public awareness and participant recruitment to attract actual clients.

Develop an operational budget and get approval of applicable persons in your organization. The budget should include both anticipated expenses and revenues for three years. Budgeting should involve repeated review of alternatives in terms of the costs and revenues associated with the services to be provided. Develop several budgets, each portraying the fiscal results of different start-up times, staffing patterns, and service packages. This process will help to ensure that the budget finally selected will be as close as possible to a realistic portrayal. Develop a budget summary that can be used in written or oral funding proposals. Chapters Nine and Ten outline factors to be considered in budgeting. Chapter Sixteen describes how budgeting can be done more easily on a computer.

Write a policies and procedures manual. The best way to start is to keep all documentation relating to decisions about the day care center. A notebook containing lists of services to be provided, job descriptions, and eligibility criteria is a rudimentary policies and procedures manual. Add detail regarding how services are to be carried out. Appendix E more fully indicates topics that should be included in a policies and procedures manual.

Mobilizing Resources

As planning proceeds and opening day approaches, there will be more and more to do. Planners must use all their management skills to organize the many tasks that must be accomplished quickly. Time management forms, such as the one illustrated in Figure 4-1, will assist in mobilizing personnel. Note that no two situations in planning for an adult day care center will ever be exactly the same. The order of the steps outlined in the sample time management form will be different from one center to the next, depending on your resources, your community, and your reasons for investigating day care.

Long-Range Planning and Program Evaluation

Planning for adult day care does not stop with opening day. The center's continued success will depend, in part, on long-range planning that never ends. Managers must look down the road to anticipate changes in the program's market, financing, and service patterns. The long-range plan then outlines responses to these changes so surprises are minimized.

Before the center opens, write goals and objectives for the program's first three years. Goal statements should be large-scale desired outcomes. Include both short- and long-range goals. Many goals will be so large that they may not be achieved in your lifetime; but we need to dream of the future or we won't work toward it today.

Sunnyside ADC Preopening Activities

Task	Staff Responsible	MO1	MO2	MO3	MO4	MO5	MO6
Renovate/decorate facility	John S.	X	X	X			
Purchasing	John S.					X	
Participant recruitment	Mary R.			X	X	X	X
Arrange meal service	Mary R.					X	
Est. transportation system	Ann J.					X	
Order phone service	Ruth P.					X	
Develop service schedules	Mary R.	X					
Write job descriptions	Mary R.		X				
Hire employees	Mary R.				X	X	
Recruit volunteers	Ann J.			X	X	X	
Develop recording forms	Ann J.		X	X			
Write Policies and Procedures Manual	Mary R. Ann J.	X X	X X	X X	X X		
Develop fee scale and bookkeeping system	Mary R. Jeff A.	X X					
Staff orientation	All staff						X
Opening day!	All staff					X	

Figure 4-1 Sample Time Management Form.

Break each goal into a series of objectives. Objectives are smaller than goals; they should be measurable, and they should be attainable in a reasonable amount of time. Indicate desired or estimated completion dates for each objective.

Outline the steps to achieve each objective. These action steps are much like a "to do" list. For each step, show who is responsible and a specific date for completion.

As an example, the long-range plan might contain the following series of goal, objectives, and action steps:

Goal: Expand service to low-income persons, while ensuring the program's financial viability.

Objective 1: Obtain Medicaid coverage of ADC in this state within the next two legislative sessions.

Action Step 1a: Mary R. will contact the following to determine their interests/priorities regarding Medicaid coverage:

- State ADC Association within one month
- State Division on Aging within two months
- Governor and legislators within three months

Action Step 1b: Within the next month, Anne J. will obtain sample laws and regulations from states that have Medicaid coverage.

Objective 2: Obtain donations to the scholarship fund in the amount of $100,000 within the next six months.

Action Step 2a: Paula R. will develop a mailing list of potential donors within two weeks.

An integral part of long-range planning is the evaluation of whether objectives have, in fact, been achieved. Chapter Seventeen describes techniques for evaluating adult day care programs. Program evaluation should include at least the following areas:

- Census growth, including demographics related to persons referred, persons admitted, and persons discharged
- Fiscal management
- Quality of care
- Implementation of optional services, expanded hours, or other program growth
- Advocacy efforts.

Maintaining Perspective

Many adult day care centers begin with funding bases that resemble patchwork quilts. At first, they may not be able to offer all the services the planners would like, or they may not be able to serve all economic groups equally well. Frustrating as this may be, it can still be a viable place to start. After all, if we do not take that first step, we may never go down the path at all.

There *is* a danger in starting a program that does less than we might have hoped: planners can lose sight of the original goals. In the early days of a new center's operation, particularly, there will be much to do. Attend to new issues as they arise, but always keep your eye on your purposes—whatever they may be. This will help you to move ever closer to the full program that you want.

Reference

National Institute on Adult Daycare. 1984. *Standards for adult day care.* Washington, DC: National Council on the Aging.

Further Readings

Mace, N.L. and P.V. Rabins. 1984. *A survey of day care for the demented adult in the United States.* Washington, DC: National Council on the Aging.

O'Brien, C.L. 1982. *Adult day care: A practical guide.* Monterey, CA: Jones Bartlett Publishing Co.

Padula, H. 1983. *Developing adult day care.* Washington, DC: National Council on the Aging.

Panella, J. Jr. 1987. *Day care programs for Alzheimer's disease and related disorders.* NY: Demos Publications.

Ransom, B. and B. Dugan. 1987. *Adult day care: an annotated bibliography.* Washington, DC: National Council on the Aging.

Weiler, P.G. and E. Rathbone-McCuan. 1978. *Adult day care: Community work with the elderly.* NY: Springer Publishing Co.

CHAPTER 5

Facilities Development

Kay Rooney Larmer and Linda Cook Webb

Adult day care centers have grown dramatically over the past decade, producing a rich variety of programs, in very diverse settings, utilizing many different types of facilities. Some adult day care programs are found in renovated buildings such as schools, churches and storefronts. Others are housed in part of a larger facility, such as a nursing home, hospital, or senior center. A few have been built with the sole purpose of providing ADC services. With these various approaches, much has been learned about the special needs of the population served and the particular environmental requirements for the facility.

In the past, the facility was seen by many adult day care planners as important primarily because of the needed space it provided. It was viewed as a passive background, having little importance to the actual program and little effect on the participants' needs and behavior. Much of this was reinforced because there was little money to renovate or specifically design facilities for the impaired older population. Research and experience are now demonstrating, however, that the physical environment has great potential for use as a therapeutic tool. A well-designed facility can be supportive to programs and activities, and may actually improve the participants' social interaction and functional capacity. This information is particularly important for adult day care providers, because evidence now suggests that the environment plays an even more significant role as an individual's level of impairment increases.

This chapter will examine the particular architectural and physical design features that are most important for adult day care centers. These recommendations have evolved through a synthesis of information from a

37

variety of day care centers, and is a compilation of ideas from individuals in the field. As you read through this chapter, please keep in mind that these are guidelines and suggestions. They may not be universally applicable, since every center will have its own goals, types of participants served, building constraints, and budget requirements. There is no "best design" or "perfect environment." In fact, creativity and imagination are two key factors that are largely responsible for the unique and successful development of centers today. This chapter should only serve as a basic construct for those aspects of design that most strongly support an individual adult day care program.

Before discussing specific design features, it is important to look at the basic philosophy of adult day care, and examine how it relates to the facility design. Day care enhances the value of human life and affirms the dignity and self-worth of the individual, regardless of age, frailty, or disability. In designing an ADC center, planners must create an environment that is sensitive and supportive to these goals. In order to do this, the following general principles should guide the design process. The adult day care facility should:

- Maximize the functional level of the participant and encourage independence to the greatest degree possible

- Build on the participants' residual strengths, recognizing their limitations and impairments

- Establish for the participant a sense of control and self-determination, regardless of the participant's level of functioning

- Assist in maintaining the physical and emotional health of the participant while preventing further debilitation

In concert with this philosophy, the following major design concepts should be considered in developing centers. Details and explanations will be presented throughout the chapter and are illustrated in Figures 5-1 and 5-2.

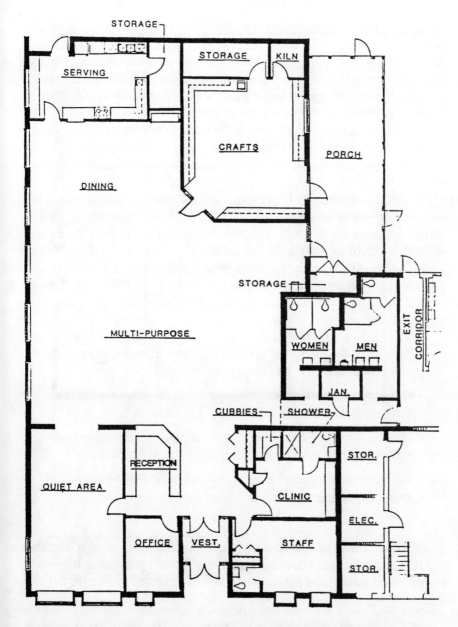

Figure 5-1 Floor Plan of Adult Day Care Center. Source: Lewinsville Adult Day Care Center, Architect David Lipp, A.I.A. (Used with permission)

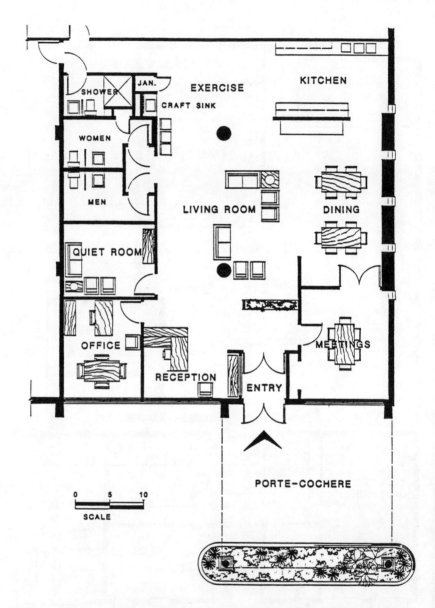

Figure 5-2 Second Floor Plan of Adult Day Care Center. Source: Eldercare Center, University of Missouri at Columbia, Architect Keith Westenhauer, A.I.A. (Used with permission)

- The safety and security of the participants must be a prime consideration in planning the facility. Persons attending ADC centers have many physical and mental impairments, and often a combination of both. These impairments can be quite severe, so the facility should be designed to avoid accidents and injuries, yet still allow for ease of movement throughout the center.

- The atmosphere should be warm and inviting. The setting should be home-like and noninstitutional. Many participants spend eight to ten hours a day in the center; they should feel comfortable and at ease.

- The facility should provide opportunities for social contact, both casual and structured, as well as the opportunity to choose privacy when so desired. This should include designed spaces, such as special rooms/nooks, as well as visual and acoustical separations.

- The environment should reinforce *orientation* and awareness of the surroundings by providing cues and information about specific rooms, locations, and functions that help participants to get their bearings to time and space. Many centers have had success with extensive use of signs and with color-coding specific areas of the facility.

- The environment should facilitate the participants' ability to perform activities of daily living. Reduction of external stressors and limiting distractions helps in this area. Complicated designs and too many alternatives impair the participants' functioning. *Simplicity, predictability, and routinization* are key words in the design of an adult day care center.

- The environment should stimulate all the senses through *visual, tactile, auditory, and olfactory assistance.* Many participants have an accumulation of sensory losses that are quite significant. The environment can play an important role in helping to compensate for these losses.

- The facility should be designed to be flexible and to provide *options and choices* for different participant needs. If at all possible, the center should be arranged to allow two activities to be offered simultaneously. It should also assist in managing certain behavioral patterns typical of day care participants— wandering, incontinence, and catastrophic reactions.

• The facility should be designed to *support staff and family/ caregivers*. While the primary concern in the design of the center should be the special needs of participants, the needs of others using or working in the facility must also be given particular attention. The stress of providing adult day care is high, and environmental supports are essential to assist staff members to maintain a sense of balance and job satisfaction. Staff need a quiet area and a restroom away from the program. The emotional strain of caregiving is also tremendous for families and other home caregivers. They should have an identified room available to be alone with staff or to have small group discussions.

Site Considerations

When selecting a location for the ADC center, certain basic information should be considered.

• Demographic information, including the current density of the population to be served, as well as the projected growth of this group in the next few years. (Chapter Three discusses demographic analysis in more detail.)

• The facility should be able to comply with all applicable state and local building and zoning codes. It should also meet standards for handicapped accessibility. (See Appendix C for more information about the American National Standards Institute's (ANSI) standards for handicapped accessibility. Other regulatory agencies such as the Department of Social Services, the Health Department, and the Office on Aging should also be consulted to determine whether the building and grounds meet any applicable licensing/certification requirements. Failure to conform to these regulations can be costly to new programs if they must go back to try to comply after construction is completed.

- The facility and site should have sufficient space to accommodate the number/types of participants to be served and the full range of services to be offered. Square footage requirements vary. Many states have regulations as to the minimum space per client for licensure or certification. The National Institute on Adult Daycare (NIAD) recommends a minimum of 40 square feet per participant, excluding hallways, offices, restrooms, and storage areas (NIAD 1984). On Lok, in California, suggests 70 to 85 square feet per participant, if dining is not a separate space (Von Behren and Gould 1985). In determining what is best for an individual program, include only those activities areas commonly used by participants. Dining and kitchen areas should be included only if these areas are used by participants for activities other than meals. Reception areas, offices, restrooms, hallways, service areas, or specialized spaces used only for therapies should not be included. It is important to note that where an adult day care center is colocated in a facility housing other services, it should have its own separate, identifiable, and measurable space (NIAD 1984).

- Whenever possible, the site selected should have easy access to public and private transportation, be close to major transportation routes and be conveniently located to critical services, such as hospitals, ambulance service, and fire station. Proximity to other community services, such as recreational facilities, shopping, and the places of business is desirable. It is also important to examine the approach roads for safety and good repair. Roads should be able to accommodate deliveries and emergency vehicles and allow for peak hours of use during early morning and late afternoon times.

- Orientation to the sun is important. Sunlight may have a positive or negative impact on the program. Sun provides natural light and warmth; but without filtering it may also cause glare, shadows, and excessive heat.

- Renovated sites have their own unique problems, particularly if the facility is old. Asbestos removal, furnace repair/replacement, and new roofing are all costly.

- Expansion potential is especially important if ADC planners do not have the immediate funds to provide the type of facility they eventually desire. The site should be selected and the facility designed to enable the entire program to grow as the budget allows.

Once a site is selected, it is important to enlist neighborhood support. Remember, most people are unfamiliar with adult day care. Especially in residential areas, neighbors may fear increased traffic and noise or they may worry that a poorly maintained facility will decrease property values. Good public relations and educational efforts will go a long way toward calming these fears. In fact, neighbors often view ADC as an asset to the community and something of which they can be proud.

Exterior

In preparing to open the center, attention should be paid to the exterior as well as the interior of the facility. Good signage is one way to market the service and say, "Welcome!" to the community. Signage for marketing is particularly effective if the center is located on frequently traveled routes. Be certain, however, that the lettering is large enough to be read quickly. Use directional signage to indicate location of the ADC center, location of parking, and location of appropriate entrances. This is particularly important if the center is colocated in a building with other services. Signage may also be used to advertise special events, such as bazaars, health fairs, and so on. It is also a nice way to familiarize people passing by with the type of activities provided at the center.

The entrance should not be located on a main road, if at all possible. Most participants will be arriving and departing at approximately the same time, thus creating great potential for traffic congestion. Planners should request that the city designate the center as a "safety zone." This will ensure adequate traffic lights, stop signs and good transportation flow. There should be sufficient parking available to accommodate staff, family/ caregivers, and visitors. A minimum of two of these spaces should be identified as handicapped parking. Handicapped spaces should be at least 13 feet wide and should be located near the entrance door. Good drainage patterns are important in the parking and main entry areas, to prevent accidents and falls. In cold climates, give special attention to drainage and surface materials that will help to prevent ice formation.

Adequate lighting around the parking lot and grounds is crucial to ensure the safety and security of participants arriving or departing during dawn or twilight hours. Fences, lower shrubs, good locks, and alarm systems also help secure the facility.

Ideally, adult day care centers will also have some provision for exterior recreation areas. These could include smooth walkways, seating for resting or watching activities, recreational space, and a garden area. The garden area should be controlled by a fence or landscaping to prevent confused participants from wandering, and it should be easily supervised by staff. Outside furniture should be stationary, sturdy, and safely arranged. Avoid picnic tables with attached benches. If benches are used, they are best placed at the edges of the area. Some seating should face neighborhood activities, as even traffic seems to be more interesting to participants than quiet areas.

Entrance and Vestibule

The building entryway should have an awning or other covering, provided from curbside to the entry door, to protect participants and visitors from inclement weather. The ideal canopy extends over the driveway, covering two car widths, and allowing at least 10 feet to 12 feet in height to accommodate buses and vans. The entrance should be well lit. The shorter the distance between the point of arrival and entrance into the center, the better.

This area could also provide seating for participants to wait for their rides when it is time to go home. Allowing participants to wait outside during pleasant weather often provides a needed diversion and helps to decrease anxieties such as "Will my family forget to come?" Obviously, it will be necessary to provide some type of supervision when participants are outside.

The vestibule provides a modulated transition between the exterior and interior of the building. On sunny days, normal interior lighting can appear quite dark to persons entering the ADC center. Older people, in particular, require more time to visually accommodate for the change. The vestibule can help in this transition. It also provides for improved temperature control within the facility, is an energy saver, and assists in maintaining the cleanliness of the center.

An ideal vestibule includes two sets of glass doors, electronically controlled to recede into the wall. The space between the two sets of doors should be large enough to accommodate a participant in a wheelchair and a second person who is pushing the chair (at least 5 feet wide by 6 feet deep). It should be heated, have a nonskid surface, good lighting, and be visually accessible to staff. Figure 5-3 illustrates a vestibule that can be supervised either from the reception area or the director's office.

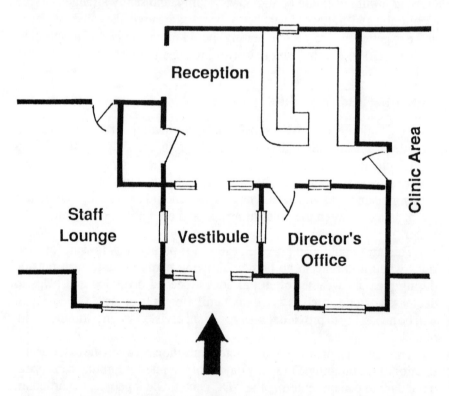

Figure 5-3 Entrance, Vestibule, Reception Area, and Director's Office. Source: Lincolnia Adult Day Care Center, Fairfax County, Virginia. Architect Cohen-Karydas & Associates. (Used with permission)

Reception Area

The reception area should make visitors feel welcome. Remember that many family members are encountering a disability for the first time with their loved one. At their first visit to the center, they are likely already to feel anxious. These family members are probably making decisions about adult day care while they are in the midst of a crisis, and they may feel uncertain about their ability to make the proper decision. Potential participants may also feel anxiety, often worrying that they are being placed in a nursing home without being told. Even visitors coming to the center for the first time may feel awkward about the experience. The unfamiliar sights, sounds, and possibly smells of the day center can seem overwhelming without some transition from the "outside world." The reception area should be an attractive and inviting transition. Special use of soft colors, comfortable furniture, plants and pictures will help newcomers to "warm up" to the center. A partial barrier between the reception area and activities areas will provide emotional protection for visitors who want to observe the center before really entering it. This barrier can be constructed with a half-height stub wall or with placement of furniture. Furnish the reception area so that it is easily identifiable as such. This cues visitors regarding appropriate behavior (i.e., take a seat and wait). If there is no receptionist, provide a means such as a bell or buzzer for visitors to get the attention of staff.

The reception area can also be used as an educational center for visitors. Pictures of center activities, awards, articles about the center, monthly calendars and applicable licenses can be posted on a bulletin board or framed and hung on the wall. This is also a good place to display center brochures so visitors will take them.

The reception desk area can function well as the control center of the ADC program. Ideally, it should be large enough for several people, have sufficient lighting for the receptionist to do close work and adequate storage for paperwork. If a counter is used, it should be rounded to avoid potential accidents. A barrier should be provided around the desk or counter to provide separation from the rest of the reception area. This barrier should be high enough to provide privacy for a person seated at the work area, but low enough to allow that person visual supervision of surrounding areas. The reception area should include room for office equipment such as a typewriter, copy machine, computer, printer, and so forth. Locking storage should be provided, either in the reception area or in the director's office, for participant charts and billing records. Do not underestimate the amount of storage for this purpose, as medical and billing records must be kept for several years, depending on length of stay of each participant and legal requirements in your state.

Storage should also be provided near the reception area for several wheelchairs. Centers should keep one or two extra wheelchairs for use in the event that a participant becomes ill, or to evacuate slow-moving participants during fire drills. In addition, many people will use their own wheelchairs only for getting to and from the center. It will, therefore, be necessary to provide storage for these wheelchairs during the day.

Coat closets present a special design challenge. On the one hand, they should be located near the entry, to encourage family members to assist with taking off/putting on participants' coats. On the other hand, the coat closet should not be visible to participants during the day, as confused individuals often worry about leaving on time. In centers with visible coat closets, participants may get their coats and try to go home right after lunch. Others will continually rummage through the closet looking for their belongings. Several new centers are designing this area with some type of camouflage. Figure 5-3 illustrates an arrangement in which the coat closet is near the door, but not visible from activities areas. If it is not possible to have a special coat closet or individual lockers, a coat rack can work well. The rack should, however, be inaccessible to participants in much the same way as the coat closet.

Participants should have the right to use a phone during the day for emergency calls, for calls related to arranging services, and so forth. Since these calls will be infrequent, the receptionist's phone is usually used. Design the desk area to allow easy use of the phone by handicapped persons. (Note that for some confused participants, it may be necessary to monitor phone calls and gently limit excessive calls to family members.)

If possible, a restroom should be located near the entry.

Handicapped Accessibility

Access to the center should be safe and barrier-free. Some basic features of the handicapped-accessible environment include:

- Ramps with a slope no greater than one foot of rise per twelve feet of length

- Wheelchair turning space at least 5 feet by 5 feet in front of the entrance doors, in restrooms, and in other applicable places

- Door openings that are at least 32 inches wide

- Doors that can be opened with one motion and that will stay open until closed

- Thresholds level with the floor

- Lever-type controls for faucets, doors, etc.
  (Knobs can be used in areas not intended for participants.)

- At least 29 inches clearance underneath lavatories, and 27 inches clearance under tables and other work surfaces

- Grab bars or safety frames at all toilets

- Angled mirrors at sinks, to allow visual access by persons in wheelchairs

For more detailed information, consult the ANSI standards for handicapped accessibility.

Security Provisions

As much as possible, provide nonintrusive methods to prevent disoriented persons from wandering off. Some centers are designed with a wall, hallway, or other barrier between activities areas and the entry door. This will discourage wandering; however, if there is no receptionist, the doorway should be visually accessible to at least one staff office.

Doors not normally used can be disguised with screens or draperies. Be certain, however, that fire exits are not obstructed.

Some type of bell or warning system should be utilized at all entrances and exits normally used by participants. A string of temple bells or an old-fashioned shop-keeper's bell attached to the door are simple, noninstitutional alarm devices. They can be quite effective, if they can be heard throughout the center.

Some centers are now installing sensor panels at entrance doors, to alert staff when participants wander. An alarm in the sensor panel is activated when a confused person wearing a sensor bracelet attempts to exit. This is an effective method to ensure participants' safety and reduce staff time in supervising the door.

Large Group Activity Area

One large activity area should be planned to accommodate all the participants simultaneously for group activities such as community speakers, movies, and exercises. Sometimes, the dining area is designated to double as the only large activities area, however, this creates problems in scheduling and furniture placement. To facilitate maximum involvement of the greatest number of participants, the large activity area should be designed for an activities circle. This circular or semicircular arrangement of chairs, no more than two rows deep, allows everyone to see and hear relatively well. An 18-foot diameter circle will accommodate 25 to 30 participants. Allow a pathway on at least two sides of the circle for ease of movement within the center.

Some new centers are installing audio loops above the area of the activity circle, to promote inclusion of hard-of-hearing participants. Audio loops are a new technology that augments the function of participants' hearing aids when the speaker is using a microphone.

In using this large area, the key word is flexibility. The large group area functions as the hub of activity. It can provide room for adapted sports, space for several small group activities (especially if acoustical dividers are used), a place for participants to walk during the day, small conversational areas, or individual seating near windows so participants can observe outdoor activities. It is also used by visitors to observe the program in action.

This space should feel like home. It should allow as much natural lighting as possible, remembering that an older person's eyes need protection from the glare of sunlight. Adjustable blinds or fire retardant drapes over the windows will decrease glare. Lined draperies are also useful, to block out sunlight for movies and slide presentations. Low pile carpet, treated for stain resistance, pictures on the walls, and comfortable furniture are recommended. The furniture should promote as much independence as possible, and be appropriate for participants with vision and mobility problems. Chairs should have high backs and raised arms, and there should be a clear kick space below the front edge of the seat. Recliners are good, if the reclining mechanism is easy to operate by participants. It is most important that a fabric sling be provided between the front edge of the recliner seat and the foot rest. This will prevent confused participants from being injured in attempting to step through the space. For chairs, many colorful fabrics can now be specially treated and vinyl-laminated to protect from incontinence and wear. Due to the potential for falls, all furniture edges and corners should be rounded. Throughout the center, safety is always a consideration, so good arrangement of furniture, careful location of electrical cords and use of high-intensity, low-glare lighting is crucial. If fluorescent lighting is to be used, special "parabolic" filters can produce good quality light for older eyes. Heating, cooling, and ventilation systems should provide comfortable conditions, regardless of the number of people present. Excessive drafts should be avoided. Noise should be controlled through the use of acoustical ceiling tiles, partitions between activity areas, and separation of noisy rooms, such as the kitchen.

As the level of confusion increases in impaired people, they seem to experience a greater need for a feeling of open spaces and less confinement. This can be architecturally accommodated by raising the ceiling in the large activity area and by reducing clutter.

Older people require more fluids than they generally drink, so it may be helpful to include a water fountain in the large activity room.

Storage is a major issue throughout the center, but especially for activities areas. Much of the equipment used in activities requires large storage areas (beach balls, adapted sports equipment, quilting frames, books, games, bingo, prizes, seasonal decorations, theatrical props, movie projector, etc.)

Special Activities Rooms

If possible, space should be designed for a quiet activities room. It should be located off of the large activity area, with doors to allow privacy if needed. This room will be used for quiet activities such as puzzles and reading, and for small group discussions. Bookcases, card tables, and even a fireplace are conducive to a restful and quiet environment.

The quiet activites room can also be used for confused participants who require individual time away from the stimulation of the group. If such a room is not available, an office, conference room, or screened area of the large activities area can make do. Regardless of its design, staff should have some visual control of this area, in order to protect participants.

Ideally, there should be a separate room for crafts and other messy activities. This room should be located off of the main activity area, but visually accessible to it. The separate room allows for projects to be left out for participants to work on when they so desire. This, in turn, encourages self-directed activity with minimal staff involvement. It also allows participants to attempt projects that will take several weeks to complete. Such projects could, conceivably, be set up in the main activities room, but this results in a cluttered and distracting appearance.

The messy activities room should be as spill-proof, stain-proof, and dirt-proof as possible. Often, the tables are left covered with newspapers in preparation for painting, repotting plants, and similar activities. This area should include as much supplies storage as possible, natural lighting from windows or sky lights, and adequate tables and chairs for all who wish to participate. If ceramics are offered, the kiln should have its own, separate, locking room with shelves. This area is an ideal location for the recreation therapist's office—separate from activities, but visually accessible.

Food Service Area

The food service areas require special consideration. Ideally, the center should have its own kitchen and dining areas located adjacent to the activities areas. Where the center is colocated in a facility with other programs, the kitchen and dining area are often shared among programs. This may be a viable means of containing costs, however, it limits participants' helping with food preparation and service. Logistically, the shared food service area creates problems in meal counts and special diets and increases staff time in moving large groups of impaired people to other areas of the facility. The dining area should be able to seat all the participants at once, and should be large enough to allow ample room for wheelchair traffic. To calculate square footage, use the following guide:

- A 42 inch by 66 inch table seating six persons requires floor space of 9.5 feet by 11.5 feet

- A 36 inch square table seating four persons requires floor space of 9 feet by 9 feet

- A 48 inch round pedestal table seating five to six persons requires floor space of 9.5 feet by 9.5 feet

Dining tables should seat no more than six persons, to facilitate conversation among participants who have hearing loss. A round table with pedestal base is safer, as the table legs do not get in the way of wheelchairs. At least five to six feet should be provided for passageway between the tables. Dining chairs should be lightweight to provide ease in rearranging the room. Stackable chairs may be especially useful. At least half of the chairs should have arm rests to assist persons who have difficulty sitting down and standing up again.

Many centers cannot have a separate dining room, so other architectural features can be used to define dining space. Dropped ceilings edged with wood, wood beams on the ceiling, or a change in floor covering (in fact, many centers recommend tile or sheet flooring for the dining area) are all ways to divide this area. A few centers have tables that are stored in the ceiling and electronically lowered for meals.

The dining area is generally a good place to hang a large wall clock. It cues participants when meals are served. It also provides reality orientation, since most people associate meals with a certain time of day.

A staging area between the kitchen and dining room will assist staff, volunteers, and participants in serving meals. The staging area can be an extended counter, table, cart, or a pass-through shelf. Many participants can help to set the tables, fill water glasses, and assist in clean-up if this area is designed to facilitate these tasks.

Kitchen

The kitchen should have a residential appearance, not institutional, although if meals are prepared on-site, an institutional stove, sink, and dishwasher will be required. (Many health departments require a three- or four-part sink for clean-up, even if meals are prepared off-site.) Adequate lighting, nonslippery floors, preferably unwaxed and solid color, and sufficient storage are important. A walk-in pantry with shelves is ideal. A fire extinguisher should be located in or near the kitchen, and staff should be trained in its use. A phone is useful for staff, as the receptionist often helps with meal service. There should be a service entrance for deliveries, with a dumpster close by for trash pickup. A bulletin board provides a good central place to post participants' special diets, menus, snacks, and serving schedules.

Many centers plan therapeutic activities in the kitchen. This provides opportunities for impaired adults to learn new life skills, and socialize while using old ones. The greater the amount of work space (either tables or counters), the better. If confused participants use the kitchen, safety latches should be on all the cabinets, especially under the sink. Other measures should be taken to ensure that all dangerous equipment, cleaning compounds, and utensils are inaccessible.

Clinic and Rest Area

A separate room or area should be available for participants who become ill, disruptive, or require rest. Often, this room is equipped with beds. It should be located away from the activities areas and near to a restroom and the nurse's office. Ideally, a handicapped shower is adjacent to this room, to serve incontinent participants. Shelves or cubbies for participants' changes of clothing should be located near this area. A locked medication cabinet/closet should be nearby. A storage area is important to store clinic and first aid supplies and other personal care or nursing supplies.

Physical therapy, speech therapy, and occupational therapy can be conducted in this room, depending on furnishings and equipment. Often, this room can also function as a treatment room for podiatrists, medical consultants, and similar people.

Restrooms

The National Institute on Adult Daycare recommends that each facility have a minimum of one toilet available for every ten participants in attendance (NIAD 1984). Experience has shown, however, that due to the special needs of participants, more toilets are often advisable. The problem is aggravated by the fact that participants tend to cluster at the restrooms during breaks between activities.

The restrooms should be located as close to the activity areas as possible (preferably no more than 40 feet from activities). Some centers use color coding for the men's and women's restrooms, starting in the corridor and leading to painted doors. Another method to assist participants in finding their way is the use of gender pictures and lettered signs on the doors.

All restrooms should be handicapped-accessible, and should be equipped with call bells for emergencies. Ideally, the restroom entrance should have no doors, only vision screens (see Figure 5-4). If this is not possible, doorways should at least be handicapped-accessible. Additionally, to provide ease in cleaning, the toilets should be wall-mounted, partitions

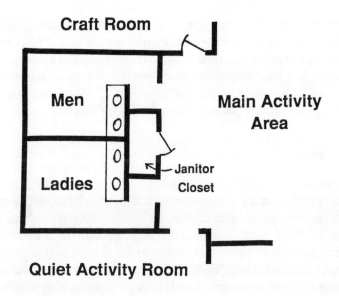

Figure 5-4 Floor Plan for Restrooms. Source: Lincolnia Adult Day Care Center, Fairfax County, Virginia. Architect Cohen-Karydas & Associates. (Used with permission)

between stalls should be ceiling-mounted, and floors should slope toward a drain. A good ventilation system is especially important in this area.

It is advisable to provide a seating area near the restroom entrance, in case participants must wait. Within the restroom, or close to it, there should be a place to store equipment and supplies necessary to assist incontinent people. Janitorial storage should be near to maintain the sanitation of restrooms, as well.

Offices

The number of offices or staff work spaces will vary in each center because the services offered vary. At minimum, the director should have a private office. Personnel records, program financial data, and other relevant information should be filed in the director's office. Ideally, the nurse, social worker, and recreation therapist or activity director should also have their own office space. The staff offices should have good visual access to entry/

exit doors and activity areas. They should be furnished comfortably and have sufficient storage cabinets to keep pertinent files and equipment.

Therapists or other consultants should have access to a desk and phone located in a quiet area. This does not, however, have to be a separate office. Families will also need space for counseling, education, and similar situations. Office space can easily be adapted for this use.

Staff Lounge

The stress involved in providing care to impaired adults is extremely high. Staff need an area to get away from it all. This area should be removed from the activity areas, and should be comfortably furnished. If staff meetings are held here, it should be large enough to accommodate a conference table and chairs, in addition to the rest area. If possible, staff should have individual mail slots, locked storage spaces, a coat closet, and a separate employee restroom. A staff bulletin board is also helpful in this area.

Porch

Although a screened-in porch, covered patio or sun room is not essential to a quality center, it does add a special dimension to the program. It enables participants to enjoy fresh air in a controlled environment. It allows the staff to provide programs outside, and encourages socializing and visiting in small groups. This type of room is also helpful in relieving restlessness found in many persons with dementia. A closet for exterior maintenance supplies and equipment such as rakes and hoses should be designed close to this area.

Storage

A truism in designing ADC centers is that it is impossible to build too much storage space. When designing room layouts, it is often hard to imagine the sheer volume of items necessary to day care programming that require storage. The following check list indicates some of these items and the areas in which they may be stored:

- Near entry

    Wheelchairs

    Coats

- Reception area

    Office machines (typewriter, copier, etc.)

    Office supplies

    Participant files

    Billing information

- Director's office

    Personnel files

    Program planning files and books

- Nursing office or clinic area

    Medications and nursing supplies

    Linens

    Therapy supplies and extra canes, walkers, and so on

- Social worker's office area

    Information on community services

    Supplies for family support groups

- Near activities area

    Activities supplies and equipment

- Kitchen

    Food for meals, snacks, and/or cooking club

    Equipment and supplies for food preparation,

        storage, service, and clean-up

- Near restrooms

  Storage for extra participant clothing

  Cleaning supplies and equipment

  Paper goods for restrooms

- Near service entrance

  Exterior maintenance supplies and equipment

  Gardening supplies and equipment

Environmental Aids

There are numerous environmental aids that assist in keeping the confused participants oriented to person, place, and time, including clocks, calendars, bulletin boards, and directional signs.

An environmental aid that is sometimes debated is color usage in the walls, floors, and furnishings. The colors that are easiest for older eyes to see are reds, oranges, and magentas. The color combinations that are easiest to see are those that are high-contrast. On the other hand, pastels in the blue, green, and brown ranges provide a calming influence for anxious or agitated persons. These two principles (visual ease vs. emotional impact) are not necessarily in opposition. For example, if dining tables are surfaced with pastel blue Formica, many participants will have difficulty seeing the edges of a white dinner plate. Introducing strong tone contrast, but keeping the blue theme could be accomplished with navy place mats. This would allow the overall color effect to be calming, while ensuring accessibility for low-vision persons. Understanding the effects of color allows ADC planners to make more informed interior design decisions, based on the types of participants served and the atmosphere most desired.

The Best Design for Adult Day Care

Many of the suggestions presented here are recommendations for approaching the "ideal" ADC environment. No center, however, is able to incorporate all of these principles in a single setting. When designing a new adult day care center or a renovation, considerations such as the characteristics of the population to be served, the projected functions of the environment, and the desired ambiance should be major factors in the decision-making process. Limiting factors, on the other hand, may include budget, existing structural features, and so forth. The best design process is to find a balance between what is ideal and what can be done.

References

National Institute on Adult Daycare. 1984. *Standards for adult day care.* Washington, DC: National Council on the Aging.

Von Behren, R., and A. Gould. 1985. *Adult day health care policies and procedures manual.* San Francisco: On Lok Senior Health Services.

Further Readings

American Institute of Architects (AIA). 1985. *Design for aging: An architect's guide.* Washington, DC: AIA Press.

American National Standards Institute (ANSI). 1980. *Specifications for making buildings and facilities accessible to and usable by physically handicapped people.* New York: ANSI.

Ansak, M. L., and R. Lindheim. 1983. *On Lok housing and adult day health care for the frail elderly.* San Francisco: On Lok Senior Health Services.

Aranyi, L., and L. Goldman. 1980. *Design of long-term care facilities.* New York: Van Nostrand Reinhold Company.

Architectural and Transportation Barriers Compliance Board (ATBCB), et al. 1984. *Uniform Federal Accessibility Standards.* Washington, DC: ATBCB.

Architectural and Transportation Barriers Compliance Board (ATBCB), 1980. *Resource guide to literature on barrier-free environments.* Washington, DC: ATBCB.

Gelwicks, L. and R. Newcomer. 1974. *Planning housing environments for the elderly.* Washington, DC: National Council on the Aging.

Padula, H. 1983. Physical Facility in *Developing adult day care.* Washington, DC: National Council on the Aging.

Panella, J. Jr. 1987. Physical Facilities in *Day care programs for Alzheimer's disease and related disorders.* New York: Demos Publications.

Raschko, B. 1982. *Housing interiors for the disabled and elderly.* New York: Van Nostrand Reinhold Company.

Robinette, G. 1983. *Barrier-free exterior design: Anyone can go anywhere.* New York: Van Nostrand Reinhold Company.

CHAPTER 6

Transportation

Paul D. Maginn

Transportation is a headache. It is expensive. It is difficult to administer. But it is vital. Adult day care programs have failed because they afforded no reliable way for disabled people to get to the center and home again (Padula 1983, 30).

How true Helen Padula's words are! Transportation is, at one and the same time, the boon and the bane of adult day care. This chapter will assist center directors with some ideas on how they might better utilize their present transportation system, as well as provide some answers for those in the midst of planning an adult day care transportation system. One of the first things the planner will note is the lack of any in-depth information on transportation for adult day care. It is noted in several publications as being essential, but only briefly described.

The national survey of adult day care centers (Von Behren 1986, 19) revealed a high number of centers providing transportation. According to the study, transportation was provided by staff in 56% of the centers. An additional 32% of the centers reported contracting for transportation, while 10% referred participants to transportation providers in the community. The staff at many ADCs agree that transportation is an essential part of adult day care.

Planning

Planning is the key to success for persons exploring the development of adult day care services in their community. Several important factors are

61

parts of the planning process: community needs assessment, analysis of your organization's needs and resources, description of the population to be served, size of the adult day care center, the geographic area to be served, and the mission and philosophy of the sponsoring organization(s).

All of these factors have an impact on how an organization can respond to the challenge of transportation for adult day care. *The Standards for Adult Day Care* (National Institute on Adult Daycare 1984, 22) describe the target population of day care centers as including "adults with physical, emotional or mental impairment who require assistance and supervision ... [and/or] adults who need restorative or rehabilitative services in order to achieve the optimum level of functioning." While the population served will vary according to the identified community need and the goals, resources and capability of the organization providing the service, adult day care serves a frail, dependent, home-bound population in need of assistance and supervision. How to transport this population from their own homes to a center becomes the key question.

To Provide, Contract, or Refer

A center must decide whether to directly provide transportation, contract for this service, or refer clients to community transportation programs. There are pros and cons with each arrangement.

The question of transportation as a program service should not be viewed solely from the focus of an organization's available resources. Rather, the first question should involve the community's need and existing community resources. Once community need and resources have been identified and defined, the adult day care planner will have a clearer idea of the need for transportation and how the center can respond.

There are several options available to the center in providing transportation to an individual participant. The center may provide transportation directly by staff or volunteers, contract with a transportation vendor, refer the need to a community provider, or have family or caregivers provide.

No one option is without its problems. The latter two options, if chosen, leave the center at considerable risk for attendance problems and difficulty of administering its daily schedule of activities, interventions, and events. The best intentioned families/caregivers have unplanned interruptions. Community transportation providers (cabs, city bus, etc.) frequently are unwilling or not equipped to meet the assistance and supervision needs of the adult day care population. Even local transit programs primarily serving the handicapped and elderly have limitations on the degree of service they are able to provide (i.e., curb-to-curb service rather than assistance out of and into the home). Many of these limitations stem from union rules and a concern for liability costs.

The question of transportation most frequently comes down to a choice between the center providing transportation directly or via a contractual agreement with a public or private vendor. As noted before, neither option is problem-free. Figure 6-1 notes some of the pros and cons of these two options.

Integrating Transportation into Program Services

Planners should look at how to integrate transportation into the total range of services provided. Not only is transportation linked to attendance, but it also directly impacts on participation and programming. Many scheduled activities have been interrupted or had limited attendance because of a vehicle running late. Similarly, a large bus run may take longer, unduly tiring participants, reducing time at the center, and reducing enthusiastic participation.

Scheduling transportation becomes of primary importance in avoiding some of the pitfalls associated with getting frail, impaired individuals from home to the center and back. Proper scheduling must consider the participant's needs while limiting the time of the trip to between 30 and 45 minutes, *and* remaining cost-effective. Short trips are important because of participants' generally low endurance and their high probability of needing a restroom. The National Institute on Adult Daycare's (NIAD) *Standards for Adult Day Care* note that trips should not last more than 60 minutes (NIAD 1984, 38). Medium-sized busses work well when individuals are grouped by location, ensuring a run near capacity, while limiting run time. Four-door station wagons work very well for picking up individuals living outside the parameters of the bus run. Prior planning should involve determination of the radius of transportation services offered. As attendance patterns change, so will the bus runs and the individual transportation offered.

Drivers can be observant about the participants in their home settings. Drivers are frequently able to identify problems before other staff members suspect that anything is amiss. The information drivers share can lead to

Staff Provided

Pros

- Ability to schedule and provide transportation enhances the center's programming

- Center activities are scheduled around the van run facilitating participant usage and staffing

- Maintain census close to capacity enhancing cost-effective delivery of service

- Trained drivers provide reliable, safe transportation and are linked with participant's family/caretaker/home situation

- Transportation can be more easily integrated into the program

Cons

- Expense of vehicles (purchase price, maintenance, gasoline)

- Drivers' salaries as well as expenses associated with recruitment/retention, training

- Limited radius of service due to expense concerns

- Length of travel time

Contracted

Pros

- Leave the hassles of weather, vehicles and maintenance, etc., to others

- Cost/benefit analysis—less expensive than staff provided

- Contractual agreement with terms to be met

Cons

- Unplanned interruptions

- Willingness and/or ability of staff to provide needed service

- Staff ability to assess participant needs and provide motivation to attend

- Ability to find suitable, reliable vendor

- Cost/benefit analysis—more expensive than staff provided

- Length of travel time

Figure 6–1 Pros and cons of two transportation systems.

early intervention or immediate referral regarding the need observed. As an example, at one center, a transportation attendant went to pick up Mrs. S one morning. He saw that Mrs. S was uncustomarily weak and disoriented, and discovered that she had turned the furnace pilot light so low that it had gone out during the night. This was in the midst of a Nebraska winter. Upon arrival at the center, Mrs. S was found to be suffering from hypothermia. Following care by the center's nurse and some special instructions regarding the pilot light, Mrs. S could safely return home. In numerous other examples, the drivers' observations have alerted day care staff to the need for safety measures (railings or wheelchair ramps) and to the need for supervision in the home (stove burners being left on or deteriorating living conditions).

Adult day care serves a frail, dependent population. Drivers who are trained, observant, and sympathetic can provide assistance to those in need and reassurance to the confused or anxious participant. Their role is frequently one of motivation and encouragement to individuals, resulting in a positive impact on attendance. (This is a fact frequently not quantifiable for evaluation and unfortunately too often taken for granted by other staff.) Drivers should have special training in responding to emergencies, as they often are alone with several participants for extended periods. During the afternoon bus run for one center one of the participants began choking on a piece of hard candy. The driver quickly brought the vehicle to a safe stop, rushed to the back of the bus, and successfully applied the Heimlich maneuver to dislodge the candy. The participant was comforted and returned to the center for evaluation by the nurse.

To maintain a cost-effective approach to transportation, some programs assign driving responsibilities to staff who also provide other essential functions, such as program aide, activity coordinator, or social worker. This type of arrangement may soon lead to problems as the number of participants increases and staff members are needed on-site full time. A better arrangement is to employ staff members whose primary function is transportation. Many programs employ part-time transportation staff who work split shifts—on several hours in the morning, off for a few hours, followed by several hours of work in the afternoon.

In adult day care centers with a strong health focus, transportation staff may justify more than part-time status by providing additional transportation for participants to get to medical appointments and other community errands. Use of staff to provide such transportation ensures that the individual is provided the assistance needed and keeps the scheduled appointment. In addition, transportation staff can act as intermediary between the nurse and family or physician to encourage intervention or resolution of needs. Some centers have developed transportation services for handicapped adults or elderly persons not involved in the day care center. This makes efficient use of drivers' "down time" and generates additional revenue. This service can be effectively offered on an appointment basis for medical, grocery shopping, and other community errands (McAuley Bergan Center 1987).

Whatever the decision of an individual center regarding transportation, bringing participants to and from the center will involve scheduling, communication, and problem-solving on an on-going basis.

Recruiting and Training of Drivers

Transportation has an immediate and direct impact on programming and attendance in adult day care. Drivers should be an integral part of a center's staffing pattern. Therefore, care should be taken regarding recruiting, training, and retaining qualified transportation staff. Skills in communication, human relations, observation, and defensive driving are prerequisites for transportation staff. Some centers in areas with significant elderly populations have had great success employing older workers for the transportation staff. In areas with colleges or universities, centers have successfully employed students. Do not overlook the availability of retired military, Veterans' Administration, or federal service employees. Frequently, the mature worker brings years of experience, skill, and employment stability to a work situation where communication and developing familiarity are essential.

Training resources in driving, first aid, CPR, and vehicle safety are available in most communities through the Safety Council, American Red Cross, American Heart Association, local school district, or the metro transit system. At the state level, the Department of Roads may offer training in defensive driving and vehicle safety.

Volunteers Versus Paid Staff

The question of using volunteers to provide transportation, either in total or as a supplement to paid staff, is worth consideration and review. Inevitably, the question of liability arises and can only be answered adequately by discussion with an insurance agent or the state insurance commissioner. The day care planner should give careful consideration to the daily schedule of the center, the needs of participants, and the special assistance that might be required, before utilizing volunteers as drivers. Volunteers can also perform an essential service of being an attendant on the center's bus run. Monitoring riders during pick-up stops and assisting the driver in emergencies are important functions.

Volunteers play a particularly important role in rural and specialized transportation, nationally, according to the Rural Transportation Reporter (RTR) (1986, 7–10). Private, nonprofit agencies constitute 84% of the 4400 transit systems receiving assistance through the Urban Mass Transit Act. Many of these systems rely on volunteers to transport clients, schedule rides, dispatch drivers, and raise money.

Resources

Community-based rural and specialized transportation systems represent the fastest growing segment of the transit industry today. Community transportation, which has developed from local cooperative efforts and from the social service arena, is the most dynamic sector within the public transit industry today. Included in the more than $1.9 billion spent annually is a combination of federal, state, and local support. More than 50% of the funds come from programs administered by departments of the federal government, such as the U.S. Department of Health and Human Services, Medicaid, the Administration on Aging, and Head Start. Approximately 7% of the total funding comes from the Urban Mass Transit Act (UMTA). Section 18 of the act provides public transportation funding for rural areas. Section 16(b)(2) provides capital assistance for elderly and handicapped transportation. It is the latter that can be a significant resource for most adult day care centers deciding to directly provide transportation (RTR 1986, 9–12).

In 1970, Section 16(a) of the Urban Mass Transit Act established a national policy that the elderly and handicapped have the same right as other persons to utilize mass transportation services, that availability of service would be ensured, and that federal mass transportation assistance programs would implement this policy. In 1973, Section 16(b)(2) authorized capital assistance grants to private, nonprofit corporations to provide transportation to the elderly and handicapped where mass transportation services were unavailable, insufficient, or inappropriate. UMTA has continued this policy to date. In spite of federal cutbacks in funding for many social services, UMTA Section 16(b)(2) funding has increased each year. The 1987 fiscal year appropriation was $35 million (a 2% increase over the previous year) (Rucker 1986, 4).

Exploration of existing UMTA funds in your state can be an excellent resource for nonprofit adult day care centers. Section 16(b)(2) provides funds toward the purchase of vehicles and equipment to be used for the transportation of the elderly and handicapped. In most states, these funds are administered by the State Department of Roads. Annually, the department announces the availability of funds and outlines the application process. Generally, this application process involves working with the local or regional planning commission in the area to ensure that the service fits in with local transportation needs and services. In many large cities, the local metropolitan transit system is represented on this commission and may, in fact, be the coordinating agency for monitoring of Section 16(b)(2) activity. With approval of the local planning group, the application goes on to the Department of Roads. It is then incorporated into the State Plan for that fiscal year. The State Plan, in turn, is submitted to the regional UMTA office for final approval.

An additional UMTA resource is the newly formed Rural Transit Assistance Program's (RTAP) National Resource Center in Washington, DC. The resource center is a national clearinghouse providing information and assistance on rural and specialized transportation. For information on transportation planning, funding, management, operations, training, coordination, and other technical assistance, call the RTAP Hotline at (800) 527-8279.

Section 16(b)(2) of UMTA provides capital assistance funding on an 80%/20% match, with the local organization picking up the 20% from its own budget. Included under capital assistance are vehicles, accessory items, wheelchair lifts, and two-way radios. In some cases, the metro transit system may provide its radio frequency for emergency use of the two-way radio. An enterprising adult day care program may be able to justify its own dispatch system or work out a cooperative agreement with an existing radio dispatch system. Either arrangement will enhance ability to provide safe, reliable, low-cost service.

In addition to UMTA funds, there are other resources that should be explored, including foundations and the United Way. While foundations are frequent resources for meeting community needs, apparently most receive few applications to fund transportation (RTR 1986, 8–11). See Appendix C for a list of specialized libraries that can assist you in locating foundations that may be interested in receiving a proposal for transportation funding.

Frequently, transportation expenditures by foundations may be hidden in other grants. Further, most foundations do not want to fund operating expenses. With that in mind, an adult day care planner interested in transportation might approach a foundation for seed money for a demonstration project, funds for coordination of existing transportation, or, where appropriate, request the 20% match for UMTA funding.

One of the nation's largest voluntary philanthropic organizations, the United Way, may be an available resource for day care programs. Traditionally, United Way has been involved in special transportation and/or the needs of the handicapped and elderly (Manlove 1986, 12–13). As part of its 1987 centennial, United Way has taken a more aggressive stance as a catalyst for resolving community human-care problems and is developing a more flexible fund distribution system to respond to changing issues. The increasing need for adult day care would seem to be of interest to a local United Way chapter. Now may be a particularly opportune time to build a relationship with United Way.

With all of the resources noted, beginning exploration as soon as possible is imperative. All resources have criteria for eligibility, a calendar for consideration of applications, and a set funding cycle. Fast action is not the norm; and funding a request may take a year or more from the time of application.

Using Existing Resources

Some communities may have additional resources that planners should explore. School system transportation programs may be able to provide some assistance, depending on existing rules and regulations. Many area agencies on aging provide or contract for transportation, and may be a valuable resource for transporting participants. Larger communities may have several taxi cab systems. One or more of these may have a contract to provide transportation to Department of Social Services clients. Many states provide Title XX (social service) or Title XIX (Medicaid) funding to transport clients to medical or health-related appointments. Adult day care would meet these criteria. As noted earlier, any of these arrangements may present problems for programming and attendance. In some cases, however, the adult day care center may have no other choice.

Families sometimes choose to provide transportation to and/or from the center in spite of other potential arrangements. Sometimes, this is a matter of geography or finances. The center may not provide transportation to some neighborhoods, or the additional cost of paying for transportation may be more than the family can afford. In other instances, family caregivers may work, and it is more convenient for them to transport their relative on the way to and from their jobs. Finally, some families prefer driving the participant, either to ensure safety or to obtain a more convenient schedule of participation.

Insurance

In an age of litigation and liability, insurance for transportation is frequently a key issue. At least 48 states have adopted two insurance rate classifications for human service transportation providers. Developed by the insurance industry and the federal government, the regulations allow local programs to purchase, at a low cost:

- Liability insurance for vehicles owned, operated, or leased to the agency conducting the program

- Excess liability insurance for vehicles owned, operated, or leased to the agency conducting the program

- Excess liability insurance for both the agency and vehicle owner when vehicles owned by full- and part-time agency employees or volunteers are used to transport program participants (Padula 1983, 105).

Each state has a department on insurance and an insurance commissioner. Adult day care centers interested in current information on liability insurance should contact their state insurance commissioner as part of their overall planning process. As you conclude your exploration of transportation, what will your decision be? Reflect on Helen Padula's words, whether you decide to directly provide or contract. Transportation is vital to adult day care.

References

Manlove, J. 1986. United Ways—A new commitment to transportation. *Rural Transportation Reporter* 4(10): 12–13.

McAuley Bergan Center. 1987. *Community connection transportation.* Omaha: McAuley Bergan Center.

National Institute on Adult Daycare. 1984. *Standards for adult day care.* Washington, DC: National Council on the Aging.

Padula, H. 1983. *Developing adult day care.* Washington, DC: National Council on the Aging.

Rucker, G. 1986. Community transit gets increases. *Rural Transportation Reporter* 4(9): 4.

Price, B. R. 1986. Start-up steps for volunteer programs. *Rural Transportation Reporter* 4(5): 7–10.

Price, B. R. 1986. Foundations and transportation: Current funding, future prospects. *Rural Transportation Reporter* 4 (7): 8–11.

Price, B. R. 1986. Community transportation: A growth industry. *Rural Transportation Reporter* 4 (8): 9–12.

Von Behren, R. 1986. *Adult day care in America: Summary of a national survey.* Washington, DC: National Council on the Aging.

CHAPTER 7

Staffing Considerations

Marianne Rawack Brannon

Various factors affect the staffing of an adult day care center. The philosophy of the organization and the type of participant expected to attend are crucial to development of staffing patterns. Local licensing rulings will also have to be considered when staffing the center. Most centers will have to adhere to a tight budget, but it is important that quality of care not be compromised. Finally, employment rates in some areas will affect the range of people available to provide needed duties.

General Requirements for Adult Day Care Staff

Staff preparation and background will have to take into consideration the wide scope of participants' needs. Participants in existing centers vary in their physical and mental states. Participants may be alert, or they may suffer from slight to severe dementias. Some may be suffering from schizophrenia or other mental illnesses. Physical ailments may run the gamut from cardiac conditions, which limit endurance, to severe handicaps, which prevent the person from performing his/her own activities of daily living (ADLs). Each of these participants requires different caregiving skills.

Staffing will set the ambiance of the center as much as the center's financial structure. Many adult day care centers are geared to an older population. In the selection of staff, therefore, the attitude of the prospective staff person toward aging and disabilities will have to be taken into consideration. Beware of staff attitudes such as those of people who:

- "Just love" old people. A true caring about elders is important. An overly sweet statement of love, however, can mask unresolved feelings about the individual's own family members.

- Want to "mother" the participants. This may lead to an approach of babying people, rather than encouraging them to be as independent as possible. Older persons are often treated as children and not given credit for the abilities they still possess because of other skills that have been lost.

- Display fear of the aging/frail population because of anxiety about what will eventually happen in their own lives.

Identifying such factors in the process of staff selection can help to prevent problems that will lead to constant staff turnover.

Personal flexibility is one of the most important qualities of good adult day care staff. Budgets are usually limited, and it is imperative that staff be able to function as an overlapping team. Often, the nursing staff is involved in toileting while aides and the social worker are serving a meal. It is therefore imperative that *all* staff be capable of employing the Heimlich maneuver and other types of first aid. Anyone in the center may have to help with serving food and cleaning up. Staff members may need to assist in ambulation, although their training before joining the center has not prepared them for that task.

Naturally, anyone employed to work with the adult day care population has to be a "people person." This is important, not only for caregiving staff, but also for clerical staff. In most centers, the clerical staff does interact with the participants. This may happen when participants visit with the receptionist at the door, or when the secretary helps with serving meals. Clerical staff who are encouraged to have this interaction will gain a greater investment in the center's success. Any of the support staff should be able and willing to step into a gap to work with the participants.

People of all ages can be excellent staff members. In general, participants seem to show no preference for people of any given age, and relate well to all of them.

When choosing staff, try to avoid individuals who are "fast movers" and like to get things done in a hurry. The type of participants served in adult day care tend to move slowly and may have to be assisted in moving. This can be extremely frustrating to the "speedy" personality.

Staff Orientation

A newly opening center should seek staff training from an existing center. At a minimum, the center's managers should spend some time in a functioning center. More and more established centers are offering consulting and training assistance for a reasonable hourly fee. If time is available, it would be advantageous for the ancillary staff to get similar exposure.

During the center's first few staff meetings, make time for each professional to explain the functions that his/her discipline serves.

As staff is hired, some of the topics to address in training sessions are the philosophy of the center, funding, general policies and procedures, specific information about particular disabilities, physical management of day care participants, psychological approaches, how to interact with the elderly, working with sensory deprivation in participants, safety measures, and fire escape procedures.

New employees should have the opportunity to observe all the disciplines—nursing, social services, activities, and therapies. This observation will be valuable when they have to assist in a setting other than the one for which they were hired. It will also help new employees to participate in care planning or case discussions.

Staff will need continuing in-service education on an ongoing basis. That education may include speakers from various community agencies. Some of these agencies may want to use the center's services or they may be current referral sources. Asking these outside agencies to provide education will make common interests apparent and help overcome some of the stumbling blocks in smooth service delivery. Speakers may also be drawn from contract personnel, who can talk about new methods of handling specific diagnoses. Safety practices, hygiene, and experiences of other centers may be additional items of interest.

The Staffing Pattern

The National Institute on Adult Daycare's Standards (1984, 28–33) outline minimal criteria for staffing patterns. The minimum recommended staff-participant ratio is one to eight. Programs with a high percentage of severely impaired participants should have a smaller staff-participant ratio of one to five. As the types and numbers of services provided increase, the number of staff should also increase. Staff time counted toward this ratio should include only that time spent in direct service with participants, not administrative or other duties. Importantly, volunteers can be included in the staff ratio only when they conform to the same standards and requirements as paid staff. The NIAD standards also state that there should be at least two responsible persons at the center at all times when there are participants in attendance. One of these people should be a staff member. This is the case even if there are only a total of two participants in the center. In an emergency, one staff member could attend to the participant in trouble, while the other person would be able to call for help and supervise the remaining participant(s). Finally, each center that is located in a facility with another service, such as a day care center located in a nursing home or hospital, should have its own separate, identifiable staff.

Many states now have regulations that govern staffing patterns in adult day care centers. See Figure 3-1 for more information. See Appendix F for sample job descriptions and an organizational chart.

The Role of the Director

The program director is needed to keep the diverse parts of the day care center functioning in unison. The individual disciplines (nursing, social work, etc.) are so different that they may have difficulty understanding each other's needs. There may be rivalry among personnel. Someone has to have final decision-making power when divergent opinions impinge on the center's smooth functioning. The director has to be someone who is comfortable with conflict. The director also has to make sure that all the rules and regulations are followed and that the paperwork flows smoothly.

The director should be flexible. In small or newly starting centers, it may often fall to the director to function as the center's "fill in person." When staff is short, the director may have to act as program aide, help out in the kitchen when meals are served, be the emergency plumber when the toilet overflows, or call 911 while the nursing staff is busy with the accident victim and the secretary has just left for lunch.

Budget knowledge and fiscal responsibility are important to the function of the director. The director should be able to prepare a budget, either alone or in conjunction with the accountant, administration, and/or the board of directors. The director has to be able to say "no" to requests that do not fit into a tight budget and must occasionally make unpopular decisions when cutbacks are required by monetary problems.

A program director should have an administrative and/or supervisory background. Prior professional functioning in a multidisciplinary team setting will help the director set the tone for the program. Many health and social services workers have not had that experience, so the director will be a unique individual. Community health experience, such as working for a health department, home health agency, or community clinic provides valuable experience. The director who has this experience can help the staff to understand situations facing the participants and their families, and will round out the staff's expertise. The director should be skilled in facilitating group meetings, since leading both staff meetings and care planning discussions are management responsibilities.

Larger programs also have an assistant director to help with the director's responsibilities and to fill in when the director is absent from the facility. If program size does not justify an assistant, the director should appoint a staff person to take over during any absence.

The Role of the Nurse

The amount of nursing time needed will vary from one adult day care center to the next. The position of registered nurse may be a full-time position, or one of a consulting nature. It will be an advantage if the nurses have had public health experience, as that will help when working with family and physicians. Some programs will supplement professional nursing time with certified nurse aides and/or medication technicians.

The professional nurse should make an initial assessment of the participant's health status, and repeat this assessment at scheduled points in time. The nurse will continuously monitor participant's medical conditions and report problem situations to physicians, and may coordinate ongoing review of participants' care plans. Nursing staff will distribute medications or assist the participants in managing their own. Some participants may need assistance in making appointments for medical care. Many families will need to be educated about the individual's health care needs. The nurse will be responsible for general nursing treatments and responding to medical emergencies. Personal hygiene and management of incontinency problems are further tasks for nursing. Since elderly individuals often have difficulty swallowing, some centers have a nurse in attendance at meals in case of choking.

Some services, such as nursing treatments, may be less emphasized in certain centers. Other services, such as personal care, can be delegated to nurse aides. Each program should design its own nursing staff to be able to adequately respond to the needs of persons admitted to the center.

The Role of the Social Worker

In small programs, a social worker may also perform the director's role. As the center grows, however, it will become increasingly necessary to employ a full-time professional social worker. The social worker should have at least a BSW degree and professional experience in a social work position. Some programs also employ LCSWs or MSWs, either on a staff basis or on a part-time contract basis.

The position of the social worker in the adult day care setting is a complex one. At the time of referral of a prospective participant, the social worker will begin an evaluation of the individual's appropriateness for admission. The assessment of the direct needs of the prospective participant, as well as those of the caregiver, will help to determine whether the participant and/or family is in need of the services that the center has to offer. If the participant cannot be accepted into the center, the social worker will make a referral to a more suitable setting. If an applicant is admitted, the social worker will discuss discharge plans with the caregivers so that they are aware of the center's service limitations.

The social worker, by being the client's initial contact, will have an advantage of getting to know the family more than the rest of the staff. It will fall to the social worker to explain the participant's background and status to the staff. During the participant's stay, the social worker will perform reassessments and join in the discussion at care planning conferences.

The social worker can also offer support groups for the participants. These groups may be oriented to assisting participants in emotionally adapting to functional limitations, or the groups may focus on enriching participants' lives. Individual counseling may be needed. Counseling may be provided by the social worker or by referral to a licensed counselor or psychologist. In some settings, the social worker may also lead support groups for the staff.

The Role of the Activities Staff

The activities program is probably the heart of the center. It is through therapeutic programming that most participants will be able to progress toward the goals established in their care plans. The therapeutic activities setting will be explored in depth in Chapter Thirteen.

Ideally, the activity director should hold a degree in Recreation Therapy or a related field, and should have experience in therapeutic recreation for the aged and handicapped. The activity director should have good organizational skills and a rich imagination to design activities that meet each participant's needs. This person will also need good supervisory abilities to manage assistants, aides, and volunteers.

The activity director's position should be augmented by assistants and aides, depending on the size and type of participant population. As an example, the Elderday Adult Day Health Care Center serves 40 to 49 participants and provides 44 hours of activities staffing per day. This coverage is accomplished with one full-time activities director; one full-time assistant; two activities aides, each at six hours per day; and four senior volunteers, each at four hours per day.

The activities staff leads groups ranging in size from four to 49 people. Small groups are led in discussion, larger groups play games, and the largest groups are led in music and parties. The activity staff, therefore, has to be very adaptable. Any of them must be able, at a moment's notice, to switch attention from a group to an individual who is disturbed or agitated. Frequently, activities staff is also called upon to help participants in the bathroom.

The Role of Therapists

Physical therapist (PT), occupational therapist (OT), and speech therapist (ST) involvement with participants varies among centers. In some programs, the therapy role is exclusively in the functional assessment of participants. In others, the PT or OT may consult on development of group exercise. In still others, the PT, OT, and ST may all be part of an intensive program of rehabilitation for selected individuals. At times, the therapist may make home visits to assess problems encountered there. The therapist will also communicate with prior therapy providers and with the patient's physician. The PT and OT assess the new participant upon admission and at reassessment. The therapists write their treatment plan and carry it out, with the help of ancillary staff.

To have all therapy hours delivered by the registered therapist can be extremely expensive. To maximize use of the therapist's time, two or three staff members may be delegated to deliver the required services during the therapist's presence. Each therapist's hour can thus be made to count double or triple. Naturally, the therapist is responsible for the quality of services delivered. The PT/OT trains each new staff member. The therapist is also available on premises while therapy is delivered. This enables staff to call on the registered professional whenever need arises.

The Medical Director

Rarely are physician services provided at the adult day care center. Most new applicants to the center will already have their own family doctors, and should be encouraged to maintain that relationship. Staff can then communicate with a physician who has known the patient for some time.

It will also be advisable for the center to have a medical director to consult in developing policies and procedures and to provide guidance to the staff. This guidance can be through informal consultations or through formal review of participants' charts. The medical director may also interact with the participant's own doctor when there is a need. There may be situations, for example, in which the participant's personal physician is not available to the staff, or times when the ADC center's desired course of treatment is not to the family physician's liking. In some cases, it may be appropriate for the medical director to take personal responsibility for the diagnosis and treatment of specific participants. In this case, the participant can become a patient in the medical director's private practice.

In some centers, the medical director is a psychiatrist who consults with the family doctors in the management of demented participants. The medical director lays out guidelines for psychotropic medications, but never prescribes without the family doctor's knowledge and agreement. In centers serving a high percentage of persons with strokes or orthopedic problems, a physician specializing in rehabilitation medicine (physiatrist) could serve as medical director.

Many professional and support services can be provided directly by staff, or contracted through other organizations. These may include accounting, dietitian services, meal preparation, therapy, psychological counseling, janitorial services, and others.

Other Staff

Other staff include the secretary/receptionist, driver, nurse aides, activity aides, custodian, and possibly additional persons. Such staff may come to the program with prior training, or they may be trained by current staff to serve the center's specific needs. It is especially important that these staff members be flexible, as they are frequently called upon to function outside their "normal" responsibilities.

The secretary/receptionist is a good example of the need for flexibility. This individual must monitor whether or not paperwork required from other staff (i.e., progress notes and requests for recertification) is done in a timely manner. The secretary must be well-organized and have a friendly but firm personality. Proper phone demeanor is vitally important, as the secretary's phone voice often forms the public's first impression of the center. Family calls to day care are frequently placed in times of stress, so the secretary should be able to give concise, slow, and repetitive directions. The primary responsibility for preparation of bills often falls to the secretary, thus requiring some bookkeeping skills. And, as if this variety of tasks did not place enough demands on the secretary, there is one more vital responsibility. Participants will frequently approach the secretary, wanting to talk. Often, they will do this just as the secretary is involved in something else that requires intense concentration. Sometimes, participants won't understand that the secretary is working under a deadline. The secretary should be comfortable visiting with participants, as time allows and should also have strong skills in gently redirecting participants when time simply doesn't allow conversation. Above all, this individual should have the patience of a saint!

Drivers, cooks, and custodians will face similar situations with participants. They must be able to find that delicate balance between "getting the job done" and treating the participant as a valued human being.

Relief Staff

Most adult day care centers have relatively small staffs. This can cause problems in maintaining desired coverage when a staff member is sick or on vacation. Two methods of developing fill-in staff have been successful in a variety of centers: the on-call staff and the cross-trained staff.

Some centers hire and maintain a list of on-call staff. These are people who are willing to work occasional, part-time hours in positions such as program aide, cook, and custodian. Some may be students or housewives. Some of the on-call staff may have been unemployed for an extended period of time; some may hold part-time jobs as in-home aides or sitters. By hiring directly, the center can avoid the high cost of using a registry or employment agency.

In many centers, it is cost-effective to cross-train the regular support staff. For instance, in one center, a driver who had free time from 10:00 to 2:00 now assists in activities when program aides are ill. The office assistant has been trained to work in therapy, and now helps out during staff vacations. The office work is then done before and after the participants need attention. This method of increasing staff hours rather than hiring other people serves a twofold purpose. The staff member is able to make extra money, while the center does not have to recruit, train, and pay benefits to another employee. Another bonus of this system is that the "fill in" person is familiar to the participants. Confused and/or anxious participants do not have to get to know another staff person, and the relief person is already familiar with the setting.

Volunteers

Most centers could not survive without volunteers. Volunteers are drawn from several sources and serve for different lengths of time. Some serve as companions and confidantes to participants. Volunteers assist with tasks, such as doing crafts and serving meals; they assist in guiding participants around the center; and can fill in for the secretary during lunch. Volunteers provide many "little extras" to brighten participants' days, such as party entertainment and gifts. They can help with fund-raising and public relations. The list goes on and on.

Volunteers come from all over. They are senior volunteers, housewives, students, working people, teens, and many others. Some individuals come as court referrals who have been convicted (usually of a misdemeanor or "white collar crime") and have been sentenced to community service rather than jail. Many are delighted to work in adult day care centers and turn out to be excellent helpers even though they have not chosen to be there.

Volunteers are not simply staff that you do not have to pay. Recruiting, training, and managing volunteers takes a great deal of time and sensitivity from paid staff. The regular staff thus has to decide the benefit of volunteer hours compared to the time invested in them. Volunteer management is a specialty in itself. Developing a strong volunteer corps within the center will be enhanced by learning from professionals in this area.

The Secret of an Excellent Staff

People who work in day care for very long are a special breed. They must have a true caring and concern for the people they serve. They must be able to withstand the pressures of working in programs that may be constantly "under the gun" financially. They must be able to trust other staff enough to develop strong communication patterns, and to sense when someone else needs help. They must truly believe that no job is beneath them. At one time or another, they all help participants in the toilet or scrub up a mess from the floor. They all become involved in activities, not out of laziness or a desire to "have fun," but because each has something special to give to the therapeutic program. They work together to serve better.

Reference

National Institute on Adult Daycare. 1984. *Standards for adult day care.* Washington, DC: National Council on the Aging.

Further Reading

Lauffer, A., and S. Gorodezky. 1977. *Volunteers.* Beverly Hills: Sage Publications.

Pell, A. 1977. *Recruiting, Training, and Motivating Volunteer Workers.* New York: Pilot Books.

Voluntary Action Center. 1981. *From here to there: Management techniques for volunteer programs.* Dayton: United Way.

CHAPTER 8

Support Staff as Part of the Professional Care Team

Linda Cook Webb

Adult day care centers often suffer prolonged financial difficulties during start up, and therefore "make do" with minimal staff. As necessity is the mother of invention, though, most centers have become quite creative in staff utilization. Day care directors have learned to maximize the abilities of staff members who do not have professional degrees or experience (i.e., aides and clerks). These "support staff" may become so skilled in their paraprofessional role that it can be difficult to tell they do not have professional backgrounds.

In many day care centers, aides learn to implement therapeutic responses to persons with mental impairments. Secretaries become adept at dealing over the phone with families' emotional needs. Drivers provide routine home assessment. Housekeeping staff help to market the center in their neighborhoods. The cook helps a participant who has had a stroke learn once again how to set the table. The examples increase with every center observed. Training support staff to fulfill expanded functions such as these is closely related to two concepts already common to other areas of health care: the team approach and the health education approach.

In the team approach, staff members each contribute their own perspective in an attempt to gain a more complete picture of the patient. They each support the total care plan, even when this means functioning across traditional discipline boundaries. Usually, the team approach refers to professionals working together. In long-term care, however, aides often

85

spend more time with the patient and therefore can contribute valuable information to the professional care planning process.

In the health education approach, practitioners teach health care consumers information that can safely be used by ordinary persons without reliance on skilled professionals. This same general process can often be used to upgrade the skills of support staff in adult day care.

The stage has thus been set, for some time, to promote development of support staff to work in areas traditionally reserved to the professional. When support staff are fully utilized in this way, it is not unusual for visitors to the center to mistakenly think that all of the staff are professionally trained. The support staff display professional attitudes and behaviors, even though they may not have the diploma to match. As a result, activities assistants may be mistaken for recreation therapists, or the secretary for a social worker. Obviously, this does not happen overnight, or without purposeful management by a sensitive director.

The Role of Support Staff

The first step in working toward full utilization of support staff is to understand their position in and importance to the center. The major role of support staff is to assist professionally trained staff to augment client services. In this capacity, center capabilities can be significantly extended. Support staff must, however, be utilized with certain cautions.

The suggestion of using auxiliary staff in expanded functions has certainly aroused anxiety in other fields, such as medicine and dentistry. Concerns regarding quality of care are often discussed. Less openly discussed, but perhaps stronger concerns, revolve around "turf" issues. When a professional has worked so hard and paid so much for the education leading to a degree, the professional may find it hard to let go of responsibilities enough to trust paraprofessionals.

A certain amount of this concern is well founded. Untrained people should not move into expanded functions without adequate training and professional support. There must be clear limits within which paraprofessional staff act. Establishing these limits is particularly important in many states because of the Professional Practices Acts. These laws regulate how frequently and under what circumstances aides can provide services. Professional staff may endanger their licenses and the center may have problems with state regulatory agencies if state provisions are not followed.

Remember, not everyone in support positions may be able to handle the added responsibility of expanded functions. A look at basic personal qualifications will tell you that while there are many eligible people, they are also very special. In addition to the basic qualifications for day care staff (discussed in Chapter Seven), the support staff member who has high potential for learning paraprofessional responsibilities must have : common sense, enthusiasm and a sense of humor, ease in communicating with others, desire to function as part of a team, willingness to "pitch in" wherever needed, willingness to learn skills necessary to help effectively, and an ability to learn technical and/or complicated skills.

Finally, we must understand that support staff can never replace professional staff. Support staff can have a significant role in supplementing and extending professional services, but they will continue to need the guidance and encouragement of professionals. For example, new drivers can be instructed to collect basic home assessment information for the nurse or social worker. Over time, additional training can increase the driver's home assessment skills. It is still, however, the responsibility of professionals to evaluate the situation and guide interventions. In spite of the limitations that must be place on development of paraprofessional involvement in day care, however, the benefits can still be significant.

Due to the nature of their duties, support staff may see aspects of participants' lives that are not normally observed by professional staff. For example, the driver sees home environments on a daily or weekly basis. Aides, in helping participants in the restroom, have an opportunity to observe physical abilities such as transfers, reaching, and bending. Often, too, the toileting experience may be stressful for the client. The aide can observe how the client responds under stress, and may be able to reduce stress levels through rudimentary counseling techniques. Secretaries, janitors, and cooks also spend time during each day with participants. Since they are not involved in direct provision of care, these particular staff members are likely to be perceived in the friend role by participants. As a result, these staff members frequently become confidantes, privy to information the participant would not normally share with professional caregivers, or perhaps even family.

Beginning the Training—Looking Within Ourselves

Training actually begins with the program director. The director must be firmly committed to the goals of full teamwork among professionals and paraprofessional staff, or the system will not work. This means beginning with a willingness to share all responsibilities among all staff—even those responsibilities that may not be much fun.

An example of the effects of sharing responsibilities is in toileting. Helping participants in the restroom can become a job done only by the "low man on the totem pole" or it can become a source of staff unity. The director sets the tone, in either refusing bathroom responsibilities or in helping occasionally. It is amazing how significant the director's helping a participant in this way can be to staff. When the director assists a participant with toileting, he or she provides a very powerful role model.

Once the director believes, and starts teaching other staff to believe, that no job is too small for any team member, the second step of developing expanded functions can begin. In this step, the director must demonstrate that all staff can contribute to the total success of the center.

Make time to listen to employees! This can be as informal as an "open door" office policy or as formal as including everyone in structured team meetings. In the beginning, let support staff tell you in their own words what they see, think, and feel about clients and about the program itself. Listen closely, and help them identify solutions. Figure 8-1 recounts this type of conversation—one in which the secretary begins to see herself as part of a solution.

Once you have established with the support staff that you value their input, work with them to develop special training. It is this training that will actually enable them to function in an expanded role.

The Role of In-Service Education

There is certain, basic knowledge all staff will need to do their jobs well. This information is probably best conveyed through in-service training programs. Not only will all staff be exposed to the same information, but by learning together, they will develop a stronger sense of themselves as a group. Use staff members to conduct some of the training sessions and you will also foster an understanding of each person's special skills. For example, the nurse and an activities assistant could jointly offer a session on "Working With a Blind Person." The social worker and a very active older aide could talk on "The Structure of the Aging Network."

Be aware that different types of learning are fostered by different types of teaching methods. To transmit knowledge, use lectures with discussion.

Secretary:	Every time I get off the phone from talking with that Mrs. Allen, I just want to scream! I have tried everything. I just don't know what to do with her.
Director:	What exactly does she do that makes you feel this way?
S:	She is so demanding. She can't seem to understand that I have other things to do. And she's rude. And sometimes downright insulting. Like this morning, she wanted me to check something about her bills, and I was rushing to get that grant proposal done for you by 10:00. I tried to tell her I would call her back, but she wasn't having any of it!
D:	Do you have any idea why she acts this way?
S:	Well, I know she's worried about her husband. We've seen him getting more and more confused, and he's got be a handful at home. I don't know...maybe she's really wearing out. She has sounded tired the last few times I've talked to her.
D:	And maybe feeling overburdened by having to take care of the household accounts alone?
S:	I think that's true! Could we ask the Social Worker to try to arrange some help for her?
D:	That's a very good idea. While she's at it, I will ask her for an evaluation of Mrs. Allen's emotional state. Weekend respite or a family support group might help, too. Is there anything you can think of that you might be able to do to help calm her on the phone?
S:	I think it will help a lot for me to just see her side of things...Maybe if I tell her that I know it must be hard at home...(shyly) Could I call her and tell her that the Social Worker can help with the insurance forms, if she's interested?
D:	That's the best idea yet! Since you are the one she has been calling about her bills, it would be natural for you to be the one to offer help. And with you making the effort to call her, she'll know that you care. Sometimes that goes a long way.

Figure 8-1 Conversation between secretary and director.

To change attitudes, use sensitivity training, role playing, and simulation games. Case studies, either in writing or on film, will encourage integration of knowledge previously gained. Repetitive practice will build confidence in a new skill. Outside speakers for selected sessions will generate enthusiasm; however, it is not necessary to rely on them all the time. Most important, encourage staff to use new knowledge or skills in their daily routines. Through individual feedback or during case conferences, help staff identify those places to put their training to work. Finally, always give generous praise for progress!

Basic in-service education topics can include:

- CPR and First Aid

- Communicating with the Deaf Person

- Working With the Blind Person

- Transfer Training

- Communicating With the Mentally Impaired

- Psychological Effects of Disability

- Family Response to Disability

- Attitudes Toward Aging

- Attitudes Toward Disabilities

- Structure of the Aging Network/Disabled Services System and How ADC "Fits In"

- Medical Terminology and Abbreviations

- Regulations

Individualized Training

The heart of assisting support staff to develop expanded functions lies in developing an individualized training program. Through this process, the director and the employee can develop joint goals for learning, identify learning methods, review progress, and reassess goals. Figure 8-2 outlines the steps in this process.

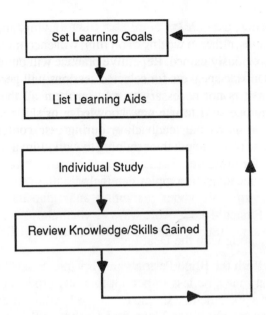

Figure 8-2 Components of the Individualized Training Program.

The supervisor can assist the staff person to set individualized learning goals by asking questions such as: Where do you want to go in this job? What do you want to accomplish here? How long do you expect to work here, and where do you want to work next? What would you like to be doing five (or ten or two) years from now? Is there a special project or activity that you would like to develop here in the center? Do you have training or skills beyond those initially required for this job, and would you like to develop them further? Is there something you have always wanted to do, and never had the chance? (Actually, these are also good questions for professional staff, to encourage them to continue developing in their disciplines!)

It takes a certain time investment to get to know employees this well, but the investment will be more than repaid in increased motivation and decreased turn-over of staff. Remember that in the first discussions of learning goals, anything should be an acceptable suggestion. Once several goals have been defined, you and the employee can set up priorities to determine which will receive the most attention.

Goals may also develop out of an employee's experiencing a problem in doing the job. For example, the secretary in the Figure 8-1 dialogue later decided she would like to learn more about family dynamics in order to respond more sensitively on the phone. A month later, she decided to add a second goal of learning to help families with insurance paperwork problems. Aides frequently set goals related to learning basic counseling skills, because as one aide said, "When one of the participants starts to cry, I don't know what to do." Activities assistants often ask to learn more about PT and OT, to make sure they are leading the exercise group properly. All are likely, at one time or another, to decide to learn more about a specific disease process or disability. If the center is having problems with low census or with inadequate budget, all staff (including professional staff) may want to learn more about marketing and financial management. Chapter Ten describes some specific ways in which staff have been helpful in both of these areas. (See Figure 8-3 for a more complete list of potential expanded functions.)

Remember that each person's goals are very individual. The content of the goal may, at times, be less important than the process of setting the working toward a goal. Include simple goals, well within the capabilities of the employee, to ensure early successes and build confidence. Encourage staff to stretch, but also be aware that some may have lower motivation or abilities, and allow for this.

Once goals have been established, develop a list of learning aids that will facilitate individual study. There are a number of readings and films which will be helpful. Supervision of the learning process by the staff professional in a related discipline should also be considered, including scheduled time for one-to-one teaching. Continuing education classes may also be of use to support staff even though they are not typically designed for the paraprofessional level. These classes are especially useful in focusing on disease processes and understanding new treatment modalities. It is not necessary for the employee to "take in" everything from the class. Give support staff permission to take away only what they can understand and use. After attending a continuing education class, it is important that the paraprofessional discuss the material with a professional in a related discipline. This confirms a correct understanding, and allows the professional to know how the support staff's knowledge and skill is increasing. Participation in community support groups, such as Alzheimer's Disease and Related Disorders Association, Stroke Club, National Head Injury Foundation, etc. is also very instructive. Employees will learn a great deal, and these groups will appreciate your organization's involvement.

Task Area	Traditional Staff	Support Staff
Patient Assessment (Especially assessing changes over time.)		
Physical	RN, LPN	
Functional (ADLs and IADLs)	RN, LPN, PT, OT, SW	All Support Staff
Mental Status	SW, RN, OT, ST	
Emotional Status	SW, OT	
Home and Family Assessment	SW, OT, RN	Driver, Secretary
Therapeutic Response to Person w/		
Adjustment Problems	SW, OT, RN	
Psychological Problems	SW, OT, RN	Aides, Secretary,
Mental Impairments	SW, OT, RN, ST	& Others
Establishing a Peer Support		
Network for Clients	SW	Activity Director
Therapeutic Response to Families'		
Emotional Needs	SW	Driver, Secretary
Assistance in Performing		
Therapeutic Exercises	PT, OT, ST	Aides
Supervision of		
Other Staff		
Senior Employment Workers	Director	All Staff
CETA Workers		
Volunteers		
Marketing	Director	All Staff
Resource Development		
Volunteer Recruitment		
Fund-Raising for		
Special Events	Director	All Staff
Obtaining Donations		

Figure 8-3 Some potential areas for expanded function.

Making Sure It Works

Set timelines for specific activities. These may be relatively immediate, or they may cover longer periods of time. Just be certain that in the press of daily responsibilities, neither you nor the employee lose sight of the eventual goal. Periodically review progress together, and continue to set new goals as appropriate. Soon, your support staff will be fully functioning members of the professional care team.

CHAPTER 9

Financial Management in Adult Day Care: An Introduction

Linda Cook Webb and Linda J. Crossman

The first hard lesson for many adult day care directors is that the program's fiscal status is just as important as its quality of care. Even though the center may be considered "not-for-profit," it still is a business and it needs businesslike management. This becomes clear with the realization that if the center continually loses money, it will not be in business at all.

In order to survive, adult day care does require strong financial management. As with many other forms of health care, the average participant cannot afford the full cost of care. ADC, however, does not have widespread coverage from either public or private insurances. This means that program income is often a patchwork of participant fees, Medicaid, fund raising, grants, contracts, private insurance, in-kind donations, and other unique funding sources. Finally, many centers use sliding fee scales that have not been well supported by outside funding. The result is a difficult financial management job.

Unfortunately, few ADC directors are prepared to meet the fiscal challenges of their programs. Most have come from health care and social services backgrounds where little was taught about the type of sensitive financial management required by adult day care centers. There have been

95

a lot of mistakes made in this area of adult day care, many of them by the authors of this volume. Making mistakes can be a form of learning, though, and many centers are now closer to financial stability than in the past.

Whose Job is Financial Management?

Many people became day care directors, thinking that their job is to manage the program—not necessarily to manage the budget. In fact, the National Institute on Adult Daycare's study, *Adult Day Care in America*, found that "persons providing the ADC services may not be involved in the fiscal aspects at all..." (Von Behren 1986, 22).

Experience has shown, however, that in successful adult day care centers, the director has become intimately involved in fiscal management. This involvement includes the areas of budget development, income generation, management of expenses, and financial evaluation of the program. By having a thorough involvement in and understanding of these processes, the director can monitor financial status more closely than a separate accounting or bookkeeping office that may have responsibility for multiple programs.

The ideal arrangement for sound financial management is to create a team of the adult day care director and the agency's accountant. If the day care center's agency does not have an accountant on staff, the director should either contract for accounting services or work with an accountant who might be willing to volunteer on the center's board of directors. In order for this team to work well, the day care director should have training in basic principles of accounting and the accountant should visit the center to learn more about the requirements of running a day care operation. This special training for both day care director and accountant will help them to communicate more effectively as a team in setting budgetary priorities and explaining financial status to agency boards.

The remainder of this chapter gives basic guidelines to directors who are beginning to learn the skills necessary to participate in successful financial management. The following chapter details specific methods of implementing financial solutions to some typical fiscal problems in day care.

A Short Course in Accounting

Two basic financial documents will provide the most help in initial forecasting, planning, and evaluation: the budget and the income statement. These two documents are structured similarly, with the budget projecting goals for the future, and the income statement recording what has happened during a specific period in the past. See Figure 9-1 for a sample budget and Figure 9-2 for a sample income statement.

In both the budget and the income statement, the first few items identify income sources. The second section identifies expense categories. Finally, net profit or loss is calculated by subtracting expenses from income.

When the "bottom line" shows a loss, three methods may be employed to improve the financial picture. First, income may be increased by the amount of the loss. Second, expenses may be decreased by the amount of the loss. Finally, income may be increased and expenses decreased, to total the amount of the loss.

Initially, it may be tempting to try a reduction of expenses. This may appear to be the easiest solution and the quickest to implement. It may also be the most dangerous, since to cut certain costs may result in cutting quality. Reduction in the quality of services may adversely affect the number of families who can be attracted to the program, and if carried to extremes may jeopardize licensing or certification. As an example, the most logical place to begin cutting expenses is in the cost category that is the largest. For adult day care centers, this is typically in staffing costs. It is important to realize, however, that in offering a service, you are dependent on quality staff. The presence of an excellent, dedicated staff is the only means of delivering quality services.

Ironically, sometimes the best way to improve financial status is to actually increase expenses to yield increased income. This may be the case when there is some barrier preventing or discouraging people from using the program. If you can spend some money, reduce the barrier, and generate more utilization, increased expenses may be well worthwhile. This principle often holds true with regard to transportation. Many centers rely on publicly supported transportation for the elderly and handicapped to bring participants to and from adult day care. Initially, this appears cost effective,

Three-Year Budget

	Year 1	Year 2	Year 3
Income			
Fees—Private Pay			
Medicaid			
Title III			
County Grant			
Foundation Grants			
Donations			
Other			
Income Subtotal			
Minus Rate Adjustments			
Minus Bad Debt			
Total Income			
Expenses			
Total Salaries and Employee Fringe			
Professional Fees			
(Therapists, Nutritionist)			
Management Services			
(Accounting, Mgmt. Consultants)			
Employee Recruitment			
Staff Mileage			
Conferences and Dues			
Rent			
Utilities			
Marketing			
Insurance			
Telephone			
Supplies			
(Office and Program Supplies)			
Meals			
Transportation			
Maintenance and Repairs			
Depreciation and Amortization			
Total Expenses			
Net Gain/Loss			

Figure 9-1 Sample budget format. Source: Sunnyvale Adult Day Care Center (Used with permission.)

Income Statement—Sunnyvale Adult Day Care Center
March 1 to 31, 1988

Income		
Fees—Private Pay		
Medicaid		
Title III		
County Grant		
Foundation Grants		
Donations		
Other		
Income Subtotal		
Minus Rate Adjustments		
Minus Bad Debt		
Total Income		
Expenses		
Total Salaries and Employee Fringe		
Professional Fees		
Management Services		
Employee Recruitment		
Staff Mileage		
Conferences and Dues		
Rent		
Utilities		
Marketing		
Insurance		
Telephone		
Supplies		
Meals		
Transportation		
Maintenance and Repairs		
Depreciation and Amortization		
Total Expenses		

Net Gain/Loss

Figure 9-2 Sample income statement format. Source: Sunnyvale Adult Day Care Center. (Used with permission.)

but in some communities it may not be. It is not unusual that these transportation systems are already operating at or near capacity. When their resources become strained, the availability and accessibility of regular transportation for adult day care may suffer. Advocacy with the transportation provider may help, but many ADC programs try to get their own van as quickly as possible. One adult day care director who managed this commented, "It worked out to be a lot more cost-effective than trying to deal with the provider and with frustrated families and with lost income."

Taking this type of action assumes, of course, that a thorough cost-benefit analysis has been done, comparing the two alternatives. Include in the analysis any expenses associated with use of the publicly supported transportation and a calculation of lost revenue from absence days. Then compare these figures to the capital and operating expenses associated with the use of a center-owned van. Expenses for the center's own van might include liability insurance, vehicle maintenance, and driver salaries. Additional income realized by an increase in attendance may well offset these costs, but such an analysis is imperative.

The most effective method for improving the day care center's financial picture is to use a combination of increasing income while ensuring that expenses are contained. Using this "combination" approach, the management team will bring the center more rapidly toward self-sufficiency.

Effecting an improvement in the program's bottom line begins with an analysis of the details included in the income statement. Note that the sample income statement includes a variety of income sources. Multiple income sources will assist a program to reach stability in funding. By diversifying, the center can more easily weather funding cut-backs or changes from an individual source.

The income statement also includes two types of expenses: fixed and variable. Fixed expenses do not change from month to month (rent, lease payments, etc.). Variable expenses may fluctuate with the season or with the number of participants attending (for example, in winter months, heating bills will go up—also, as you serve more participants, food costs will increase). The largest expense category for day care centers, staff paychecks, may include both fixed amounts (salaries) and variable amounts (wages for relief staff).

The difference between fixed and variable expenses can sometimes explain seemingly wide variations in monthly expenses. For example, food and transportation costs can be expected to go up during a month in which attendance increases. There may also be months in which winter heating bills coincide with quarterly insurance payments.

Fixed and variable expense categories are also used in calculating break even levels. The basic formulas used in determining break even levels are:

Price per Unit – Variable Cost per Unit = Contribution to Overhead
and
Total Fixed Costs / Contribution to Overhead = No. Units Needed To
Reach Break Even

Figure 9-3 shows how these formulas would be applied to an adult day care center.

Projections of cash flow will also be important to financial management. Typically, many expenses (such as salaries) must be paid out before payment for services is received. For example, if payday is every two weeks but families are billed monthly, there may be a strain on the center's bank account. Centers intending to heavily rely on Medicaid should realize that in some states, payment may arrive at the center 60 to 90 days after services have been delivered. There may also be cash flow problems if grant sources change their method of payment. New centers, particularly, should track cash flow carefully.

Familiarity with other accounting practices (such as accrual versus cash accounting, balance sheets, etc.) will enhance the day care director's ability to function well in the financial management team. This information is available in basic accounting courses through local colleges and continuing education programs.

Developing the Budget

Ideally, the first program budget should be developed early in the center's planning process. Prior to working on the budget, program planners should have completed a community needs assessment to determine two things. It will be necessary to know how many people in the area may need the program, and of these, how many can be expected to actually use it. Techniques for estimating these figures can be found in Chapter Three. Planners also should have measured the area of the center to determine its maximum capacity. It is important that these steps be done before the initial budget, to ensure that the center can break even within the maximum number of people who may use it or within the maximum number that the space will allow. If it is determined that the most people who will ever use the center at one time will be 20, and the program cannot break even with less than 35, the staff and board of directors will need to do some serious evaluation of goals.

Necessary Data:

Daily rate, including meal and transportation	$32.50

Total variable expenses for the past year (VE)	$56,768
Total participant days for the past year (PD)	5421
VE / PD = Variable expenses per participant day	$10.47

Total fixed expenses for the past year	$160,186

Total working days available	260

Calculation:

Daily Rate - Variable Expenses per Participant Day = Contribution to Overhead, or

$32.50 - $10.47 = $22.03

Total Fixed Expenses / Contribution to Overhead = Annual Participant Days to Break Even, or

$160,186 / $22.03 = 7,271.27

Annual Participant Days / Working Days Available = Average Attendance to Break Even, or

7,271.27 / 260 = 27.97

Figure 9-3 Sample calculation of break-even for an adult day care center.

The initial budget will be in two parts: the preopening start-up costs and the operational budget representing income and expenses after opening day. At best, the adult day care director and the accountant will be guessing at most of the income and expense figures for the first operational budget. If possible, review current budgets from similar day care centers that have been in operation for a while. This may assist in making a more educated guess about income and expenses for your center. Once your program has been functioning for a few months, actual historical information from the income statements will help to refine future budgets. Some simple guidelines, however, will assist in making more accurate estimates the first time around. Figure 9-4 illustrates a budget development worksheet that incorporates the following guidelines.

Before beginning the budget, develop monthly census goals for the start-up period. Be conservative in estimates of how long the center will take to achieve full capacity. One of the biggest problems for new centers is in assuming that the center will fill up quickly. Nationally, many centers require three to five years to get to a full census.

In addition to a slow start-up, expect seasonal variations in attendance levels. For example, in areas with harsh winters and very hot summers, the center may see predictable census declines in January and August.

A third factor affecting census build-up is the monthly variation in number of working days available. Due to holidays and short months, some months may have only 19 working days while others may have as many as 23. This can cause a dramatic difference in the total number of participant days. For example, average participant days per working day equals 20 for two months in a row. In month one, with 19 working days, total participant days equals 20 x 19, or 380. In month two, with 23 working days, total participant days equals 20 x 23, or 460. If fees were $30.00 per day, the difference in revenue between month one and month two would be $2,400.00!

Similarly, decide whether the center will be open five days a week or less. Some centers have found success by starting with either two or three days a week. Once those days fill up, they then expanded to a fourth or fifth day. The decision to open with two days or with five days can be guided by an analysis of the families whom the program will serve. For example, if you will be catering to working families, five days a week coverage may be necessary. Resources in your area and the composition of the target population will determine the number of days a week that the center should be open.

Year One Budget Worksheet

Projected Census	Month 1	Month 2	Month 3		Year Total
Income					
Fees—Private Pay					
Medicaid					
Title III					
County Grant					
Foundation Grants					
Donations					
Other					
Income Subtotal					
Minus Rate Adjustments					
Minus Bad Debt					
Total Income				(Continue columns for a total of 12 months.)	
Expenses					
Total Salaries					
Professional Fees					
Management Services					
Employee Recruitment					
Staff Mileage					
Conferences and Dues					
Rent					
Utilities					
Marketing					
Insurance					
Telephone					
Supplies					
Meals					
Transportation					
Maintenance and Repairs					
Depreciation and Amortization					
Total Expenses					
Net Gain/Loss					

Figure 9-4 Sample budget development worksheet.

After projecting monthly census during the start-up period, give some consideration to the center's fees. At this point, the financial managers should go back to the agency's mission statement, and should also discuss financial goals with the board of directors. Many nonprofit agencies, for example, have a strong commitment to serving the low-income elderly. If this is a priority for the adult day care center, it will be necessary to obtain significant outside funding in the form of grants, donations, and scholarship support to subsidize the cost of care for these individuals.

Some centers, in fact, choose not to charge fees to any clients and rely instead on voluntary contributions. This requires a major commitment to fundraising by the board of directors and staff. Even with this commitment, there will be financial uncertainty from year to year, as funding sources shift priorities or have fewer funds to distribute. Providers who have had the experience of moving from voluntary contributions to fee-for-service will attest to how many problems are involved in such a transition, both for the clients and the provider. To ensure the program's long-term stability and viability, serious considerations should be given, at the outset, to a fee-for-service system.

The structure of the fee scale guides further analysis of income from charges. Some centers structure the fee scale to bill all services together under a "daily rate" charge. Other centers bill some services separately. (The following chapter describes some of the rationale for billing meals, transportation, and therapies as separate services.) If some services will be billed separately, project the number of units of each service that will be billed for each month during start-up.

Establish a tentative fee structure, and using the projected census rates, calculate fees revenue. Add in donations and other projected income to determine income generated during start-up time.

From this income subtotal, subtract an allowance for rate adjustments (reductions in private pay fees) and subtract an allowance for bad debt (usually 2% or less of fees revenues). This will yield the total projected cash income.

Now, look to expenses. The budget analysis form shows sample expense categories. Any particular center may not use all of these categories, or may use additional ones. Be prepared to do a fair amount of research into the agency policies regarding salary increases, bonuses and staff benefits, costs of equipment, supplies, and insurance, and funding to support a good marketing campaign.

In calculating expenses, be sure to allow for those costs that will be offset by volunteer staff hours, donated materials, or other in-kind donations. Some centers elect to show in-kind donations on their budgets and monthly income statements, while others prefer to keep a separate accounting. Either way can be effective, as long as in-kind donations are monitored as closely as other types of income.

Once expenses have been calculated and totaled, you can review the net profit/loss figures for each month during start-up. If this line shows intolerable losses, rework the budget, using the techniques from Chapter Ten, to increase income while decreasing expenses. This process of "number crunching" can be done quite easily on a personal computer, using spreadsheet software. (See Chapter Sixteen for more information on spreadsheets.) With a little bit of perseverance, it can also be done successfully with pencil and paper.

Including Staff in Financial Planning

At a minimum, successful fiscal management in adult day care depends on solid teamwork between the center director and the accountant. That team approach can also be successfully expanded to include the adult day care staff.

Try sharing the income statements with staff and educating them as to what each revenue or expense category involves. This process can be spread over several weeks or months. With the staff, look at how each category within the income statement is coming into play on a day-to-day basis in the center. Some staff people are likely to develop excellent ideas for changes which can positively affect the bottom line. Some of these ideas will be new to the director and accountant, and the employees will feel good about being able to contribute. Adult day care staff people have usually been selected, in part, for their creativity and dedication. When they apply these skills to the center's financial picture, you may be surprised at the solutions that emerge!

Looking Down the Road

Once the program is operational, the income statements may begin to show losses higher than the agency can tolerate. In this case, financial managers can use a variety of techniques to assist in improving the bottom line. Some suggestions are contained in the following chapter, "The Road to Self-Sufficiency."

Reference

Von Behren, Ruth. 1986. Adult Day Care in America: Summary of a National Survey. National Council on the Aging, Washington, DC.

Further Reading

Johnson, G.L., and J.A. Gentry, Jr. 1980. *Finney and Miller's principles of accounting.* Englewood Cliffs, N.J.: Prentice-Hall, Inc.

CHAPTER 10

Financial Management in Adult Day Care: The Road to Self-Sufficiency

Linda Cook Webb and Linda J. Crossman

What is "the road to self-sufficiency" in adult day care? For many directors who have struggled for years with inadequate resources, financial management has often seemed like a journey down the yellow brick road. In the midst of dealing with families who can't afford day care and a Medicare system that doesn't fund adult day care, self-sufficiency may look like the mythical land of Oz.

Unfortunately, no one has found the wizard with all the answers. We can learn, though, from each other and from professionals in the field of financial management. This chapter will incorporate much of that knowledge in a discussion of the pitfalls and problems, as well as the solutions with which many adult day care centers have experienced. First, it is important for the day care center to have a team of financial managers, which includes an accountant and the day care director. Several of the following techniques actually require this teamwork in order to be effective.

Techniques for Improving Income Levels

Establishing Fees

There is currently little uniformity in the way that adult day care centers handle fees. "Centers may charge by the hour, the day, the week or the month. There may be two sliding fee schedules or fixed rates, and a number of centers have both. In addition, centers may have no charge or accept donations only" (Von Behren, 1986, 24). Many of those centers that have operated on a donation-only basis in the past are now moving to a fee structure of some type. This section will focus on the considerations faced by centers that do have fee scales.

The first step toward increasing income is to perform an analysis of the fee structure. One way of analyzing fees is in terms of whether charges are lumped together in one daily rate or whether they are broken into separate charges for separate services. For example, meals, transportation, and therapies can be assigned separate charges from the base daily rate. A model for how to structure this type of fee scale comes from experience with family planning clinics.

Originally, the clinics charged patients the exact cost for both family planning education and for birth control pills. Their main goal was to provide education. Selling the pills was just a convenience to patients. What clinic managers discovered was that patients wanted to buy the pills cheaply and not come to the family planning classes. In order to have positive impact on their financial situation and also motivate their patients to come for education, the clinic's managers shifted the charges. They increased the price of pills significantly, but still kept charges below those of local pharmacies. The managers also lowered charges for family planning classes. Then, they said, "You can only get the pills if you come to the classes." Patients understood that when they paid for pills, they were getting something, and were quite willing to pay more for the pills. They were even willing to come to classes in order to get what they saw as a "bargain" on the pills.

Applying the family planning clinic experience to adult day care, we find some interesting patterns. People are used to paying for meals and transportation when they go to a restaurant or ride in a cab. Furthermore, they understand that it will cost more to eat in a restaurant than to put a meal on the table at home. Most of us, however, are not used to paying to be able to join in a discussion group. As an example, one center's financial managers made the following changes from a flat daily rate. The actual cost for the meal was $1.75, so the charge for the meal was set at $3.00. Because the meal was separated out from the daily rate, the day's charges were reduced by $2.00. This change resulted in more work for the staff, because it required more complicated bookkeeping and billing procedures. On the whole, though, it was quite worthwhile. The new fee scale was more attractive to many potential clients, and census increased.

Absence days may also be an issue for analysis in the fee scale. There are many ways to charge for days a participant is absent, if you choose to do so. You can charge for unexcused absences only. You can charge for all absences. (An excused absence might be for illness, while an unexcused absence might be for family vacations.) You can also charge full fee for the first day of an unexcused absence, and a partial fee for another two or three days, until it becomes an excused absence. For example, some centers charge the same rate for all absences as for days attended, just as child care centers do. The problem with that is that in adult day care we are dealing with a chronically ill population. Because some absences cannot be avoided, a full-fee charge for absence days may be seen as penalizing people for their illness. It is not the same as child care, in that sense. Each center must, however, assess its own situation to define its policies and devise a workable solution.

A final issue for analysis of the fee structure is in terms of whether the admission assessment is a billable service. Most adult day care centers do not charge for assessment. Others, in contrast, have followed the model of child care centers and charge $25 to $35. This one-time fee is usually payable in advance, and is usually charged whether or not the applicant is accepted.

Billing Issues

Once analysis of the various parts of the fee structure has been completed, financial managers can consider the timing of billing. Most centers bill for care after services have been delivered. In this way, bills are sent to families, insurances, and other payment sources at the same time. Other centers, however, have elected to send bills to families in advance of delivery of care. In this second system, the family and participant contract for a specific level of services. Payment is expected on or before the first of the month for the entire month's activity. If the center does not bill for absences, that amount is credited against the following month's bill. In centers that have a diversity of payment sources, advance billing may become complex. Medicaid and other insurances, for example, will not accept bills until after services have been provided. This means that some bills would be sent prior to and others after service delivery. Another situation to be addressed by centers using advance billing is the budgetary constraints of families who may have to "save up" to afford the first month. Once a family is established on advance billing, though, they should not feel any more financial pinch than if they were billed at the end of the month. The advantage of advance billing to the adult day care center is that it provides a healthier cash flow for the center, with monies being available earlier.

Remember, throughout the analysis and restructuring of fee scales, that charges must be based on two factors:

- The actual cost of providing care *must* be covered by the total of all income sources (including fund-raising and other sources)

- Charges should be evaluated in terms of how they compare to fees for similar services in the area

Sliding Fee Scales

Another method for analyzing charges is in terms of whether a sliding fee scale is in use. Many centers fall into the temptation of using an unfunded sliding scale (i.e., where there is no funding source to subsidize those clients who are charged less than the actual cost of providing services). The major hazard of this situation is that every participant admitted on the unfunded sliding scale increases the center's losses. If, for example, the center has an additional cost of $120 a day for each ten people served, and families are paying only an average of $8, the center is losing more than $10,000 a year for each additional ten people admitted. That is not a wise tactic and it's best to change the fee scale so that charges are at least covering variable costs. (Figure 10-1 provides a more detailed discussion of this concept.)

When establishing or changing sliding fee scales, it is important to do a detailed analysis, not only of the variable costs of providing care, but also of the distribution of clients along the scale. If the bulk of participants' families are paying near the bottom of the scale, they are not contributing much toward fixed overhead costs. This will mean that in order for the center to remain financially stable, someone will have to do major fund-raising activities.

Note that there are a number of ways to develop sliding fee scales. They can be based on the client's income alone or on income plus assets. If assets are counted, a flat allowance can be deducted (i.e., the level of assets

In the early days of program operation, we believed that as the program expanded, we would continue to reduce our deficit, and eventually reach a break-even point. It seems to make sense. The fixed costs would be spread over more participant days and therefore the average cost per visit would go down.

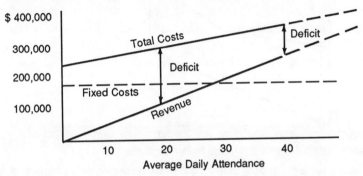

However, there are a number of circumstances in which this is not true. In fact, as more people are served, the deficit may actually increase. These circumstances are outlined below.

1) The average fee does not cover the additional variable costs.

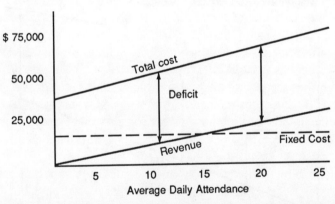

As services are expanded, the fixed costs remain unchanged, but other costs increase. Additional staffing, transportation, meals, and supply costs are increased as more people are served. If the average fee collected does not at least equal these variable costs, then serving additional people will cause the program to go deeper in debt—*despite the fact that the average cost per visit may still be decreasing.*

Figure 10-1 "The more people you serve, the more money you lose": When this is true and when it is false. Source: Ann Iversen, Associate Director, Marin Adult Day Health Services. San Anselmo, CA. (Used with permission.)

2)   The variable expenses may increase at a higher rate at higher utilization levels.

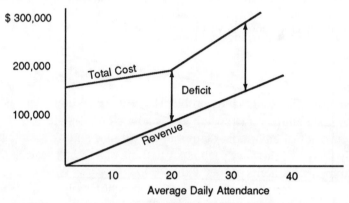

In some instances, a great deal of in-kind may be available as a program is first begun, (i.e., volunteers, grant subsidies for transportation or meals). As the program expands, these additional services may have to be paid for, thereby increasing the program's costs.

3)   Finally, increasing capacity to serve more people will result in an increase in fixed costs which may also increase the deficit.

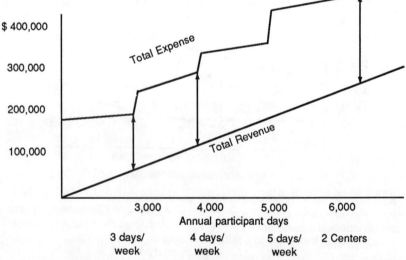

Capacity may be added by increasing the number of days of operation or the number of centers. In both cases, fixed and variable costs will be increased. The added revenue from such an expansion may or may not cover the added costs.

Figure 10-1, continued.

allowed for purposes of determining Supplemental Security Income eligibility—see Figure 10-2). Alternatively, you may want to prorate assets over the life expectancy of the participant. An example of this approach, using actuarial tables, is shown in Figure 10-3.

Scholarships

Another potential solution to problems with the sliding scale is to abandon the scale entirely and switch to a scholarship program.

There are a lot of emotional factors in the terms, "sliding scale" and "scholarship fund." We all have a tendency to think of a sliding scale as this wonderful thing that benefits people without a lot of money. We don't think about where the money comes from. With a scholarship, it's clearer topeople in general that there is a specific fund. There is a set amount of money, and when funds run out there are no more scholarships available until additional money is raised. (Note that an unfunded scholarship won't work any better than an unfunded sliding scale. It is important that fundraising activities occur and that money actually be deposited into the fund *before* scholarships are awarded.)

Use of a scholarship encourages both clients and staff to be creative in order to minimize use of the limited scholarship dollars available. For example, if the basic fee scale bills meal and transportation as separate services, the family may elect to provide transportation rather than request more dollars from the scholarship.

Staff should take the responsibility of monitoring the success of family-provided services. For example, if the spouse commits to provide the meal, staff should watch nutritional content. Sometimes, this can be a way of monitoring the meal planning in the home. Some family members simply do not know how to select nutritious, well-balanced menus. In that case, education is in order. On the other hand, some families do not have the money to be able to afford adequate nutrition. If this is the case, the center director can decide to assign more scholarship assistance to the particular participant.

Scholarship monies can be assigned in a variety of ways. Some centers use a formal application process in which the family must disclose their income and expenses. Scholarship dollars are then allocated based on the staff's evaluation of financial need. Other centers use a less formal process in which they allow the family to assess their own finances and request a specific level of assistance. Both methods have advantages and drawbacks.

1. Participant's Name: _____ Date: _____

2. Case # _____

3. ASSETS: List all liquid assets (current savings, bank balances, current market value of stocks, bond and mutual funds) (Self and spouse)

_____ $_____

_____ $_____

_____ $_____

                                    Total (A)_____

    DEDUCT: Asset Allowance
              ($1500 for 1; $2000 for 2) $_____

                                            Total (B)_____

Divide (B) by 12 (Enter result on line (C) Record   3.   (C)_____
Amount on Line (C) Below**

4.   GROSS MONTHLY FAMILY INCOME: (Self and spouse)

Social Security	$_____	Asset Value From 3(C)	$_____
S. S. I.	$_____	Total 4(A)	$_____
Pensions Annuities	$_____	Total Income	$_____
Interest/Dividends	$_____	Less: (Monthly Mtce.	$_____
Other Income	$_____	Allowance-$560 for 1;	
Total 4 (A)	$_____	$1,039 for 2)	
		Adjusted Gross	
		Monthly Income .... $_____	

I affirm that the statements made herein are true and correct to the best of my knowledge.   /s/ _____

Figure 10-2   Sample form for determining sliding fee scale using an asset allowance. Source: Marin Adult Day Health Services, San Anselmo, CA. (Used with permission.)

Fee Schedule

For the Period Starting_____(Date)

A.G.M.I.	ADHC (%)	Community Care (%)
$1,800- Up	100	100
1,500- 1799	90	90
1,200- 1499	70	70
1,000- 1199	60	55
800- 999	45	45
600- 799	Minimum	30
0- 599		Minimum

Send Bill to: _____

Rev. 8/87

Figure 10-2, continued.

Sliding Fee Scale For Non-MediCal Participants

All figures should reflect assets, income and expenditures of applicant and spouse.

Liquid Assets

Cash on hand	$_____
Savings/hecking Accounts	$_____
Stocks/Bonds	$_____
Total:	$_____
Less Asset Allowance ($1,500 for one/ $2,250 for two)	$_____
Total:	$_____

Life expectancy from IRS
   actuarial tables _____
Total Assets Pro-rated Annually $_____
Monthly Asset Allowance $_____

Figure 10-3 Sample form for determining sliding fee scale using actuarial tables. Source: Marin Adult Day Health Services, San Anselmo, CA. (Used with permission.)

Income

Social Security Check(s) per Month	$_____
Other Pension check(s)	$_____
Interest Income	$_____
Rental Income	$_____
Other Income	$_____
Total Monthly Income	$_____

(A) Monthly Asset Allowance
    and Total Monthly Income $_____

Expenditures

Rent/Mortgage	$_____
Food/Utilities	$_____
Clothing/Miscellaneous Household	$_____
Uncovered Medical Expenses	$_____
Other Expenditures (Describe)	$_____
_____	$_____
_____	$_____
_____	$_____
_____	$_____

(B) Total Monthly Expenditures $_____

Disposable Monthly Income
(A) minus (B) $_____

Interviewed by:

_____

Figure 10-3, continued.

When the center staff assign the level of assistance, families are not put "on the spot" to make decisions about whether they may be requesting too much money. Some families, on the other hand, seem to prefer the trust implied in being allowed to do their own financial assessment. It is extremely rare that a family requests unreasonable amounts of financial assistance. In fact, directors using this system report that the danger is actually in the opposite direction; families may not ask for as much as staff would have assigned.

Staff have to be prepared to handle this delicately, and may want to suggest to specific families that additional funds can be made available. The method of allocation of funds that will be most successful in a particular center may be, simply, the method the director prefers.

Policy decisions should also be made regarding the term of scholarship assistance. Many directors using a scholarship tell the families that assistance is available only for a specific amount of time (ranging from three months to one year). At the end of that time, new determinations of assistance will have to be made based on the amount of money then available. This protects the center and forewarns the families that the fund cannot be overspent. If the total amount available decreases, then less assistance can be given.

Increasing Utilization

Increasing attendance may initially seem like an obvious way to increase income. As with other techniques of financial management, however, it is important to analyze the effects of any changes. If, in fact, each new participant's fees or reimbursement are less than the cost of care, then increasing utilization will actually have a negative effect on program income. Before marketing for new participants, it will be necessary to establish a fee scale and a reimbursement pattern that ensures, at a minimum, that:

- No new participant enters the program without funding to cover at least the variable costs of providing care

- The average participant pays or has reimbursement for a fee amount that will contribute toward fixed costs

- The budget includes a reasonable amount for marketing activities

Once an adequate fee structure has been established, marketing to increase the program's census is helpful. Chapter Eleven describes many techniques for increasing participation in the adult day care center. In addition, two financially oriented marketing techniques may be helpful. First, the center can give a reduced rate for people who attend more days a week. Second, families can be educated about the costs of their alternatives with a flier that outlines local charges for home care and nursing home services.

Marketing Fee Changes

It is easiest to start out charging a flat fee and trying to raise money for scholarships, as it can be very difficult to increase fees later. If the center has started with donations only, beginning to charge is even harder.

The success of a new fee structure will depend, in part, on the staff's reaction to charges. Frequently, staff come from a background of working in social services and poverty programs. They may sincerely feel that clients cannot afford to pay or should not have to pay more than a nominal amount for services. Staff needs to be aware of what the budget is and what the cost of operating the program is. They need to know what the costs of those services are, and they need to look at their own time. When staff complain about fee increases, the director can respond, "One hour of your counseling (or nursing or therapy) is worth $___ (name the figure). And we're only charging $___ for the entire day." Educate staff about looking at their own value.

One of the other unique features about educating staff is that the same people who are doing intake are concerned about the service needs of the client. It becomes very difficult for the staff when fees begin to be a barrier since their whole thrust is to get as many people as possible to come into adult day care. Often, clients need to be enticed to at least try the program. It's very difficult for professional staff to then turn around and say, "This is the fee." So the staff need a lot of support when the center is going through these changes. Give staff an "out," by allowing for exceptions to be made. If a client says, "I know this is where I fall on this fee scale and I just can't afford it" that case can be referred to the director or other administrative staff. At least it's one step removed and the decision is being made by administrative staff.

Families and participants may also need some preparation and explanation of why charges increase. Honesty usually proves to be the best policy. Clients can understand and sympathize with a simple explanation, such as, "The only way we can keep our doors open is to increase our fees." In one center which did this, daily charges increased by $5 to $10 per day, and only one client out of 125 initially left the program. That participant is back with them now, enrolled in the program a year later. Center staff found, though, that they really had to market the program more to existing clients to help prevent people leaving. Part of that marketing involved making certain that the families were aware of their options. Many of them were already aware that they couldn't get someone to come into the home for $4 or $5 an hour (what they were actually paying for day care on an hourly basis), not to mention the cost of nursing home care. To these families, that cost comparison was really the trade-off.

Another side of increasing fees for adult day care is that we are dealing with a population of older people who have a unique financial background. They grew up in the depression, have made their own way, and don't like the idea of accepting charity. We all know the fear that older people have of ending up on welfare or Medicaid. Some older people won't even come to a program when it is free or the fee is too low, because they feel they really need to pay for the service. We need to recognize that.

Creating a Package of Reimbursement Sources

Medicaid, Medicare, and private insurances will all pay toward adult day care charges—but only under certain circumstances.

Medicaid (Title XIX of the Social Security Act) is a program of health care insurance for low-income persons with medical need. It is funded in part by the federal government and in part by each state government. Because of this organization, specific eligibility and coverage can vary from state to state. Adult day care is one of the services that can be covered by Medicaid, according to each state's option. About half of the states now have provisions for Medicaid coverage of adult day care and/or adult day health care. In order to obtain Medicaid reimbursement, a day care center must be located in a state that has Medicaid coverage *and* the center must apply for certification as a Medicaid provider. Details about this program are available through the state agency that administers Medicaid.

Medicare (Title XVIII of the Social Security Act) is a federal program of health care insurance for older persons and some handicapped people. Medicare Part A, hospitalization insurance, is provided free to persons who qualify. Medicare Part B, outpatient and physician insurance, is available at an extra cost to persons who have Part A. Some adult day care centers that provide a lot of medical or rehabilitative services may qualify to become certified as Medicare providers. The two applicable types of certification are:

- The Outpatient Rehabilitation Facility, which can bill for Physical and Speech Therapy

- The Comprehensive Outpatient Rehabilitation Facility (CORF) which can bill for Physical, Occupational, and Speech Therapy as well as rehab nursing, social work, and some other related services

Note that neither type of facility can get reimbursement from Medicare for maintenance-oriented therapies. Details of these two programs are available through the federal Health Care Financing Administration. At the time of the writing of this book, bills allowing Medicare to specifically cover adult day health care are before Congress. For more information on this possible future coverage, contact the National Institute on Adult Daycare.

Some centers are having success in negotiating private insurance coverage for part or all of day care services. You have to be careful in approaching the insurance company, though. Do not call the insurer and say, "Mrs. Smith needs adult day care. Will you pay for it?" The response to that question will almost always be "no." Start by doing some research. Look at the insurance policy to determine if any of the services that will be provided by the center could possibly be covered. Nursing treatment and therapy are two good options. Some plans will also cover private duty nursing, home health care, and/or nursing home services. Contact the physician to determine what the options for this patient would be without day care. Many doctors will be willing to sign a statement to the effect that without adult day care, one of the covered services would be indicated. Armed with all this information, call the insurance company and advocate for reimbursement. Explain that they will be paying for these services anyway, or that they may be at risk of having to pay for services more expensive than the day center. The insurer may want to "study the situation," but many centers have had good success with this approach.

The Veterans' Administration will, in some instances, reimburse for adult day health care for veterans. This reimbursement is available under a model project and may be expanded in the future. (See Chapter 18 for more information.)

Organizations devoted to the care of specific diseases sometimes provide partial funding for eligible persons. These agencies may include the Muscular Dystrophy Society, Easter Seals, and others.

Government Contracts

Federal, state, and local governments regularly contract with community agencies to provide certain types of services. The process of applying for a contract is much like the process of applying for a grant, with two major differences. First, grants may be awarded to not-for-profit organizations only, whereas contracts may also be awarded to for-profit ventures. Second, grants are usually designed to fund a one-time demonstration or start-up period, whereas contracts may be designed to fund on-going services, year after year.

The following programs are the contract programs used most often by adult day care centers:

- Title IIIB of the Older Americans Act (note that in some areas, these funds are administered as grants, not contracts)
- Title XX of the Social Security Act
- County funds that support services for senior citizens and/or handicapped persons
- Health Revenue Sharing of the Public Services Act

The department on aging at the State level will be able to tell you who administers the Title IIIB program and should also know application procedures for other locally available contract programs. Other sources for information on these programs may include the state agency overseeing Medicaid (this varies from state to state), the Health Department (state, county, or city), and the regional office of the Administration on Aging. (See Appendix D for addresses.)

Each type of contract uses a specific bid cycle. Applications are only accepted at predetermined times for specifically defined services. Agencies interested in seeking a particular contract may request a bid packet that defines the services to be contracted and instructs bidders in how to complete the application process.

Since Title IIIB is a major funding source for so many adult day care centers, it deserves some special comment. Program directors often labor under one of two misunderstandings about Title IIIB programs: Some people believe that Title III-supported programs are prohibited from charging any fees to any participant, and some people believe that a program accepting Title III funds cannot serve younger adults (as many day care centers do).

Interpretation of the regulations may vary from one area to another; however, in many areas neither of these prohibitions is necessarily in force. The main point of misunderstanding has to do with the way in which the money is handled from an accounting perspective. If Title IIIB money is deposited into a scholarship fund account, rather than used for general overhead, the program may charge fees and may admit persons under the age of 60. Some restrictions would still apply. IIIB scholarship dollars can *only* be used for persons who are IIIB-eligible. Further, on the days that a participant's services are covered by IIIB, the day care center may not charge a fee for that person's care. The center may, and is often encouraged to request donations on those days. On days *not* covered by IIIB, the program may charge a fee. Finally, there can be no means testing to determine IIIB eligibility (i.e., no assessment of assets and income).

For example, Effie Schmaltz may come to the center five days per week. She is 85 years old, although some of the others attending the center are young adults. Monday, Wednesday, and Friday, the cost of Effie's care is covered by Title IIIB. Once a month, she is given an envelope which she can use to make donations to the program. Effie's charges for Tuesday and Thursday are billed to her daughter.

Not all programs may wish to use IIIB money to support a scholarship program. If this is the case, Title III funds could go toward supporting administrative overhead or a specific service, such as transportation. This would, indeed, prohibit the center from accepting younger people. The prohibition on charging fees would still be in place; however, the center could develop a system of strongly encouraging donations. Some adult day care centers ask families to "pledge" a certain amount to be donated each month. A pledge statement can be sent to the family, as a thank-you for last month's donation and a reminder of this month's pledge.

It is important to be aware of local variations in interpretation and implementation of the Older Americans Act (OAA). Some agencies administering OAA funds may be quite willing to work out special arrangements, while others may be more resistant. Frequently, terminology may contribute toward this willingness or resistance. For example, in some areas the pledge arrangement is called a sliding scale donation, with no negative reaction from the OAA agency. In other areas, however, the OAA agency might see this as conflicting with the interpretation that Older Americans

Act programs are supposed to be delivered without any type of financial assessment. Be prepared to negotiate to find terms agreeable to both the OAA agency and the adult day care center.

Many county funding programs for the aged may also seem to have prohibitions on serving young adults. Frequently, the scholarship approach will help the day care center to maneuver around this barrier. Informal negotiation with county personnel can help to clarify limitations.

Grantswriting and Fund-Raising

A few, simple guidelines apply to grantswriting and fund-raising, whether you are writing a foundation proposal for $100,000 or asking an individual for $10.

First, know your targets. Learn something about what they want and why they might give to your program. Find a way to stress the idea that they will get something substantial in exchange for their donation, such as publicity or the opportunity to have an association with a creative and exciting new service. It may be the feeling that they have gotten a bargain for their donation (i.e., "For every $10 you give, we can provide $30 worth of services.") Each organization or individual is likely to have slightly different priorities. Be sure that your request is specific to the priorities and needs of the donor.

Review your program's goals, services, staffing, and benefits, as well as the larger context in which the center developed. It often helps to compare your situation to that of other day care centers across the country. For larger proposals, be prepared to review your budget and in-kind summary. You may also be asked to project your budget for the next three to five years.

Many donors will want to know your other sources of support. Keep accurate records of the monetary value of assistance already received. Indicate those other organizations that support the concept of your program. In a formal proposal, include letters from related agencies stating the benefits of your center to the community.

In seeking potential donors, look first to the donors to your agency's other programs. Watch the news to see which foundations, corporations, and churches give to related programs. If a current or past donor is unable to give the total amount required, ask them for suggestions of other sources to approach. They may even make the initial contact for you.

Groups to approach include local and national foundations, churches, service groups (Kiwanis, Soroptimists, etc.), sororities and fraternities, businesses in your immediate neighborhood, major local corporations, and United Way.

Foundations libraries located throughout the U.S. can be of particular assistance in identifying major donors and consulting in the development of grant proposals. A list of these libraries is contained in Appendix C. Public libraries may also offer directories of foundations and books detailing successful techniques for soliciting funds.

Many of us may be shy to ask for financial help for our programs. Remember that you are not begging. Slant your proposal in terms of the benefits that the donor's giving will promote. Tell why yours is an exciting program. If you are turned down once, don't let it stop you. Go back again with a different proposal. If you are given assistance, definitely go back again! Keep you supporters apprised of good things happening in the program, and especially let them know of future needs.

Generating Other Income

Sometimes, centers have resources that may be valuable to others in the community. These resources can be extended to other agencies in exchange for a fee. As an example, most day care vans are in use only during the early morning and late afternoon hours. Would another agency like to have access to the van during midday, evening, or weekend hours? In calculating charges, consider whether you will allow the van to be driven by the other agency's personnel, or if you prefer to require that van and driver be contracted together. Sometimes, hospitals may be interested in this alternative to transport their dialysis and chemotherapy patients. Churches, scouts, and other groups may be interested as well.

Many centers receive requests from other organizations thinking about starting adult day care. Some of them will be willing to pay a consulting fee for substantial assistance. Others that are not so serious will not monopolize your time so much when they hear that there is a fee. Many center directors feel a certain obligation to provide free assistance to new centers because they got a certain amount of free advice when they were new to day care. A good compromise arrangement might be to say that the first hour of consulting is free, and that the charge applies after that. The consulting fee can also be made low enough that it won't prohibit serious day care developers from asking for help.

There may be other resources that you have. Perhaps you have space that would be appropriate for use by some other organization in your community. Maybe your staff is able to provide contract services that other people or organizations will pay for. Several centers are now experimenting with sharing music therapists and recreation therapists. One center could hire such a person full-time, use their services parttime, and contract out the rest at slightly higher than actual salary plus fringe benefits.

Techniques for Decreasing Expense Levels

Reducing Staffing Costs

Salaries will always be the largest expense category for adult day care centers. It is, therefore, the first cost category to examine in attempting to decrease expenses. Most day care centers are not over staffed, so it is not usually safe to reduce total staff time. There are, however, several techniques for maintaining staff capabilities while decreasing cash costs.

Contracts for specific professional services may help to reduce total cost. Many centers contract with a local home health agency to provide therapy services. The contract can stipulate that therapists will be provided for as much time as needed by the participant population, and that the home health agency will bill the center only for the actual amount of therapy time delivered. (This arrangement will be more to the center's advantage if the contract states an hourly rate rather than fee for service. When home health agencies charge a fee for service, they typically use a fee scale based on Medicare reimbursement, which can be quite high.) Contracting prevents the center from having to hire a therapist who might, at times, not have much to do. Therapy services provided by independent therapists may be another alternative for contracting. A comparison of therapy costs when provided by staff (including benefits, if applicable), home health therapists, and independent therapists is useful in determining the most cost-effective way of using therapists.

Related agencies in the community may be willing to provide in-kind services. For example:

- The community mental health center may provide a psychotherapist or clinical social worker to consult with staff and/or provide

counseling for participants/families. Often, these services can be
provided free of charge or at an extremely reduced cost.

- Junior League members may provide board training, PR training
  or consultation, and/or assistance with grantswriting.

- Marketing or advertising firms may develop marketing plans,
  design brochures, and similar functions.

- Nursing schools, medical schools, dental schools, and the health
  department may provide screening/health education programs
  for participants and in-service education for staff.

Students in professional disciplines (both undergraduate and graduate
level) frequently need to do an internship or field placement as part of their
educational requirements. Vocational schools may also wish to place
paraprofessional interns at the center for periods up to one year. While not
as expert as someone who has been in the field for a time, students can bring
good skills into the center. It should be recognized, however, that students
are not free labor. For the placement to be successful, job responsibilities
must mesh with the student's individual educational goals *and* the center
director must spend extra time evaluating and guiding the student's progress.

Salaries for specific staff can be subsidized by Title V of the Older
Americans Act and by other government training programs. This may be a
way of funding positions such as aides, secretary, bus driver, and janitor. Be
aware that sometimes the training programs have a delay in being able to
provide workers, and that these workers may need a great deal of supervision and support. Also understand that workers are placed with an agency
for training only, and that the placement is expected to enable the worker to
move into competitive employment. Subsidized workers may only be with
the day center for a year or two, but they can be quite valuable during that
time.

Volunteers can be a great help throughout the program. The range of
areas in which volunteers can assist is great. Traditional volunteer jobs
include receptionist, activity assistant, nurse, and dining assistant. Some
volunteers can also develop and carry out creative independent projects. For
example, a person with interests in journalism might produce a monthly
newsletter for the center. A volunteer with good public speaking skills

might talk to local community groups about what the day care has to offer. The opportunities are endless. Organizations that may provide or recruit volunteers include:

- Voluntary Action Centers (VAC)
- Retired Senior Volunteer Project (RSVP)
- The Senior Companion Program, through ACTION
- Scouts, Campfire, 4-H Clubs
- Service groups, such as Junior League, Rotary, or Optimists
- Churches or other religious groups
- Sororities or fraternities
- Corporations that give employees time to volunteer on their lunch hour or normal work day.

Volunteer recruitment and management is a specialty in itself. See Chapter Seven for more information and a reading list.

Reducing Costs of Equipment and Supplies

At times it may be easier to obtain donations of actual furnishings, equipment, and supplies than it would be to recruit donations of money to purchase these items.

Get to know the purchasing agent and the head of maintenance at the local hospital. These people can be a tremendous resource for donated beds, nursing/therapy equipment and supplies, office furniture, and even paint. Let them know that you are willing to take their cast-off items, and you will be likely to get substantial donations two or three times a year.

Physicians (especially those who refer many participants) may donate blood pressure units, *Physician's Desk Reference* and other books, or samples of over-the-counter drugs. Durable medical equipment companies (DMEs) may donate wheel chairs, canes, emergency oxygen units, and other medical items. Sporting goods stores may agree to give games and adapted sports equipment.

The public library will often set up a rotating stock of books on loan— and usually these are large-print books. Department stores can be good sources of furniture, stereos, and TVs. Locally owned stores may be easier to approach.

Families of current participants frequently like to offer birthday party supplies and small items for the activity program. Families of participants who have graduated or died may want to send medical equipment and supplies, lounge chairs, and clothing for use in emergencies. Organizations that use small everyday items imprinted with advertising may be good sources of pens, pencils, note pads, calendars. Any organization that might have unclaimed freight can be a good source for a TV, furniture, and other items.

Remember that in recruiting these donations, the techniques of successful fund-raising often come into play. Do some research to learn a little bit about the person or agency you will be approaching. Have specific suggestions of the items you want. Always thank people who have made donations. Then go back and ask them again.

Two other techniques for reducing costs for equipment and supplies deserve note, but may have less total impact on the budget. These are competitive bidding and making equipment.

If your agency has used the same equipment supplier for a long time, you may not be getting the best prices. Shop around a bit to test the waters of current pricing. If you feel you can get a better deal, develop a bid package and let all suppliers know that it is being widely distributed. Sometimes, this brings out competition among suppliers and helps you to get a better price. One caution in using this technique: Suppliers serving nonprofit agencies may feel that they are already giving reduced prices because they like what the agency does. If this is the case, handle purchasing decisions extremely gently. You may also want to investigate group purchasing arrangements with other nonprofit organizations in your community. By getting bids for bulk purchases you may be able to get significantly reduced prices. In some states, if an agency is receiving state funds it may also be eligible to buy supplies through the state's purchasing office.

A few pieces of equipment can be easily constructed for much less than they cost to buy. Exercise tables, for example, involve simple workmanship and can be made for several hundred dollars less than the purchase price.

Decreasing Fixed Expenses

Sometimes expenses can be moved from the category of fixed costs to the category of variable costs to decrease total expense level. For example, more and more centers are hiring on-call aides who are willing to work on an intermittent temporary basis when census is high or when regular staff aides are on vacation. This allows a lower total for staff salaries, while targeting the staff hours to the times they are needed most. Other expenses that have been treated as fixed expenses may be treated this way, as well.

Doing Without

Even though doing without may be a difficult alternative, it is sometimes one which must be realistically considered. If a program really must do without, it still is not a good idea to nickle and dime all aspects of the service. It will be much more workable to cut back a day or cease to offer specialty services *rather than compromise the entire program.* Before considering any reduction in services, however, perform a careful analysis of how the reduction will impact revenue. For example, there may be no net gain by cutting back a day of operation because you will also lose that day's revenue.

Financial management of adult day care is not easy. To be done well, it requires a team approach from the center director, the accounting staff, the board of directors, and sometimes the day care staff. Many of us have, at various times, been tempted to perform drastic cost cutting to try to reduce program losses. That alone, however, is not the way. The answer is much more complex. Above all, you have to have confidence in what you do. You have to believe in your program. And then you have to take action.

Reference

Von Behren, R. 1986. *Adult day care in America: Summary of a national survey.* Washington, DC: National Council on the Aging.

CHAPTER 11

Marketing Adult Day Care

Linda Cook Webb and Greg Newton

The fellow who tries to attract business without marketing is like a fellow who throws his sweetheart a silent kiss in the dark. He knows what he's doing—but nobody else does (Paraphrased from William Jennings Bryan).

Many of us in service industries tend to be very humble about our programs. We often share the feelings of a Wisconsin adult day care director, who tells about her first experiences in fund-raising: "I felt apologetic, asking for money, until local civic leaders said, 'You have something really special there! Be proud of it, and ask for what you need.' "

This "confidence principle" holds true, whether you are seeking funds, trying to recruit participants or advocating for new licensing standards. Each situation presents unique marketing challenges within adult day care.

What is Marketing?

It may be surprising to think of fund-raising and advocacy as marketing issues. This will be especially true, if you think of marketing as being the same as selling. Selling is certainly a part of the marketing picture, but it is a very small part. Selling involves only those activities which occur at the point of sale, and it focuses on the product to be sold. Marketing, in contrast, begins with finding out what people want and planning a product or service to satisfy those wants. It starts with people. It continues with producing, packaging, pricing, promoting, and distributing those want-satisfying goods to a customer who is willing to give something in exchange. In short,

133

marketing includes all those activities involved in getting a product or service from the maker to the consumer. It is the process of solving someone else's problem. The best example of this is the principle of the Buffalo Bridle: "You can make the buffalo go anywhere, just so long as they want to go there" (Weinberg 1985).

What Are We Marketing?

The McDonald's chain has built their success on the principle of the Buffalo Bridle. They may sell hamburgers, but they are in the business of marketing relief and convenience. Their slogan names their product: "You deserve a *break* today, so get up and get away, to McDonald's."

We in the day care field would do well to see our services in the same light. Our business is *not* adult day care. How do we know that? Because no uninitiated family member has ever spontaneously said, "I need adult day care."

If our business is not adult day care, then what is it? We can easily make assumptions about others' perceptions, but we will often be wrong! To find out, listen to what people say to you when they request services. Usually families want "help" or "relief" or "the security of knowing Mom is OK while I'm at work." Participants may want "friends" or "a chance to get out of the house." Donors may want to invest in a tax benefit.

Who Are Our Publics?

To find out what our business is, we need to turn to the people who comprise our market. Since those people are not all the same, it is helpful to think of the many different groups within the market. These groups, called "publics," include our referral sources, such as other day care centers, nursing homes, physicians, and information and referral agencies. The public also includes the families of our participants, such as adult children, spouses, siblings, and parents. The public includes the government, such as inspectors from regulatory agencies and legislators. Finally, the media, including TV, newspapers, and magazines are part of the public, as well as the employees of the facility.

It can be helpful in identifying our publics, or markets, to look at a formal definition of a market, i.e., people who need or want something similar and are willing to give something in exchange.

It is easy to understand how families form a market. Families need help and they are willing to pay (at least in part) for that help. Other markets may not seem so clear cut. For example, we know that the participants have needs we can satisfy; but what do they have to give? The answer is simple: Without participants, we would not be in business. They can give or withhold their consent to come to the center. The family may override the individual's negative response initially, but if center staff cannot motivate the participant to a more positive attitude, length of stay may be shortened. Conversely, if the participant comes to treasure the days spent at the center, that individual's attendance may increase from part-time to full-time. Figure 11-1 outlines some additional markets for adult day care.

Figure 11-1 Additional Adult Day Care Markets

People	With Needs	And Something to Give
Social Workers	Referrals that work	Potential participants
Physicians	Concise, professional communications	Medical information
Media	Informations, leads	Stories, PSAs
Foundations	A place to give money to	Money
Agency Administration	A successful program	Approval of new plans
Employees	Recognition for a job well done	Creation of positive center atmosphere
Legislators	Voter support and publicity	Support of licensing or funding bills

As you can see, each market has its own distinct wants, needs, and motivations, as well as its own special set of "goodies" to offer. This understanding is important because, in essence, we should be marketing our product in different packages to each of our different publics.

It is sometimes easiest to focus on the market by trying to think of the individuals that comprise it. Buell comments (1970),

> The market is not a single cohesive unit; it is a seething, disparate, pulsating, and antagonistic, infinitely varied sea of differing human beings—every one of them is as distinct from every other one as finger prints; every one of them living in circumstances differing in countless ways from those in which every other one of them is living.

Look, for a moment, at a particular target market, and try to think not about the group, but about the individuals which comprise it. This process will help you to develop a customer profile statement. We'll use as an example, hospital social workers. Now visualize individuals within that group. Who are they? How old are they? What gender are they? What do they want? What do they need? What frustrates them? What gives them joy? What do they do during the day? At night? How do they see themselves? With whom do they associate? Whom do they respect? Whom do they fear?

Many hospital social workers are women wanting a professional career, but balancing that with family demands. They are usually overworked. Many are frustrated that they cannot give the time and attention to the caring which they have been trained to do so well. They probably like the feeling of making referrals to quality services, and knowing that the referral will work out well. They are apt to be frustrated by referrals that "bomb." They may suffer personal embarrassment when confronted by a dissatisfied family member.

To get a more sensitive picture of the market, you really must talk to people directly. This type of market research can be conducted either by individual interviews or through focus groups. The focus group is simply a group of current or potential customers from one market who are asked to give their opinions and perceptions of a current or potential service, or any one aspect of that service.

Focus groups of hospital social workers often provide startling comments. A common statement has to do with the individual's personal feelings toward patients and their families. Social workers have gone into their profession because of a caring for people. In the hospital environment, they may establish a close relationship with the patient, only to have that person "disappear" after discharge. They seldom get to hear about the patient's life after the patient has gone home.

How simple for the adult day care center to answer that need for information! One of the most effective marketing activities for ADC is to give feedback to the people making referrals to the center. Send a thank-you note for the referral. Call to explain why the person was admitted or denied. Call back again after a few months to give an update, or to tell a touching story about the participant's progress. Invite the social worker to the participant's birthday party. You will be meeting the social worker's personal needs, while providing a reminder about your services, and educating the social worker to be able to make better referrals in the future.

At this point, it will be tempting to go directly to questions of promotions design. For most people, the fun part of marketing is promotions— "getting the word out," being interviewed for the newspaper, designing a brochure, and so forth. You can greatly increase the effect of your promotions, however, by first doing some basic analysis of what you are promoting and to whom.

Market Research

Effective marketing is based on "the five Ps"—product, publics, price, place, and promotions. You need the right product, offered to the right person, at the right price, in the right place, for promotions to be totally effective.

Let's start with the product. A good exercise to use in defining your product is to write a description of it. No matter how simple you think your product is, write down all of its attributes and all of the things it can achieve. A classic exercise of this sort is to write a description of a pencil. A description of the pencil can involve many different types of features and benefits, such as:

- Basic features (it's yellow, with black lead inside a wooden tube)
- Detailed features (the rubber in the eraser comes from South America)

- Practical benefits (our pencil last 20% longer than theirs)

- Emotional benefits (it gives the security of being able to erase errors easily, and peace of mind in knowing that the pencil will not leak or stain)

- Fantasy benefits (with this pencil, you might write a beautiful play, develop a brilliant business idea, or compose a touching love sonnet)

- Self-image benefits (by using a pencil, you will impress your friends with your frugality and the courage to admit that you can make mistakes)

(Adapted from Nash 1986)

Use this exercise to describe adult day care in general, and your center in particular—remembering that different audiences will receive different benefits. Especially describe the negative aspects of your center, and turn them to the positive (as in the pencil description, with "the courage to make mistakes").

An ADC center located in the basement of a downtown high-rise provides a good example. The lack of windows was a definite limitation, but the center's staff emphasized the positive in their marketing. The advantage of being in the basement was that it was exceedingly difficult for wanderers to get away. Minor modifications in the staffing pattern and doorways were made and the staff promoted the fact that this center was the only one in town that could accommodate wanderers. The effect was amazing. Not only did the staff get referrals of wanderers, but other referrals increased as well! What they had discovered was that people appreciated the staff's willingness to serve those with "hard to handle" needs.

It is important to evaluate what you have to offer when describing your product. The best way to do this is to ask your various publics what they think of your services. The following are just some suggestions of areas of questioning. Focus on those additional issues specific to your center or community.

Product Questions

Is adult day care really needed in the community? Try to estimate market demand, using the techniques for community assessment described in Chapter Three. Are there enough handicapped and frail elders in the area to justify the size of program you are attempting? Also conduct a competitive analysis. Are other programs or services already filling the need? What makes yours different?

Does the service package match specific service needs? Is the predominant need for a highly medical or rehab program, or is the center in an area with primarily frail, isolated persons?

Are services performed in a quality manner? Do all staff have adequate training? Do staff have the equipment they need to do their jobs properly?

Price Questions

Price can involve not only direct charges, but also indirect costs and psychological costs. Direct costs are those paid in hard cash for the service such as ADC fees. Indirect costs are those which are incurred in attaining or using the service, over and above the direct costs. If an applicant must have an examination by a physician before being considered for the program, it may entail payment to the doctor. This would be an indirect cost. Psychological costs are those "paid in the mind" (including risk, lost opportunities, time, and others). Usually, psychological costs are the most important to reduce in human services marketing. In adult day care, psychological costs can be high. For example, the family may initially feel that they are admitting defeat by seeking outside help for their relative.

What costs are involved in your publics deciding to "buy" what you have to offer? Are costs affordable? Are they perceived as affordable? Perceived value is what the product or service is worth to the customer. It is dependent upon the needs and wants of the customer, and has little to do with the dollar cost. Ironically, charges which are too low may create a perception of a service which is of low value. Does the consumer perceive a value in the service which outweighs the costs? These questions should all be applied to the three types of costs.

When charges may not be affordable for many families, does the center have arrangements for insurance coverage, scholarships, or sliding scale? If an all-inclusive daily rate sounds very high, can you "unbundle" services by establishing separate rates for separate services (day rate, meals, transportation, etc.)?

Are there indirect costs you can reduce? For example, can intake assessments for working families be arranged during evenings or weekends? This would reduce the cost to the family of days lost from work.

Can you affect the perception of psychological costs? A significant psychological cost to families may be the resistance of their family member to considering day care. Sometimes, a cheerful visit from a day care staff member will help to reduce this resistance, and thereby decrease the family's perception of psychological cost.

Some questions can bridge across categories. For example, if there is inadequate public transportation for participants, how do you address this problem? A poor transportation system can form a price issue in that the headaches of dealing with unreliable scheduling are a psychological cost. Transportation is also, however, a place issue in that a good van system can bring the beginning of each day's service right to the participant's front door.

Place Questions

"Place" involves not only the physical location and facility of the center, but also the distribution system for services.

Some place questions that you might want to ask include:

- Is the center in a part of town accessible to transportation?

- Does a special transportation system allow handicapped persons to attend?

- Does the center's area of town have a positive image?

- Is the building accessible to the handicapped?

- Are signs necessary to find your way through the building?

- Does the facility present a positive image?

- Is the facility comfortable (visually, furnishings, heating and cooling)?

- Are some services (i.e., intake, home assessment) delivered in the client's home, or are all services restricted to the center?

Promotions

Once you have analyzed publics, product, price, and place, you will be ready to plan promotions. Promotional activities that are quite successful in one community may be totally ineffectual in another, similar community. The keys to which promotions will work for your program lie in the answers to the questions you have asked in the marketing research process. Promotions must center on presenting the information that your public needs, and in a way that will get their attention.

Six simple steps will help you to develop promotions that are targeted to those people you hope to reach:

- Determine who you want to reach with this specific promotion. People frequently ask, "Should I have a separate brochure for each market?" The answer is "Yes!" Each promotion should attempt to reach only one market at a time.

- Outline the needs of the specific public. What problem are you solving for them? What benefits are you offering?

- Determine what message you want to send. Link the message as closely as possible to the needs and problems of the specific public. Remember to sell the benefits!

- Consider what promotional tool will work best. Will this audience take the time to read a brochure? Under what circumstances? What do these people normally do during the day, and can those activities point the way to effective promotions? Promotional tools can include ads, public speaking, special events, newsletters, and many more traditional approaches. They can also include many normal activities of your day. For example, in scheduling speakers for the activities program, be sure to invite people who might also be referral sources. It is a way of saying, "We value you as a person" while also getting them into the center to see it for themselves. The secret to effective use of promotional tools is in the rule of

"The synergy of $1 + 1 = 3$."

This means that one type of promotion combined with another type of promotion has the total effect of three approaches. Variety and repetition of marketing tools thus results in the best public recollection.

- Outline where and when the promotional tool will be used. Try to time your message so that the audience can pay attention to it and/or at the time that they are most likely to have the problem! If you are trying to reach families of persons with Alzheimer's disease, late night TV or radio Public Service Announcements may be perfect.

- Request a specific and immediate action from the audience. This can be the familiar "for more information, call today..." or some other more specific request. It will reinforce your message strongly, for those who do respond. (Francis and Poertner 1986).

Be aware that marketing services is not the same as marketing tangible items. In traditional product marketing, the product exists before the sale takes place. Customers who are responding to the company's marketing efforts get to see, touch, feel, smell, and maybe even try the product before they decide to buy it. If you buy a car, you first get to sit in it, drive it, kick the tires, or whatever you need to do to convince yourself that it is a good idea. With services, such as adult day care, there is no way to "kick the tires" until after you have taken the risk of buying. This often gives our publics a feeling of frailty, of being at our mercy (Ambrosius 1986, 32).

Providing ways for our publics to "kick our tires" is one of the most challenging aspects of marketing adult day care. Paradoxically, "tire kicking" promotions tend to garner greater results than most other promotions. As much as possible, invite your publics into the center. Once they are there, arrange for interaction with staff and participants, or for observation of therapeutic activities. Use bulletin boards with pictures of activities, to describe a "normal day." Take a slide show about the center to community groups. Tell stores about individual participants' progress (having, of course, obtained permission first). Do whatever you can to give visitors the feeling that they have gotten a "free sample" of the full service.

The Long-Range Marketing Plan

Developing specific, written goals for marketing will help you to know when you have succeeded, and when promotions are not accomplishing their purposes. Start by sorting out program goals. Where should the center be in one year? In three years? In five years? Or, if that's too much to handle, where should it be in six months? Or three months?

Your goals for the program will tell you something about what marketing goals should be. Marketing goals usually fall into one or more of the following categories:

- Participant recruitment (increase use of services)

- Public education (increase general awareness and knowledge of adult day care)

- Image-building (develop image of professionalism with physicians)

- Advocacy (obtaining funding or services)

We are often told, "Do something, even if it's wrong!" Sometimes we should just get started, not worrying about whether what we do is absolutely "right." We have to take that risk. In marketing efforts, this is particularly good advice. The best marketing approach is often the one that is different, the one that is untried. This means that if you develop a fear of failure, you may not accomplish anything. As you start out, remember that the most effective marketing of adult day care is based on those skills which, as health and social service providers, we have already developed well: informing, motivating, advocating, and communicating.

References

Ambrosius, R. et al. 1986. *Marketing is not a four-letter word.* Sioux Falls, SD: Phoenix Systems.

Buell, V., ed. 1970. *Handbook of modern marketing.* New York: McGraw-Hill.

Francis, D. and Poertner, J. 1986. Marketing adult day care. Paper read at the 13th annual meeting of the Mid-America Congress on Aging, Mar 19-22, at Chicago, IL.

Nash, E. 1986. *Direct marketing.* New York: McGraw-Hill.

Weinberg, G. 1985. *The secrets of consulting.* New York: Dorset House.

Further Reading

Cooper, P. 1979. *Health care marketing.* Germantown, MD: Aspen Systems.

Marcus, B. 1986. *Competing for clients: The complete guide to marketing and promoting professional services.* Chicago: Probus Publishing Co.

Stanton, W. 1978. *Fundamentals of marketing.* New York: Dorset House.

CHAPTER 12

The Intake Assessment, Plan of Care, and Discharge Planning Process

Kathryn S. Katz and Paul D. Maginn

Target Population and Eligibility Requirements

Before the center is ready to admit its first participant, many decisions should have been made regarding the target population and services to be provided. The decision will have been made whether to have an adult day care center that serves a specific population (i.e., persons with Alzheimer's disease) or whether the center will be accepting individuals with a variety of problems. Based upon these initial decisions, eligibility requirements can be established for participants' age, presenting problems, rehabilitation potential, and so forth. Eligibility requirements may be determined by the center's host/sponsoring agency; by a needs assessment of the community; by the limitations of the facility; and/or by the blend of skills and traits of the staff. Eligibility requirements may also be affected by local, county, state, or federal regulations. If an adult day care center serves only Medicaid-eligible participants, then the participant will have to meet the requirements of both the center and the Medicaid program. Therefore, when developing a center and establishing eligibility requirements, be sure to take into consideration the requirements imposed upon the center by governing bodies as well as third party reimbursement systems. If the new center has private funding sources, this may provide planners with the ability to be flexible in their approach to the participants who are accepted. This flexibility will enable the center to be creative in working with a variety of individuals and assist in determining the center's niche in the community's continuum of care.

The Care Team and the Individual Plan of Care

The strength of the services in adult day care centers usually grows out of a strong team process. In this teamwork, distinctions between the various disciplines (nursing, social work, physical therapy, etc.) tend to blur, allowing a true multi-disciplinary approach. Often, professional assessments are supplemented by information from paraprofessional employees and perhaps volunteers. Families and sometimes other agencies, are drawn into the assessment and care planning process due to the need for consistent follow-up at home. Thus, there may be times when people outside of the day care staff become part of the center's extended treatment team.

The following review of the intake assessment, plan of care and discharge planning process assumes that the center is using this team approach.

Overview of Participant Progress in Adult Day Care

The National Institute on Adult Daycare's *Standards for Adult Day Care* (1984) define an individual plan of care as an essential service component of adult day care. The standards state that each participant will have an individualized, written plan of care that includes assessment, a plan of service, progress notes, reassessment, and a discharge plan. The plan of care is one of the distinguishing characteristics that differentiates adult day care from other services for the elderly.

Figure 12-1 graphically depicts the client's progress through the center's assessment, plan of service, and discharge planning process.

The center will be in a position to accept referrals after determining eligibility criteria. Usually a referral is handled by initial telephone contact, by either the family member or a referring community agency. This initial contact is an excellent opportunity to market the services of the center. An initial intake form, with basic demographic information, as well as a description of the presenting problems and needs of the participant, is usually completed. An application form for the center may be sent to the prospective participant or family member. To expedite the application

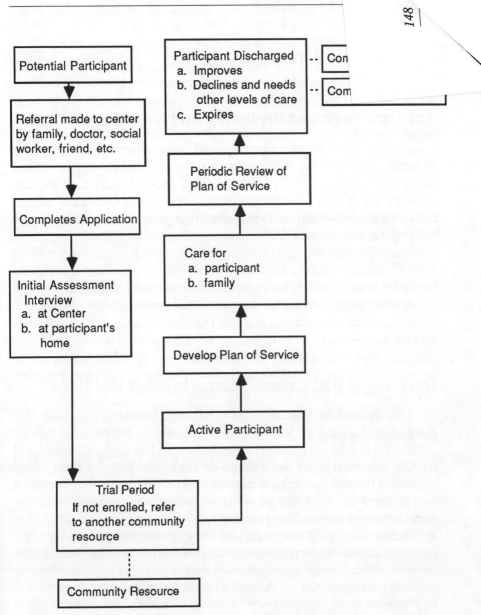

Figure 12-1 Flow Chart of Participant Progression at an Adult Day Care Center.

process, some centers do not mail the application form. Rather, they invite the applicant to come for a visit or they go to the applicant's home to complete the application. This is especially productive if a center is having census problems and does not want to risk losing an interested applicant. Most centers will arrange an intake interview upon receipt of the completed application form. The intake assessment interview may take a variety of forms:

- The interview may be conducted in more than one session, and in more than one place.

- The interview may include a visit of the prospective participant to the center.

- Adult day care staff may visit the participant's home.

How intakes are handled is a decision each center must make individually, as the intake process is a time-consuming and costly process.

Some centers have initiated a nonrefundable application fee. This fee (usually $25 to $35) helps to defray the initial assessment cost. This is primarily done in centers where the rate of assessment is significantly above the rate of participants who become active in the program, or when a number of participants are being admitted for short periods.

Initial Assessment

The components of an initial assessment will vary by the type of program. Over the past decade, professional literature cites various scales that assess the individual's activities of daily living, social adjustment, mental status, and so on. Many of these are used in adult day care. The initial assessment assists in identifying treatment goals and determining how best the center can assist the participant and the family in meeting those goals. Assessment is an on-going process that starts at the time the initial inquiry is made, and ends at the time the participant is discharged from the program.

According to *Standards for Adult Day Care*, "An initial written assessment shall be made within thirty (30) days of enrollment. The assessment shall identify the individual's strengths and needs and a determination shall be made as to how the center shall serve the individual." (National Institute on Adult Daycare 1984, 34).

Components of the initial assessment should include the following:

- Demographic information: name, date of birth, place of birth, marital status, etc.

- Social history: family of origin, family history, marital history, work history, hobbies

- Why are they seeking services at this time? What services do they need/want?

- Source of referral

- Primary health problems: diagnosis, medications, medical history, hospitalizations

- Activities of daily living: ability to walk or wheel unescorted, bathe self, toilet self, dress, etc.

- Instrumental activities of daily living: Ability to prepare own meals, do housework, do laundry, handle phone, etc.

- Emotional status: ability to cope with life changes, past experiences in handling change

- Mental status: review of memory, judgement, etc.

- Financial status: expenses, income, assets, financial assistance, who pays bills, etc.

- Support system: who assists individual? What is availability and frequency of contact? What is their health? What other responsibilities do they have? What agencies assist?

- Goals: What hopes and expectations do the participant and the family have for the day care experience?

In addition to the intake assessments, each of the professionals working with the participant will need to do an assessment. For example, the social worker will do an in-depth psychosocial evaluation, the nurse will do a physical assessment and therapists will also do their own assessments. It is also important that the participant's medical records and hospital history be included as part of the intake materials. Some centers also require a doctor's order for participation in the program.

An excellent resource regarding assessment of the elderly is the ind-depth work, *Assessing the Elderly: A Practical Guide to Measurement*. It reviews physical, mental, and social functioning, as well as composite measures. It notes that readers should bear in mind the purpose of each measure: description, screening assessment, monitoring, or prediction (Kane and Kane 1981, 23).

The Participant Record and the Individual Plan of Care

Many centers use a problem-oriented record so that the intake assessment provides the basis of the participant's record. Problems are outlined and numbered. For each problem, SOAP notes are developed. The SOAP note is a type of progress note that is structured around *s*ubjective observations, *o*bjective data, *a*ssessment, and *p*lans. The development of the participant's plan of care at the center would be the outcome of the intake assessment and development of the problem-oriented record. The following example illustrates these sections from the records of a participant, Elizabeth S.

Participant Case Illustration: Mrs. S

Profile. Mrs. S is an 80-year-old married woman who resides with her husband in senior housing. The couple receives physical and emotional support from their married son and daughter. Mr. S has been caring for his wife, but due to the advanced stages of cancer, his abilities to handle her increased wandering have diminished. In a family meeting, the decision was made to have Mrs. S attend adult day care two times per week.

Participant's Current Problem List

1. Dementia

   - Decreased mentation: mental status quotient (MSQ) is 1/10

   - Semidependent in instrumental activities of daily living (IADL)

2. Caregiver stress

   - Spouse terminally ill
   - Daughter and son supportive
   - Family considering eventual nursing home placement

Progress Notes, Using SOAP Format

Problem No. 1

S: According to participant's husband and daughter, Mrs. S's failing memory has been a problem for some time. Spouse reports that Mrs. S is able to ambulate without assistance, and sometimes "just leaves the house." Family fearful that Mrs. S needs additional supervision to ensure her safety. Mrs. S acknowledges that "I sometimes forget."

O: Mrs. S was evaluated at local geriatric assessment clinic and findings indicated that she has a progressive dementing illness. ADC staff observe a healthy, well-nourished, neatly attired woman. Pleasant and sociable. Has difficulty following instructions such as "hang your coat in the closet," but can follow one-step instructions such as "open the closet door." Often cannot find way around ADC center and has been observed to wander while at the center.

A: Mrs. S has significant cognitive deficits. She needs a safe, secure environment, as she has a tendency to wander.

P1: Activities coordinator will involve Mrs. S in mentally stimulating activities, provide opportunities for social interaction, and experiment with various recreational activities to determine areas of interest/skills. Include in the "Scheduled Walk" program.
P2: Nurse will monitor overall health status, as Mrs. S is not capable of expressing physical needs/changes.
P3: OT will further evaluate cognitive/ADL/IADL skills and recommend course of treatment.
P4: All staff provide warm, supportive, safe environment. Utilize normal precautions re: wandering. Assist with ADLs, as needed. Provide Mrs. S with praise and encouragement when she does try activities.

Problem No. 2

S: Spouse states that he is in end stages of cancer, and that Mrs. S does not know this. Son and daughter state that, "We help as much as we can. We want both Mom and Dad to live at home as long as they can, but we've already started to look at nursing homes." Son says that Mrs. S could live with him, in the event of his father's death.

O: Caring and supportive family. Both son and daughter are married, with children, and both work.

A: Mrs. S needs increasing supervision as her husband becomes weaker. Family realistic about their options for the future, but still needing much education and emotional support to deal with their situation.

P1: Provide ADC as respite for spouse and children.
P2: Encourage family to consider increasing ADC time from two up to five days per week, over the next month. This will establish a regular routine for Mrs. S that may help her to compensate for upcoming changes in her living situation.
P3: All staff be alert to Mrs. S's needs when her husband dies.
P4: Social worker provide counseling for adult children, and evaluate grandchildren's needs.

This case example was developed for illustrative purposes only. Each center will develop its own style of record keeping. In many centers, the disciplines (nursing, social work, recreation, etc.) use one record and have composite SOAP notes, as is the case with this illustration. Alternately, in some centers each discipline has separate sections in the participant chart. Centers will also need to decide whether they prefer shorter, more concise notes or a longer narrative style.

The importance of the individual plan of care is underscored by Helen Padula, who writes,

An individual plan of care says we are dealing with a unique individual and with a program tailored to that person's needs, preferences and pace (1983, 37).

Trial Period

Some centers use trial periods of one to three weeks for new participants. It is during this time that the initial plan of care is developed and discussed with the participant and the family. The trial period is mutually beneficial for the center and for the clients. It is during this time that all parties get to know each other and determine the appropriateness of the placement.

Using a designated staff member as the primary care person can be particularly effective in assisting a new participant's adjustment in day care. The primary care person is designated prior to the initial day of attendance, and is assigned responsibility for monitoring progress or problems until completion of the initial assessment. Specific responsibilities may include:

- Introduction of the new participant to other staff, volunteers, and current participants
- Orientation of the new participant to center facilities and routines
- Review of daily activity calendar
- Regular meeting times to answer questions and concerns

The primary care person notes, on a special form, the problems and progress of the participant in activities and routines. For example, items recorded could include:

- Activity level and types of activities in which person becomes involved
- Ability to orient to facility and routines
- Interactional styles and sociability
- Eating habits
- Successful ways of relating to participant

The primary care person takes an active part in the initial assessment and becomes a key person in formulation of the individual plan of care. This person should also be the key contact person for family members who have questions about the participant's situation or care.

If, upon conclusion of the trial period, the participant is becoming adjusted to the center and is appropriate for the type of care that can be provided, then a mutually agreeable plan of care is developed between center staff and the family. Some centers will have clients sign a contract, while other centers will simply discuss the arrangements verbally.

Active Participation and Periodic Reviews

Upon the successful conclusion of the trial period, the prospective participant has now been fully admitted to the adult day care center and is considered an active participant. The participant is becoming fully acclimated to the center, the staff, other participants, and daily routines. The person's problem-oriented record has been established. Medical and hospital records have been obtained; and additional participant paperwork has been completed.

For many new participants, a major adjustment should occur as the person becomes accustomed to being part of a group. Most new participants have spent much time at home, prior to their ADC admission. As Helen Padula states,

> The sense of belonging to a group and acceptance by it, are among the most important ingredients of ADC. The goal of any ADC should be to help people help themselves (1983, 47-9).

As in our case illustration, Mrs. S acclimated well to the center. She enjoys the daily opportunity to be with her new friends. Since her enrollment, the activities coordinator has had Mrs. S try a variety of activities. So far, the activities she enjoys best are baking, painting, music, and of course, the "scheduled walk" program! The nurse and OT have also spent time with Mrs. S to complete their initial professional assessments and to develop their baseline data. Since her admission to ADC, Mrs. S's husband did die. The social worker met with Mrs. S and her son and daughter to discuss their feelings about Mr. S's death and Mrs. S's relocation to her son's home. The family currently has no intention of placing Mrs. S in a nursing home, but is pleased to have that alternative, "in case the need arises." Within a very short period of time, Mrs. S had to cope with many changes: the death of her spouse, relocation to her son's home, and adjustment to ADC. Fortunately, her enrollment in the center occurred two months prior to her husband's death, so the ADC has provided Mrs. S and her family the continuity of a routine and supportive environment, which is so necessary in times of stress.

As staff members have worked with Mrs. S and her family, the participant record has been frequently updated to reflect these changes. This center uses a 60-day review schedule. Therefore, Mrs. S's entire problem list has been reviewed, modified, and updated every two months. As problems became resolved, they were considered "inactive." If a new problem surfaces, then that problem is listed on the problem list and a SOAP note is written.

All centers should have a regularly scheduled staff meeting at which the plans of care for each of the participants are reviewed. The frequency of these periodic reviews is dependent upon the center's quality assurance standards, as well as some funding source requirements (i.e., Medicaid). Some funding sources require a monthly review, while others require it less frequently. If specific times are not required by regulatory bodies, then each center may determine its own monitoring schedule—this may be every 60 or 90 days. As changes occur in the plan of care, these changes should be documented in the participant's record. Monitoring schedules may need to be more frequent than 60 days, depending upon the participant's medical/ rehabilitation/management needs.

Discharge Planning

As the participant's condition changes, discharge planning will need to be reviewed. As stated at the beginning of this chapter, discharge planning is an on-going process. For many participants, the intent of the day care placement may be a long-term community-based plan of care. These participants may be with the center for a number of months or perhaps even years. Mrs. S's case was an excellent illustration of how discharge planning is very much an active part of her plan of care. Her family is fortunate enough to have alternatives available in case changes in Mrs. S's condition warranted her discharge from ADC.

Sometimes, especially in urban areas with a number of day care centers, participants may be discharged from one center to another. For example, Harry J was admitted to the church-based day care center nearest his home when he first developed the problems of Alzheimer's disease. The ADC staff warned his family that the church setting could not accommodate people who were incontinent, and that should this problem develop, Mr. J would have to be discharged. Together, the family and staff investigated alternative services that might be needed in the future. Several months later, when Harry J began to become incontinent, he was discharged to a day care program specializing in serving people with Alzheimer's disease. Mrs. H, on the other hand, began her day care experience in a rehab-oriented program after her hip replacement surgery. When she completed her physical rehabilitation, she transferred to a day care center that was in a senior center near to her home. She was recently discharged from day care entirely, and is now active in the senior center.

There will be some participants who are admitted to rehab-oriented centers with every hope that improvement will be significant enough to allow discharge to sheltered employment. Others who show significant improvement may prefer to be discharged to their own homes, where they can use new skills to care for themselves. One gentleman reached his maximum rehabilitation potential in an ADC and was subsequently discharged from the program. He now serves as a Title V senior companion and assists other senior citizens! That is definitely a success story for everyone.

For participants who deteriorate, much assistance may be needed in working with families regarding other types of care, including implementing or increasing assistance within the participant's home. These resources may include Meals-on-Wheels, homemaker or companion services, or perhaps home health aide services. Each center should be responsible for knowing what community resources exist for their clientele. In other instances, the participant and the family may need to begin exploration of nursing home placement. This is often a difficult decision. When they receive guidance from the day center staff, however, many families are comforted in knowing that they have assisted their family member as much as possible.

One of the strengths of adult day care centers is in their ability to accommodate a wide variety of participants who have very special needs. Coupled with the ADC's view of the participant, using a holistic approach, is the center's professionalism exercised in its assessment, development and implementation of diverse plans of care and documentation skills.

References

Kane, R.A., and R.L. Kane. 1981. *Assessing the elderly: A practical guide to measurement.* Massachusetts: Lexington Books.

National Institute on Adult Daycare. 1984. *Standards for adult day care.* Washington, DC: National Council on the Aging.

Padula, H. 1983. *Developing adult day care: An approach to maintaining independence for impaired older persons.* Washington, DC: National Council on the Aging.

Further Reading

O'Brien, C.L. 1982. *Adult day care: A practical guide.* Monterey, CA: Jones Bartlett Publishing Co.

Walker, H.K., et al. 1973. *Applying the problem oriented system.* New York: MEDCOM Press.

Weiler, P.G. and E. Rathbone-McCuan. 1978. *Adult day care: Community work with the elderly.* New York: Springer Publishing Co.

CHAPTER 13

Planning a Therapeutic Activities Program

Linda Cook Webb

You all taught me that, even with this wheelchair, I am still a person—that I can still do things and have friends—and that it makes a difference to somebody. You gave me back myself. (Comment from an ADC participant).

Activities are frequently undervalued or written off as "fun and games." In reality, adult day care centers can only be truly successful when they provide therapeutic activities programming based on a great deal of thought, planning, and creativity. Therapeutic activities enable the withdrawn person to look outside of him or herself. Activities help the confused person feel some contact—if not with what we consider reality, then at least with our friendship. Activities offer the physically handicapped person a fun way to master new skills, and they lend support to the person with new limitations. Above all, therapeutic activities help to maintain some sense of normalcy for all participants.

Hamill and Oliver (1980, 3) point out, "The purpose of therapeutic, in contrast to diversional, activities is to stimulate changes in the participants' abilities from dysfunctional to functional." To accomplish that goal, they outline three objectives:

- Using the participant's current abilities
- Preventing further deterioration
- Improving function to the highest degree possible.

159

An additional benefit is that "an individualized recreation plan can provide real motivation and impetus to a participant to return to the center to receive other therapies that may not be as pleasant but are equally as important" (Weiler and Rathbone-McCuan 1978, 93).

A variety of factors impact upon development of therapeutic programming, including abilities of the staff and limitations in space or equipment. The most important factor, however, is the participant. Development of the activities program must begin with individual assessments of each person's needs and interests. The resulting goals guide a personalized program of therapeutic endeavor. Staff must monitor participants' responses to activities to establish program effectiveness. As individuals change (becoming either more or less capable) programming should adapt accordingly.

In true therapeutic programming, staff are not in control. Rather, staff only guide activities to follow the beacon that participants provide. With assessment, staff try to "see inside" the participants' world enough to discover their needs and resources. In the end, though, success of the activities is dependent on participants. Staff can try to predict, but can never guarantee the outcome. In a way, that may be the most fascinating aspect of designing therapeutic activities; there is always another surprise of the human spirit waiting around the corner.

Assessing Participants' Status, Needs, and Interests

Activities assessment should include input from all caregivers (nurse, therapist, social worker, aides, family, and any others) as well as personal observation by the activities director.

A complete participant assessment, allowing thorough planning of therapeutic activities, will include:

- Physical status, limitations, and goals

- Mental status, limitations, and goals

- Emotional status, limitations, and goals

- Functional status, limitations, and goals (assessment of activities of daily living, such as eating and dressing, and instrumental activities of daily living, such as shopping and telephoning)

- Dietary limitations

- Social history and current supports
- Positive aspects and personal strengths in the individual's present life
- Current and past interests
- The participant's personal goals
- The family's expectations

The participant's physical, mental, and emotional status will point to specific goals that should be addressed by activities. Frequently, many participants will have similar needs or at least will have goals that can be met through similar activities. Goals may relate to any area of an individual's life, as the following examples will show.

Thomas R is a 65-year old man in the early stages of Alzheimer's disease. He is experiencing depression and fear about his future, which compounds a mild disorientation. In this case, a goal might be to decrease his intense focus on his limitations. Activities supporting that goal would reinforce remaining abilities and provide an atmosphere of friendly acceptance of his true limitations. Additional activities might provide an outlet for Mr. R to express his fear of what the future holds—and find out that he is not alone in being fearful.

Mrs. B is a 72-year-old recently retired school teacher recovering from a stroke. She is now paralyzed in her right arm that shows no potential for return of function. Mrs. B misses teaching, but she is accepting of her situation and wants to learn to care for herself with her left hand (i.e., feeding, grooming). Her primary goal could be to increase coordination in her left hand. Appropriate activities, in the beginning, would emphasize large controlled movements. A secondary goal is to work toward replacing some of Mrs. B's accustomed pursuits. Activities that require leadership or educational skill are most attractive to her.

Miss M is a 50-year-old woman who has just come to the center. She is still experiencing anger over the recent diagnosis of her chronic illness. At times, she slams a book or other object down on the table with excessive force. Her family is concerned, but has no history of talking about their feelings. One goal could be to provide more appropriate outlets for Miss M's anger. Two types of activities would be helpful here: Those that encourage expenditure of large amounts of energy and those that facilitate her talking about her anger and her illness.

Beginning to Plan

Helen Padula (1983, 47) points out that,

the most important stimulus…is a quiet atmosphere of expectation. It consists of respect for the latent strength (regardless of how small) in all human beings…. Impaired old people are thought by many to be on a downhill course. Not much can or should be expected. Why put pressure on them or set up unreal expectations? Neither is proposed. No one will be pressured…. No one will be considered a failure. But what happens when nothing is expected? We *invite* nothing to happen….

Within this attitude of quiet expectation, the activities planner can make use of some fairly simple general guidelines. The following guidelines apply to specific activities that will be discussed later in the chapter.

All activities should be capable of adaptation for people with different goals or different levels of ability. One way to accomplish this is through task analysis. Break each activity into its simplest components, and identify which goals those components address. For example, repotting a plant involves the following steps:

- Gather the plant and all supplies onto the table
- Select a new pot from those available
- Put pebbles and dirt in the bottom of the pot
- Remove the plant from the old pot
- Loosen dirt around the roots
- Place plant in new pot
- Fill pot with dirt
- Fertilize and water
- Admire the plant in its new pot

Some steps require carrying and lifting (gather supplies), while others require fine motor skills (loosen roots.) Still others require judgement (choose new pot) or knowledge (how to get the plant out of the old pot.) If repotting is done as a group activity, participants will all have the opportunity to participate at their own level. In this context, admiring the plant becomes an important task because it may be the only way that some individuals can participate.

In general, alternate physically oriented activities with more restful ones. Avoid exercise for one-half hour after meals. If you are working with confused or agitated participants, be certain to provide consistency of scheduling from one day to the next. It is particularly helpful to start each day with the same activity. Figure 13-1 depicts a sample monthly activity plan.

As participants become more independent, it is important to rely on *their* abilities. Some may want to lead discussion groups or demonstrate flower arranging or bring in a grandchild to dance for the group. The resources represented by participants can be amazing, as this story from a day care director in Kansas illustrates:

> I will never forget Herman, on the day he declared his independence. Herman had had a stroke and was extremely weak on his left side. He wore a brace and used a cane and could still barely hobble around. One day I came into the center when Herman was setting up chairs for the exercise group. I thought, "Poor Herman, it's going to take him forever to do this," so I said, "Here, let me help you." He put up with my help for a while, when he finally came over and said, "You're doing it wrong! It's so much easier if you just let me do it." That made me feel so good! Here was this man who could hardly walk, telling an able-bodied person that he could do this work best. I am still in awe of Herman, not because he is so unusual, but because he is so typical of what day care folks can do.

Keep in mind that therapeutic activities should serve the special needs of all participants, not just the majority. ADC staff have, on occasion, developed a whole new activity specifically because a particular participant had needs that were not being met.

The therapeutic program should include at least some special activities for particular types of people within the group. Give special attention to the needs and interests of men, confused participants, persons with language barriers, and extremely frail participants. It is often difficult to plan activities for these groups, and they therefore may be ignored in programming.

Time	MONDAY	TUESDAY	WEDNESDAY	THURSDAY	FRIDAY
8:00	Coffee and Conversation			Cooking Club	
9:00	Newspaper Reading and Current Events Discussion				
10:00	Break				
10:30	Exercise Group				
11:30	Break (Selected Participants Assist with Setting Tables)				
12:00	Lunch				
1:00	Break (Selected Participants Assist with Clean-Up)				
1:30	Health Education or Reminiscence Group	Adapted Bowling	Sing-Along	Special Events: Birthday party/Dance/ Outside Speaker/Outside Entertainment	Movies
2:45	Break				
3:15	Walking/Wheeling Club				
3:45	Individual Activities				
5:00	Center Closes				

Figure 13-1 Sample Activity Plan.

Finally, remember that as participants' needs change, the activities should also change. The therapeutic approach includes regular evaluation and updating of programming.

Matching Goals and Activities

Once participants have been assessed and goals identified, you can proceed to structure activities. The three participants described in case studies earlier could all work toward their diverse goals through two types of activities. Sports, such as balloon volleyball or adapted bowling, would reinforce Thomas's remaining physical abilities, while training Mrs. B in use of her left arm, and allowing Miss M to appropriately discharge angry energy. A discussion group centered on the topic of feelings about disabilities would allow Thomas to express his fear, while showing Miss M that it might be OK to talk about her anger. Mrs. B, a very calm person, could be a stabilizing force in the group, and could therefore resume some of her old leadership roles. (Note that such a discussion should be led only by an individual with special training to respond therapeutically to the emotions that might be expressed.)

Figure 13-2 lists several needs that participants will experience at one time or another, and links those needs to related activities.

Sensory stimulation is particularly important to those persons who are withdrawn, isolated, severely confused, or vision/hearing-impaired. Sensory stimulation games involve isolating each sense to identify common objects, sounds, smells, and so on. For example, the "Feelie Mealie Bag" is a tube of cloth used for isolating the sense of touch. A staff person holds an object inside the bag. A participant reaches in from the other side and attempts to identify the object by holding it. Music, visitors, and many other activities also involve stimulating the senses. Last—but not least— don't forget hugs!

Exercise is especially important to the person with physical limitations. Often, large movements, such as those required for chair exercise or balloon volleyball, are easier for participants than small muscle movement. Be certain, though, that the specific exercise activities chosen are helpful—not harmful—to participants. For example, a stroke victim should not be encouraged to do grasping motions, and heart patients with angina should not lift their arms above their heads. The activities director should work as closely as possible with a nurse, physical therapist, or occupational therapist

Need	Related Activities
Sensory Stimulation	Feelie Mealie and other sensory stimulation games Pet visitation Movies Music, Singing, Dancing Field Trips Gardening
Physical Exercise (Large motor movements)	Exercise groups Walking or wheeling club Dancing Bowling (adapted) Balloon Volleyball
Physical Exercise (Fine motor movement)	Cards and board games Piano playing Rolling cancer bandages Setting the table
Health Promotion	Health education groups Walking club Goal-setting group
Competition	Games, contests Puzzles, word games
Socialization	Discussion groups Parties Intergenerational programs Remotivation Therapy
Intellectual Pursuits	Discussion groups Spelling Bee Memory games Logic and reasoning games Educational lectures
Creativity	Music, singing, dancing Drama Writing
Generativity	Intergenerational programs Autobiography Oral history
Life Review	Reminiscence groups Autobiography Oral history

Figure 13-2 Participant needs addressed by selected activities.

Need	Related Activities
Emotional Expression	Pet-facilitated therapy Pre-school visits Peer support groups Reminiscence, discussion groups
Emotional Support	Peer support groups Reminiscence, discussion groups
Community Contact	Field trips Speakers Community service projects
The Need to be Needed (Service and Responsibility)	Participant Council Volunteer projects for community organizations Work-type activities Gardening Setting the table
Self-Determination	Participant Council Goal-setting groups
Leadership	Participant Council (officers) Assisting in leading activities
Devotions	Bible reading or discussion Volunteering on mission projects Choir Meditation Memorial services, funerals
Positive Body Image	Barber/Beauty days Cosmetics demonstrations Fashion shows
Fun	Parties, games "Bring Your Favorite Hat" Days Telling Jokes

Figure 13-2, continued.

in developing exercise programs. Fine muscle exercise can be incorporated into a variety of activities, from playing cards to setting the table. Beware of encouraging arthritics to use their hands for extended periods of time, as this may actually be harmful. As with large motor movements, the activities staff should seek guidance from a therapist or nurse.

Health promotion involves learning about how to take better care of ourselves and becoming motivated to do those things we should. Often, just having the support of a group in learning and setting goals can be helpful. One popular activity for more alert participants is the "hospital seminar series." Once a week, for six weeks, various hospital staff talk about their roles in health care. Speakers should include at least a nurse and social worker, but everyone from the chief executive officer to the janitor could be good speakers. These series are so successful because most participants have been hospitalized and expect that they might be again. This is their opportunity to ask, "Why is it done this way?" and to understand more about their own health care.

Some people have a stronger need for competition than others. Games and contests can foster a sense of meeting a challenge and winning. Remember, too, that competition may be with others or with one's self. For example, a walking group could allow people to work toward increased endurance without increased heart rate. In this case, the challenge would be very individual.

Socialization activities are particularly important to persons who cannot or do not visit with others on their own. Be aware, though, that the severely withdrawn or depressed person may be threatened by a group. If that is the case, observation of a large group or participation in a smaller group may be successful. Note that for the withdrawn person, socialization may be easier with animals or with children. Visiting programs are therefore very successful.

Intellectual activities help to promote a sense of adult pursuits. When one's body seems to be falling apart, it often becomes that much more important to the individual to know that the mind is intact. Activities that encourage participants to use their intellect include discussions, lectures, and spelling bees.

Creativity is a stronger need in some people than others, but almost everyone enjoys music. Dramatic presentations are usually surprisingly effective, as well. Crafts are not included under creative activities because crafts are often the least successful activity. Being old or handicapped does not automatically make a person interested in crafts; in fact, many participants couldn't care less. Further, crafts that can result in an adult-looking product are often either too difficult for many participants or relatively expensive. Crafts may be more successful when used on an individual basis or in facilities with liberal budgets for staff and supplies. Many people do not agree with this philosophy about arts and crafts; some centers have successfully developed a strong crafts component. For further guidance in this area refer to *Therapeutic Activities for the Handicapped Elderly* (Hamill and Oliver 1980).

Generativity is the need to pass on something of your own life to succeeding generations. Since this need is often very strong in older people, storytelling, and taping or writing autobiographies are very successful activities. The person with mental impairments may need assistance with recording an autobiography, but your efforts will be well worthwhile. This is a good activity to be conducted by volunteers.

Life review is the need to assess one's own life, take credit for the successes, and come to grips with the failures. This need is also often very strong in older people, and can sometimes be met by the same activities related to generativity.

Most participants are feeling some sort of negative emotion when they first come to the center. They may be angry or depressed about a new handicap. They may feel isolated, and as if they have the worst problems in the world. Whatever their situation, it will help for them to express these emotions. Often, these people do not need psychiatric attention. Rather, they need to find out that others share their feelings.

Giving and receiving emotional support is particularly important to persons needing long-term care. Successful adjustment to frailties, handicaps, and losses is often dependent on the presence of a confidante. Peer support and discussion groups can enable participants to express their feelings and receive positive feedback. Establishment of friendships will do the same thing, on an individual basis.

Arranging for community contact will promote a feeling of normalcy for persons who cannot participate in the community on their own. Field trips to local attractions or events allow participants a wider view of their community. Frequently, theaters, bowling alleys, civic groups, and other organizations will arrange for free admission for participants and their helpers. Some field trips can be scheduled for the evening, to involve family members. The community can also be brought into the center. Local political candidates may be willing to speak to participants. Theater groups may visit the center to perform scenes from their repertoire.

We all need to be needed. Activities in this area can be group or one-to-one. This is an area in which the janitor, driver, or cook can bridge over into activities responsibilities. Often, men like to help with sweeping the floor or pushing people in wheelchairs out to the van. These jobs may be done successfully, even by individuals with some dementia—although they must be supervised. Setting the table and cleaning up after lunch are usually big activities in day care centers. These familiar activities can be reassuring to older women who feel the loss of the housewife role.

The need for self-determination develops early in all of us—the need to make choices about ourselves and our environment, and to somehow control our own destinies. For the severely impaired person, self-determination is often minimal; sometimes refusing to participate in activities is the only area of choice that appears available. The more participants are encouraged to participate in decisions, the more active they will tend to be. A participant council can encourage this process by providing individuals a means to offer feedback about activities, meals, and other services.

For many handicapped elders, loss of prior leadership roles is a real problem. Some participants like to feel that they are leaders, but may not have the ability to carry through an entire activity. In those cases, the individual can assist staff in some special way. Mr. H, for example, is very frail and somewhat confused. His job is to "lead" the adapted bowling. He looks to make sure that the pins are set and that no one is standing in the way of the bowler. Then he says, "OK, take your turn." Mr. H takes his job very seriously, and won't be stand for sloppy pin-setting.

If encouraged to do so, some participants will be able to take full responsibility for planning, organizing, and carrying out specific activities. Dorothy decided that the time right after lunch was "too dead." Staff was usually busy with supervising clean-up after the meal and with helping people in the restrooms. Many of those participants who were not busy liked to have some quiet time after eating, and did not want to enter into activities. But Dorothy was determined. She decided, with some feedback from the staff, that she wanted to start a small singing group. First, she recruited her friend, Barbara, to play piano. Then the two of them started a routine of singing for about half an hour after lunch time. One by one, Dorothy asked other women to join them. Soon, the center had regular entertainment!

Even people who do not consider themselves to be very religious may feel a need for some type of devotional activity. Be particularly sensitive to different participants' beliefs and protect their rights to those beliefs. If at all possible, develop some sort of devotions or ritual to use when a participant dies. Some day care centers arrange for a few of the remaining participants to go to the wake or funeral as representatives of the center. Others develop memorial services that are conducted in the center. The specific activity is probably less important than the act of giving heed to a friend's passing.

Frail and handicapped people often develop a negative body image. This can be compounded by the fact that it can be hard for some of these people to wash their hair at home. Many day care centers now bring barbers and beauticians into the center once a month. Others arrange transportation to take participants to the barber or beauty shop on a regular basis. Barbers and beauticians often welcome this business, and may give discount coupons to participants. Manicures, cosmetics demonstrations, and fashion shows can also help to improve body image.

Finally, there are times that we all need to have fun! Often, the sillier the better. Halloween parties, complete with costumes, are among the most successful day care activities.

Don't Forget the Men!

Developing activities for women is generally thought to be easier than programming for men. This may be because, in long-term care, caregivers are usually women, and they usually serve a predominantly female population. We should remember, however, that men's need for therapeutic activities is just as great. In fact, it may be greater, simply because the men are so frequently in the minority. A gentlemen who used to come to adult day care once said, "When I was a child, my mother told me what to do. Then I got married, and I tried to please my wife. She died, and now I live with my daughter, and have to abide by her house rules. Now, I come here, and there are more women telling me what to do. I have had it!"

Ideally, the recreation staff should include men. These may be paid employees or volunteers. If other staff members are male, they should also be encouraged to work with the men participants in developing activities. Pursuits that are generally more attractive to men may include: work-type activities, sports, fishing, games such as poker and pool, and crafts such as woodworking and tile work. Intergenerational activities with boys and young men, in which the older man can be a mentor are especially successful. Development of leadership positions in the center and continued contact with men's clubs, such as Rotary or Kiwanis may also be very important to some men.

Many of these suggestions will also be attractive to women, and can be built into programs for everyone. Others should be reserved pretty much to the men, so that they feel they have something of their own. Sometimes, the best men's activity is simply a good old-fashioned "bull session," when the guys can get off on their own to talk.

Not Everything is Group

At times, we all need to be alone. This is no less true of people attending day care. No one should be forced to join in group activities. In fact, programming should specifically include some activities that are designed to be done individually or in pairs. These activities may include walking programs, certain crafts, games such as solitaire, puzzles, reading, writing, oral histories, and some work-type activities, or community service projects.

Integration of Activities

In addition to the specific needs already discussed, people also have a need to integrate various aspects of their lives. Activities that address one set of needs at a time will be successful. Building bridges among activities will be more successful.

At one center the participants read during newspaper discussion that a man in a wheelchair had burned to death in his home. (It was actually one of the participants who brought the article for discussion.) This turned the group's thoughts toward practical questions of "How would I get out, in case of a fire?" The article prompted good discussion that day, but the group didn't leave the issue there. The activities director arranged for the fire marshall to speak about fire safety in the home. Later, the group made fire extinguishers out of old coffee cans filled with baking soda. (Sprinkle the baking soda above the fire to put it out.) The day care director also began to involve participants in planning monthly fire drills. After each fire drill, the whole group discussed what went right, what went wrong, and how to do better next time. Thus, what could have been simply the reading of a sad story became instead the impetus for more responsible action by participants.

"Wear Your Favorite Hat Day" is a good way to integrate past and present experiences. Once, Glenn, who had been quite hostile and complaining as long as he attended the center wore, three-foot long rabbit ears for his hat. It turned out that, for years, he had been the Easter Bunny for the local children's hospital. By being able to bring that memory into his current experience with stroke, he began to soften and show his kinder side.

Integrating activities can take place in a number of ways. If the group has been practicing a play or musical piece, arrange for them to perform at local churches or civic events. If a regular participant is in the hospital or has moved away, ask members of the group to talk into a tape recorder, describing recent events at the center. Then send the recording to the absent person. Arrange events that will attract families to the center (picnics, parties, talent shows, etc.) This will help to bring the participant's life at home closer to the life in the center, and vice versa.

Measuring Progress

Documentation and reassessment of participants' progress are necessary to development of therapeutic activities. Often, seeing a participant every day makes it difficult to measure progress. Through written records, however, progress can become more obvious, pointing the way to changes needed in activities programming.

Ongoing documentation should include both records of frequency of participation and progress notes. These should be charted at least monthly, by the activity director or assistant. The original participant assessment should be repeated every six months, or at least once year.

The "participation in activities" form in Appendix G is an easy check list to record each participant's activities. Activities are divided according to categories of participant needs addressed rather than specific activities. This allows great flexibility in programming without having to change the recording form. It will also assist in analyzing progress and identifying gaps in programming for specific participants.

Space, Supplies, and Other Support

To carry out an activities program, activities staff will need space as well as equipment and supplies (see Chapter Five for architecture and interior design recommendations.) The staff will also need input or guidance from related disciplines (i.e., nursing and therapy.) These can all range from quite sophisticated to very informal, and still result in a quality program.

Some centers may have access to generous staffing and funds for activities. Others may rely more heavily on sharing resources with related divisions of the agency. Still others may look to community support or use creative means to extend those resources they do have.

Ideally, a day care center should have a variety of large and small activities areas so that participants can move around during the day. Since many centers operate with limited space, some "sleight of hand" can be helpful. Make use of all possible areas within the facility for activities. If the facility does not have a variety of rooms available for activities, at least move around the main room for different activities during the day. Sometimes, just facing the opposite direction provides the "feel" of being in another room. Centers that do not have outdoor activities areas have even had success with using the fire drill as an activity. It gives everyone a chance to get away from their accustomed surroundings and walk outside briefly.

Every activities program should have access to monies earmarked for supplies and special events. Amounts can range up to several hundred dollars a month, but even $10 per month can help to support an excellent activities program.

If the center does not quite have adequate resources, don't despair. Many communities are supportive with donations of funds, supplies, and volunteer time. Families will often be willing to donate for special events or projects, too. Make sure that you let people know what you need— whether it is party refreshments, or money for special entertainment, or professional volunteers as consultants to your program.

Evaluating Therapeutic Programming

Established programs should be evaluated at least every year, and should introduce new activities as needed during that time. Evaluation can be done by the activities director, another staff person, or an outside party. Figure 13-3 is a sample evaluation format, to which you may wish to add your own specific questions.

Activities programming is the heart of adult day care, as it has a strong impact on the overall atmosphere of each center. Goal-directed activities contribute toward a therapeutic climate in which each individual and the group as a whole attempt to do all that they can. And, after all, that is what adult day care is all about—encouraging the human spirit.

Name of ADC:_____

No. of Participants:_____   No. of Activities Staff:_____

Have all clients' interests, abilities, and needs been assessed?_____
    How many charts include a written assessment?_____
    How many charts include regular reassessments?_____
    Do Progress Notes make reference to assessment information?_____

Is participation documented in all cases?_____
    How many charts include a completed "Participation in Activities"
    form?_____
    How many charts include regular and up-to-date Progress Notes?_____

What percentage of the total client population is involved in activities?
    Daily_____
    Weekly_____

Who is involved in specific activities (i.e., men, women, alert, confused)?
Are any groups underserved?

How are participants involved in planning activities?

Do activities address a wide range of human needs?

Are adequate space and equipment available for activities?

Are volunteers used in activities?   How?

How can the activities program be improved?

Figure 13-3   Activities program annual evaluation. Source: D.L. Webb & Associates, 1981. Kansas City, Mo.

References

Hamill, C.M., and R.C. Oliver. 1980. *Therapeutic activities for the handicapped elderly*. Rockville, MD: Aspen Systems.

Padula, H. 1983. *Developing adult day care: An approach to maintaining independence for impaired older people*. Washington, DC: National Council on the Aging.

Weiler, P.G., and E. Rathbone-McCuan. 1978. *Adult day care: Community work with the elderly*. New York: Springer Publishing Co., Inc.

Further Reading

Brubaker, S.H. 1983. *Workbook for reasoning skills: Exercises for cognitive facilitation*. Detroit: Wayne State University Press.

Burnside, I.M. 1978. *Working with the elderly: Group processes and techniques*. Belmont, CA: Duxbury Press.

Kaplan, J. 1972. Satisfying use of time. In *Working with older people: A guide to practice, Volume III: The aging person: Needs and services*. Department of Health, Education, and Welfare, 45–49. Washington, DC: Government Printing Office, Pub. no. HSM 72-6007.

Olszowy, D.R. 1978. *Horticulture for the disabled and disadvantaged*. Springfield, IL: Charles C. Thomas, Publisher.

Panella, J. Jr. 1987. *Day care programs for Alzheimer's disease and related disorders*. New York: Demos Publications. 39–66.

Rathbone-McCuan, E., and J. Levenson. 1975. Impact of socialization therapy in a geriatric day care setting. *Gerontologist* 15: 338–342.

Ross, M.A. 1984. *Fitness for the aging adult with visual impairment: An exercise and resource manual*. New York: American Foundation for the Blind.

Sincox, R.B., and P.S. Cohen. 1986. *Adapting the adult day care environment for the demented older adult*. Springfield, IL: Illinois Department on Aging. 23–28.

CHAPTER 14

Family Services in Adult Day Care

Kathryn S. Katz and Paul D. Maginn

Adult day care serves older persons and other handicapped adults, but its impact also touches the families and caregivers of those individuals. Rathbone-McCuan (1976) reported that families benefited psychologically from involvement of a family member in adult day care. Similar findings have been reported by Zimmerman (1986), who found that ADC enables families and caregivers to better attend to their relatives' needs, as well as their own. In the process, familial relationships are improved.

The National Institute on Adult Daycare (NIAD) recognizes the importance of services to families and caregivers as an integral part of day care, through providing support, respite, and education. The NIAD *Standards for Adult Day Care* define counseling as an essential service component. "Counseling should be available to each participant and should involve appropriate family members...If staff is not sufficiently trained to handle intensive therapy, arrangements should be made for the services of a trained professional as necessary" (NIAD 1984, 38-9). Centers faced with limited resources due to tight budgets may need to explore available professional resources in their communities to meet the intent of the NIAD standards. Such resources may include local family service agencies; social work, psychology, guidance and counseling programs at local colleges; mental health centers; hospital-based social workers; or private practitioners. Centers can establish cooperative work agreements or enter into formal contractual arrangements. A review of the community, the center resources, and center philosophy will help a center determine the best course of action.

Defining Family

From the first moment in which you say "hello" on the telephone, you have begun to provide services to the participant's family member. The initial phone contact will provide both the family member and the center personnel with a significant amount of information about each other. The family member will be able to detect the warmth, caring, and accessibility of the center. The center staff will begin to obtain basic information about the potential participant and learn about the family situation, as well as their expectations of the center.

The definition of family in this chapter is quite broad. Family members can include the participant's spouse, adult children, grandchildren, siblings, nieces or nephews, and in some cases their own mother and father, as well as many other blood relatives. Adoptive relatives, in-laws, ex-spouses, and stepchildren may also enter into the picture. Those who have worked in adult day care agree that the term "family" or "caregiver" can be quite broad. In addition to the relatives just outlined, a caregiver can also include persons who are not kin such as a neighbor, the attorney, trust officers, church people, and friends. For the purposes of this chapter, these caregivers will be included in the terminology, "family." Perhaps the most important definition of a family member is the individual who cares for the participant in a physical or an emotional manner. Throughout the balance of this chapter, we will use the term "family" in its broadest sense.

Center Resources and Philosophy

Before discussing specific services that adult day care centers can provide to families, it is important to review administrative issues such as:

- What family services can be provided within the context of the center?

- Who will provide these services?

- When will family services be provided?

- Will a separate fee be charged for family services?

The determination of the amount of family services the center is able to provide will be based upon its philosophy regarding this issue. The center's family services may range from minimal contact with families to working with families around very specific participant-centered issues (e.g., should Mom be placed in a nursing home?) Some centers provide a very broad service package that includes *any* counseling needs of the family (delinquent grandchild in the home, drug abuse by son-in-law, and so forth). The molding of the center's services will be related to the center's philosophy regarding how broadly they define the client to be served. The decision regarding the center's philosophy will then dictate how much staff and time is devoted to family services.

The decision as to who will provide the family services is dependent upon the range of services offered, the skill and expertise required to perform the services, and the necessity to comply with regulatory bodies. Family services can range from basic information and referral assistance up to and including psychotherapy. Obviously, the skill level required to provide these vastly different types of family services will point to the types of staff who will be providing each service. Centers may utilize an on-staff social worker for many of the family services, but may also use a consulting psychiatrist or psychologist for additional clinical expertise. As stated earlier, cooperative working agreements with local agencies and practitioners may also meet the center's needs.

The scheduling of family services should be negotiated, dependent upon the modality used and the number of schedules to coordinate. If family counseling is the modality, the meeting time can be easily negotiated between the family and the staff members. However, if a group meeting is the modality, then members will have to be polled to determine the best meeting time and date. It is *not* an easy task to coordinate very busy caregiver schedules, so the decision is usually based upon when the majority of people will be available. If evening or weekend family services will be offered, then staff should be hired with this in mind. Staff who will be working most directly with the families should expect to maintain flexible schedules that can include some evening meetings.

Often, expenses for providing family services are included in the center's general operating budget and are hence reflected in the daily charge. However, if a center has assumed additional expenses, (e.g., hired a consultant), then they may consider passing this cost on to family members who use these additional programs. Some centers also feel that charging even a nominal fee helps families to appreciate the services and recognize it as a professional service being provided. An important factor will be to know the family members and have a sense of whether a fee will inhibit their ability to participate. As another alternative, if the center's costs are not covered, perhaps a local foundation or corporation would help to underwrite the costs.

As stated at the outset of this chapter, family services begin with the first "hello." When the initial referral is made to the adult day care center, the presenting problems may be stated as follows:

- "I feel that Mother is very lonely and needs companionship."

- "My wife has begun to wander, and I fear for her safety."

- "Since my brother had his stroke, he is not able to get around like he used to."

These are only a sampling of the types of initial inquiries that are made to an adult day care center. While the caller will often identify a need of the participant, the needs of the family member are also included in these statements. These needs may range from the heartbreak of experiencing dramatic changes in a loved one, to the frustration of caring for a family member who has reached maximum rehabilitation potential. Therefore, when the initial telephone inquiry is made, the staff member is not only beginning to make an assessment of the participant's needs, but also the family's needs and its ability to cope with the situation.

Assessing Family Needs

When assessing family needs, consider the family's ability to cope with its relative's physical or cognitive changes. This will help to determine whether the individual remains at home or is placed in an institutional setting. For example, many families say, "If Mom could have slept through the night and hadn't disturbed my husband and children, we could have kept her at home with us." Also look at expectations within the family. The pattern of caring has traditionally been dictated by cultural mores and familial patterns. These traditions have been changing and families are seeking alternative community-based means of caring for their loved ones. The acceptance of these changes in caregiving patterns often produces much intergenerational stress. For example, Mother may say, "*I* cared for *my* mother until she died, and I always thought you would do the same for me."

With these factors in mind, one can begin to develop the framework for assessing the family's needs. The initial intake interview provides the center with an excellent opportunity to learn more about the participant *and* the family. It is during the initial interview that much information about the participant and the family is gathered, and this is when a level of trust and sharing begins to develop. The first service the center will provide to the family is that of supportive listening at this stressful time. Many families view seeking assistance outside of the home as a sign of their own inability to handle their loved one. These feelings may be hidden well below the surface of information that is presented. However, staff with training and experience can detect and address these feelings. While learning about the potential participant, staff will also learn much about the family relationship and how caregiving responsibilities have been handled in this family system in the past.

During the initial interview, it is important to explore the participant's early life experiences, as well as caregiving responsibilities the participant may have had within his or her family or origin. Note the family member's description of the onset and course of the participant's illness or condition. It is interesting to see how these descriptions compare or differ with the physicians' medical histories.

It is important to explore the family member's previous relationship with the participant. Has it been close? Has it been distant? Is it now close by necessity? How has the decision-making process occurred in the family in the past?

In the interview, the family members should describe their current situations, including other responsibilities, jobs and careers, civic and social endeavors, as well as their own personal needs. Inquire whether other family members are involved with the participant. Finally, discuss what the participant's plan of care has been, what plans are currently in place, what has occurred to precipitate this referral to ADC, and what plans or expectations the family has regarding the future.

These basic components will provide an overview of the depth of involvement by family members, their willingness to be partners in caregiving responsibilities, and what their hopes for the future may be. The answers to these initial questions will provide a basic guideline for future interventions by center staff. Experience has shown that once the participant and family become comfortable within the interview, these basic components are often readily obtained from conversation.

The Family as Treatment Team Member

It is important to realize that family members are a crucial part of the treatment team. A case in point is that the occupational therapist may work with the participant on a daily basis to encourage range of motion exercises and independence with activities of daily living. While the participant is at the center, the staff members will be encouraging use of these newly learned skills. If the individual goes home and does not continue these new skills or exercises, the amount of progress will be minimal. Therefore, it is important to educate and encourage family members to be actively involved in the care of their relatives and to work as team members. This type of involvement is equally as important with the memory-impaired participants. For example, if the ADC staff work all day to let the participant know that it is Monday, and then the grandchildren at home kiddingly say that it is Wednesday, this can only increase confusion. Therefore, it is important to engage all family members as part of the treatment team.

There are many additional ways in which day care centers provide services to family members, ranging from very formal to quite informal. On an informal basis, families who transport their relatives daily to the center will have the most interaction with staff members. They will begin to view the staff as part of their own family, just as staff will begin to view them as very much a part of the center. There is usually much information given at the time participants are dropped off in the morning and picked up in the afternoon. We often hear whether Mom had a good night, whether she has been able to do things for herself, whether she needs her hair done today, and so on. In the afternoon, the family member will usually learn from the staff whether Mom has eaten her meal, whether she received therapy today, as well as other anecdotal information. Even though these family members participate in an informal way with staff, they truly do feel a part of the team.

Another opportunity for informal services to families is by finding opportunities for them to participate. Staff can invite families to attend entertainment or educational events, and/or some family members may want to volunteer at the center. Often, family members use the days the participant is at the center as time to do things for themselves (have their hair done, go grocery shopping, or just rest!) Therefore, some people may feel that when their family member is at the center, it is very much their own private time; those people will want to safeguard their time. Other family members, however, will be eager to share of themselves with the adult day care center. They can be readily counted upon to volunteer at outings, annual picnics, and similar functions. As it seems appropriate, discuss volunteering with family members. The opportunity to volunteer occasionally and give of themselves is often a way in which a family member shows appreciation for adult day care.

Individual, Family, and Group Counseling

In addition to informal family services, formal means of providing services can be done on an individual, family, or group basis. There may be families in which all three modalities will meet the needs at various stages. These modalities are as follows:

Individual Counseling

A lot of information is gleaned during the initial interview. Each practitioner will determine how to conduct the interview. Some prefer to talk with the participant and family together, and some prefer to talk with them separately. Still others use a combination of methods. It is usually during this initial interview, however, that much sharing of information occurs. In addition, the ADC staff member is providing much information about center services and additional community resources that can assist the participant or family. This information may include suggestions on how to obtain third party reimbursement for day care, or how to find companion sitter services for respite at home. After the participant is enrolled, many centers use family meetings to discuss the treatment plan. In addition, centers may ask the family to meet with staff on a regular basis to discuss the progress of care and changes in the treatment plan.

Another form of individual counseling involves providing emotional support in family caregiving responsibilities. The care of a loved one may be an overwhelming responsibility. Many family members will need an opportunity to share their feelings and concerns about the type of care they provide at home. Their feelings may include a wide range including guilt, frustration, and anger. During these individual counseling sessions, much support and information is often shared with the family member. Again, centers will need to decide whether to concentrate counseling efforts on issues regarding the participant's home care, or whether the center will also engage in counseling family members with nonrelated or chronic counseling needs.

Family Counseling Services

Often, entire families will seek the assistance of counseling services when they are unable to reach mutual agreement on major issues. These major issues may revolve around distribution of caregiving responsibilities, or the question of when to seek institutional care for their relative. These situations are usually very emotional and may cause long suppressed feelings to surface. Most of the family counseling sessions are done with family members and have not usually included the participant. However, if appropriate, the participant may be a part of the family counseling session. Marital counseling may be included under this category. An example is the case in which Mrs. W's husband was diagnosed as having Alzheimer's disease. She sought assistance regarding future financial planning, and discussed the feasibility of whether to legally divorce her husband to ensure financial viability for both of them in the future. As one can see, the issues that confront ADC staff members are complex and varying.

Group Counseling Services

Group therapy can be used as an independent modality, or in conjunction with either individual or family counseling. Therapeutic groups often focus on a central theme, such as spouses of participants, grandchildren and the participant, Alzheimer's disease, or stroke.

Education and Information-Sharing Groups

Family members are frequently more willing to participate in what they view as a "nontherapeutic" group setting. Providing an educational meeting, initially, will help to determine which family members would benefit more from a therapeutically directed group. In order to help ensure family members' attendance, centers may consider providing activities for participants during group meeting.

Educational meetings may be as structured or informal as the staff deems appropriate. The adult day care center may sponsor a semiannual family night series. The family night series is composed of six to ten evening sessions that deal with topics that are most relevant to the family members. A questionnaire is sent to family members prior to the first meeting. This questionnaire requests basic demographic information, the family members' willingness and availability to attend meetings, their descriptions of the participant's problems, and what topics or speakers would most meet their needs. After this information is obtained and analyzed, the staff plans the family night series. This responsibility could be shared with a volunteer family member. A family night series might include evening discussions with a physician, attorney, physical therapist, occupational therapist, and the program nurse, as well as a social worker from one of the local nursing homes. One popular evening is when family members have the opportunity to experience the handicap of their family member. This usually is a collaborative effort between the physical and occupational therapists, as well as the program nurse. Each of these three professionals develops experiential opportunities for the family members. For example, by using petroleum jelly on old eyeglasses, people can experience what it is like to have cataracts. In another example, the dominant hand is immobilized and then the person attempts various activities of daily living. Therefore, the combination of information sharing and experiential exercises can provide family members with much insight and helpful information to assist them in coping with caregiving responsibilities.

Other Means of Reaching Families

Several other means of reaching families should be noted. These resources may be particularly helpful for families unable to take advantage of other center services. They may also be helpful to centers with limited staffing.

Peer support groups are different from therapeutic or educational groups because they are led by group members, not staff. Day care centers can be the catalyst for formation of such groups for adult children or caregiving spouses. In either case, the day care center may merely furnish the space or actively assist with development. The benefits of support groups for families and other caregivers are well documented (Lidoff and Harris 1985; Lidoff 1985).

Newsletters can be effective means of providing information to families or caregivers, especially if work schedules or other obligations limit the time available to visit the center. Health information, behavior management tips, book reviews, resource identification, and information on financial concerns can be communicated to families in a way that meets their needs and ultimately helps the participant. Quarterly newsletters can be timely and manageable, even where budgeting is tight.

Health screenings sponsored or conducted by the center can be another means of reaching families. Health information can be distributed to those who attend the screenings. One or two evenings a year can be managed by most day care centers and are an excellent way of involving other community professionals in a joint effort promoting community health issues.

Auxiliaries may be attractive to those families who seek a more collaborative role with the center, beyond the needs of their relative. Several centers successfully channel this enthusiasm for day care into positive ways of enlisting public support through the auxiliary group. An active auxiliary can be an effective way of disseminating information, while building a base of interest and influence in furthering the development of day care.

The types of services available to the family are quite diverse. Though they range from informal conversations in the morning to a highly structured individual counseling session, the main theme of all family services focuses on the center's ability to assist families in their caregiving responsibilities. The more ways in which the center is able to support the family, the more ways the center will also achieve its goals of providing opportunities for independent living for the participants they serve.

References

Lidoff, L. 1985. *Supports for family caregivers of the elderly: Highlights of a national symposium.* Washington, DC: National Council on the Aging.

Lidoff, L., and P. Harris. 1985. *Idea book on caregiver support groups.* Washington, DC: National Council on the Aging.

National Institute on Adult Daycare. 1984. *Standards for adult day care.* Washington, DC: National Council on the Aging.

Rathbone-McCuan, E. 1976. Geriatric day care: A family perspective. *The Gerontologist* 15, 517-521.

Zimmerman, S.L. 1986. Adult day care: Correlates of its coping effects for families of an elderly disabled member. *Family Relations* 35:305:311.

Further Reading

Mace, N.L. and P.V. Rabins. 1984. *A survey of day care for the demented adult in the United States*. Washington, DC: National Council on the Aging.

O'Brien, C.L. 1982. *Adult day care: A practical guide*. Monterey, CA: Jones Bartlett Publishing Co.

Padula, H. 1983. *Developing adult day care*. Washington, DC: National Council on the Aging.

Panella, J. Jr. 1987. *Day care programs for Alzheimer's disease and related disorders*. New York: Demos Publications.

Ransom, B. and B. Dugan. 1987. *Adult day care: An annotated bibliography*. Washington, DC: National Council on the Aging.

Von Behren, R. 1986. *Adult day care in America: Summary of a national survey*. Washington, DC: National Council on the Aging.

Weiler, P.G. and E. Rathbone-McCuan. 1978. *Adult day care: Community work with the elderly*. New York: Springer Publishing Co.

CHAPTER 15

Record Keeping: Burden or Measurement of Progress?

Linda Cook Webb

Everyone in health care and human services has probably struggled with recording requirements at one time or another. In the midst of busy days caring for people, we tend to find it hard to take the time to record what we have done. Somehow, filling out forms just doesn't seem as worthwhile as our "real work" of being with the people. It becomes easy to see record keeping as a burden imposed by some bureaucrat who doesn't understand what we really do. Sometimes, that is the case. Far more often, however, good documentation proves to be to our benefit and to the benefit of the people we serve.

At the level of the participant chart, recording can help establish practical goals and evaluate progress toward those goals. In adult day care, this is particularly important. The progress we see with our participants is often very slow—so slow, in fact, that we may not realize from day to day that change is happening. If we document the participant's actions, however, we can look back one month or six months and realize that there has been major progress. This realization will help us—and our participants—to be more energized and focused in what we do. By the same token, decline can be so slow that no one notices. With recording, however, staff can more quickly catch problems that may need special attention or even medical care.

Administrative recording requirements may not be so clearly to the benefit of the people served. In a round about way, however, they are. For example, incident and accident reporting forms collect information necessary

189

to identify patterns of problems. Is the same type of accident occurring repeatedly under the same conditions? We then know that the conditions must be changed for the future protection of all involved. Perhaps (although this is rare) the family may bring suit as a result of an accident. By having proper documentation, the center will be in a better position legally and will reduce the amount of time and money spent in the courts. That time and money saved will then be available for taking care of people.

Financial records may even help the people we serve. By carefully tracking earned income, donations, in-kind services, and expenditures, it will be easier to convince foundations that the program should be funded. This, in turn, ensures that service will be there for the people who need it.

Documentation of referrals, admissions, and discharges will help analyze whom we are attracting and whom we are serving versus whom we want to serve. Often, this information can guide positive changes in the marketing plan and eventually result in more people being served.

Keep It Simple

Design the recording system to be as simple as possible, while still collecting needed information. The simpler and more straightforward forms are, the more likely staff will be to document. The more complex forms are, the less chance there is that they will be completed.

Evaluate how each piece of data will be used. If you are collecting certain information because "it might be handy someday," documentation has probably become too complex.

Carole O'Brien (1982, 307) offers helpful criteria for developing a simple, yet effective record system:

- It should possess suitable uniformity to provide for easy recording and tabulation, which permits interunit and interservice [evaluation]

- It should require the minimal amount of time consistent with the record's purpose

- It should be quickly obtainable to the service provider

- It should be subject to coordination on those parameters considered important for planning and evaluation

- It should provide for a participant's privacy

In addition to these guidelines, remember that there will be legal requirements for documentation to be performed by professional staff. For example, all states require that administration of medication be documented. Similarly, there will be specific nursing and therapy treatments that must be documented in a specific way. The center director should work with the other professional staff in developing the recording system.

Keeping Everyone Informed

In designing the recording system, give thought not only to what type of information to collect, but also to who should have access to that information. Staff may be primarily interested in participant progress notes and administrators may be primarily interested in financial reporting. Each, however, needs some knowledge of the other aspects of the program. Staff need a general awareness of the fiscal status of the program so that they can better understand purchasing decisions (or limitations). Administrators (particularly if they do not work in the same facility as the day care center) need to know how the program is changing people's lives. If administrators of new centers see only program financials, they may feel that adult day care is a failure. They need practical reminders that success is not measured only in dollars.

Confidentiality

In considering whom to inform, remember that some people should not have access to records. Establish confidentiality policies and procedures that indicate how and when access to records will be limited. This may involve storing records in locked filing cabinets or desks. It should certainly involve policies about where records may be taken. Participant charts, for example, should be restricted to the clerical area and/or offices. Charts should not be opened or left unattended in activities areas. Under no circumstances should staff be allowed to take charts home to catch up on recording. Staff and volunteers should also be trained in the principles of maintaining confidentiality outside of the center. Even for professionals, it is sometimes difficult not to share "that great story" from the center—but it is important to realize that the participants involved may not want the story told. If staff wants to tell about participants as part of marketing the center, they should first consult the individual and the family.

What to Record

Adult day care center records generally fall into three categories: the participant chart, administrative records, and employee records. The following list indicates the types of data that will be helpful in each category. Appendix G gives samples of some forms for collecting this information. The participant chart should include:

- **Referral and intake data.** Who made the referral and how did they find out about the center? What did the referral source say about the individual's functional status and needs? Was the person admitted? Why or why not? This information can assist in evaluating and planning marketing activities. The face sheet of the chart should record the participant's and family member's name, address, and phone number. Instructions for finding the client's home are also included if applicable. The face sheet also includes basic demographic information, such as gender, date of birth, and source of payment. The back of the face sheet can easily contain intake and referral data.

- **Admission assessment.** The center's professional staff should assess the prospective participant's needs, abilities, and resources. This section of the chart should also include basic medical information from the individual's family physician. See Chapter Twelve for more suggestions for contents of the assessment.

- **Referrals.** Record when referrals are made to other community services, such as companion sitter, homemaker, and medical specialists. Indicate the contact person, agency, address, and phone, for each provider, as well as services to be delivered.

- **Individual care plan, attendance and progress notes.** These items will guide the participant's care and will indicate family contacts during the length of service.

- **Physician's recertification.** Physicians should periodically be asked to review the participant's care plan and make any necessary changes in medical orders. Changes in medications should be closely monitored.

- **Discharge plan.** Indicate the reason for and date of discharge, as well as to whom the individual was discharged (family or referral to another agency).

- **Other information specific to the program.** For example, some centers will have records of lab work and others will not. Correspondence related to the case should also be kept in the chart.

Administrative records should include the following:

- **Participant attendance records.** These records contain information for billing and will be helpful in program evaluation.

- **Fiscal records.** A professional accountant should be consulted in setting up the bookkeeping system and in evaluating what the numbers in the financial statements mean.

- **Incident/accident reporting forms.**

- **Preventive maintenance records.** This may be as simple as checking electrical cords for fraying or as complex as testing the water in a whirlpool tub.

- **Annual reports.** These reports should summarize goals for the past year, progress toward those goals, and new goals for the coming year.

- **Other information specific to the program.** If the program has its own van, you may wish to track mileage and gas usage.

Employee records should include:

- **Face sheet.** Employee's and emergency contact's name, address, and phone number. Job title, entry pay level, and date of employment.

- **Application for employment.** Education, prior experience, and references. Standard forms can be obtained in many office supply stores. Some applications are designed to double as a face sheet.

- **Records of references checked.**

- Health reports.

- Attendance, evaluations and pay changes.

- Licensing and continuing education records for all professional staff.

- Records of disciplinary counseling.

Using Computers in Documentation

Many of the records required in adult day care involve copying information from one location to another (i.e., attendance data should be in the participant chart, in daily attendance summaries for the center, and in bills). Because of the need for repetitive recording, more and more centers are using computers to record and analyze information about services, finances, and other aspects of program operations. Chapter Sixteen describes the ways in which the computer can aid in documentation and outlines the steps involved in selecting a computer system.

Structuring Progress Notes

Most records that should be maintained by day care staff are fairly straightforward. The lists in this chapter and the sample forms in Appendix G should be sufficient to guide the bulk of record keeping. Documentation of participant progress, however, can become more involved. For this reason, it may be helpful to provide staff with a format for charting participants' progress. This will ensure that all applicable information has been included, as well as give consistency from one person's notes to another's.

One effective charting method is the problem-oriented record. This method is presented as an example only, as a few other methods can be similarly effective.

The problem-oriented record system was developed in 1969, and has since become a widely accepted standard for the health professions (and to a certain extent, social services). Four basic components of this system form an effective and comprehensive recording tool. They include the accumulation of a data base, the development of a problem summary, the development of a plan for each problem, and the utilization of progress notes in a SOAP format for follow-up and evaluation (O'Brien 1982, 316).

In adult day care, the admission assessment forms the data base. From this data base and from personal observation in the center, the day care staff should work as a team to develop the problem list. A problem is any area of concern (present or potential) for the participant, the family, the day care team, or other service providers. These concerns may involve functional status, emotional condition, mental status, physical health, living conditions, or finances. The problem list serves as an index to all charting on the participant because each problem is numbered. This numbering system is then used to organize records of treatment plans and progress seen with the participant. The problem list is usually filed near the front of the chart and is updated periodically as long as the participant is active in the program. (Frequency of periodic reviews can range from 30 to 90 days, depending on the program. See Chapter Twelve for more information.) Thus, the initial problem list may include six items. By the time the individual is discharged, the list may show problems numbered one through twenty-three, with twelve of those having been resolved. Problems are always dated, both at the time the problem is first recorded and at the time of resolution.

Once the care team has developed the problem list, all team members should contribute to the plan of care. A plan should be developed for each problem listed. In developing these plans, team members should consider the "collection of additional data, procedures to be followed, and proposed client education" (O'Brien 1982, 318).

Progress notes in the problem-oriented system include narrative summaries and a discharge summary. When recording progress, staff should indicate the date of documentation, the number of the problem to be addressed, and the narrative summary. The summary should include *s*ubjective observation, *o*bjective data, *a*ssessment, and *p*lan (SOAP). Subjective observations are usually stated in the form of quotes from clients. Objective data includes measurable or verifiable information about clients. The assessment is a brief evaluation of the present situation. The plan indicates what the team or the individual staff member proposes doing about the situation. See Figure 15-1 for an example of a SOAP progress note.

Chapter Twelve discusses the discharge plan and gives a more detailed example of documentation in the problem-oriented record system.

3-19-88   #3   S: "I like to sing. We used to sing in church."

O: Mrs. J joined in a sing-a-long today. This is the first time she has participated in activities since admission, one week ago.

A: Mrs. J's depression and withdrawal appear to be decreasing.

P: Continue gentle encouragement to join activities. Focus on music and devotional activities.

(signed) Pat Cartwright, BSW

Figure 15-1 Sample SOAP progress note.

It is important to note that the success of the problem-oriented system depends on close teamwork among persons of various disciplines (nursing, social work, activities, etc.) Only by synthesizing these various perspectives can the staff gain a fuller picture of the participant, the family, and all that they may be experiencing. Because of this, most organizations using the problem-oriented record also use an integrated record. In an integrated record, the chart is not divided according to nursing, social work, and activities. Rather, it is divided according to baseline data, the problem list and initial plans, and progress notes.

All staff, no matter what their discipline, have input into each of these sections. This may be done in one of two ways. Notes may be a joint result of case conferences. Alternately, individual staff may record progress notes in a unified, chronological format.

The problem-oriented record system involves not only a set format for documentation, but also includes record audits and correction of deficiencies. The record audit can either have the objective of determining whether recording has been carried out according to the predefined system, or it can be done to assess the quality of care delivered based on descriptions contained in the record. Program staff can use checklists to audit themselves according to the first objective. Frequently, the second objective requires input from a professional outside the care team. The center's medical director (if there is one) or consultants from other community agencies can fulfill this role. Results must be communicated to all staff once the audit has been performed. This will enable the staff to modify their behavior toward the ideal, both in documentation and in their care of participants.

There are many reasons that the problem-oriented record is popular. It encourages an interdisciplinary team approach to services by developing greater communication among staff. It allows all staff to critique and give feedback on each other's assessments and care planning, thus upgrading everyone's skill levels. The technique promotes early detection of problems and fosters a preventive approach to care. Finally, the problem-oriented record is organized in a manner that lends itself to program evaluation and research efforts.

Good documentation cannot create good services, but it can certainly contribute toward the delivery of better services. It can help us to be more aware of what we are doing, when, how, and with whom. Good documentation and good practice go hand in hand.

Reference

O'Brien, C.L. 1982. *Adult day care: A practical guide.* Monterey, CA: Jones Bartlett Publishing Co.

Further Readings

National Institute on Adult Daycare. 1984. *Standards for adult day care.* Washington, DC: National Council on the Aging.

Padula, H. 1983. *Developing adult day care.* Washington, DC: National Council on the Aging.

Panella, J. Jr. 1987. *Day care programs for Alzheimer's disease and related disorders.* New York: Demos Publications.

CHAPTER 16

Computers and Adult Day Care

David S. Webb

The field of adult day care is rapidly growing into a new professionalism. As the service has expanded throughout the nation, center directors have had increasing opportunities to learn from each other and to fine tune their skills in program management. Adult day care directors are no longer in the position of having to reinvent the wheel (as they were only a few years ago). Financial management, marketing, and long-range planning are all areas in which day care is benefitting from a new expertise. In this respect, ADC directors are following in the footsteps of other types of health care services.

Hospitals, for example, have long recognized the importance of accurate, timely information about project income, costs, quality, and effectiveness. This information contributes to capable management and accurate long range planning, a goal that can be difficult to obtain using manual systems. Hospitals are increasingly using computers to collect, analyze, and communicate information for more sophisticated management.

Other community-based health and social service organizations, however, are just now beginning to make use of data processing. Some of the reason for this centers around the cost of computers. Until just a few years ago, it truly was not cost-effective for a smaller agency to purchase a computer. With the recent availability of high quality personal computers, however, smaller agencies are beginning to purchase computers.

Adult day care can benefit significantly from computerization. Through electronic data processing, the adult day care center can obtain more timely and more accurate information about participants and the services they are using. The center's financial managers can use this information to create more accurate and workable budgets. The director can write grant proposals more quickly, and fund-raising letters can be generated in larger quantity.

What Can the Computer Do?

A complete computer system can do many things. You might want a computer to:

- Organize and store many similarly structured pieces of information (i.e., addresses containing a family member's name, street address, city, state, and ZIP code.)

- Retrieve a single piece of information from many stored ones (i.e., find the address of family member, John Smith.)

- Insert retrieved information into a new format (i.e., print a bill into which John Smith's name and address have been inserted.)

- Perform complicated mathematical computations quickly and accurately (i.e., calculate the budgetary effects of increasing attendance by 20%.)

- Print information quickly and accurately (i.e., attendance reports)

- Perform the same activity almost indefinitely and precisely the same way each time (i.e., print 100 original copies of the same fund-raising letter.) (Stewart and Shulman 1984, 2)

Day care directors can use these capabilities to assist in creating management solutions. We have all, however, heard the horror story of someone who got a computer and had nothing but problems. Avoiding problems starts before the computer is ever purchased, and involves developing an understanding of what the computer will not do. The computer will not,

- Clean up a mess in the office. (The mess will only get worse if you try to computerize it.)

- Remove demands on your office staff.

- Produce some information instantaneously.

- Define the jobs that must be done. (The computer can help get those jobs done, but the jobs must be well-defined first.)

- Exactly fit current methods of getting jobs done. (You must be willing to listen to new ideas on solving problems or you will not be able to install a computer successfully or at a reasonable cost) (Stewart and Shulman 1984, 3).

Additionally, don't expect the computer to be able to work all by itself. The machine, alone, is not capable of functioning in a way that will be helpful in a day care setting. You must be sure you match the proper machine with the proper instruction package (software program), and properly train the staff in computer use for the computer system to be helpful in a day care setting.

The Most Important Part of the Computer System

Although a computer system is composed of many parts, the most important part of a successful system is the user. Users can include managers, bookkeepers, secretaries, nurses, and social workers—in short, anyone who uses the computer or the information from it. People are the most important part of the system, because all the computer's capabilities mean nothing if they do not serve human needs. In deciding how, and even whether you should computerize, always remember the needs of the people who will be using the system.

Becoming Computer Literate: Software

The needs of users are communicated to the computer via software. Software is a set of programmed instructions, recorded on disks, which directs the computer in accomplishing specific functions. It is second in importance only to the people using a computer system. Since software instructs the computer to do those things that users need, it should always be selected before the machine. There are many types of software, as described here.

Operating System software

The operating system gives the machine the ability to perform basic functions, such as write to a file, read from a file, and perform addition. With these basic building blocks, programmers can construct many types of useful software. The most widely used personal computer operating system is MS-DOS.

Application Software

Application software gives the computer instructions for performing tasks with practical application to business or other functions. Application software is found in the form of shelf software, customized adaptations, and custom-written software. Shelf software is produced to respond to generic business needs or to the specific needs of a particular industry. It has the advantage of being reasonably priced, but may not respond totally to the special needs of your setting. Customized adaptations begin with a shelf software package, and make minor programming modifications to bring the functioning closer to special needs. Custom-written software is programmed from scratch, with the purpose of totally addressing particular requirements in an individual setting. It tends to be the most expensive software available.

Several shelf software packages now on the market apply directly to some of the needs of an adult day care center. Most of the following types of packages can be purchased and used directly.

Word processing is the new replacement for a typewriter. Word processing allows easy correction of errors and editing before a document is printed (e.g., when drafting and producing letters). It also can assist in producing several similar documents without retyping entire pages (i.e., grant applications).

Desk top publishing goes one step beyond word processing to allow production of type styles and page layout similar to those from a print shop. This software can help you to produce newsletters, brochures, and other documents.

The spread sheet allows projection of many "What if...?" situations that involve numbers and calculations such as for budget development. By entering formulae rather than numbers, the user can instruct the computer to perform necessary recalculations quickly. This makes detailed budget planning much more practical, as it saves the planner an immense amount of time in recalculating and rewriting a series of budget scenarios.

A data base is a means for creating files to hold specific types of data. The information contained in the files can then be retrieved quickly, and in a predetermined order, such as a mailing list produced in zip code order and printed on mailing labels.

Accounting software functions similarly to manual accounting systems, except that the computer performs all calculations and produces all reports. Modules usually available that will apply to adult day care centers include general ledger, accounts payable, and possibly payroll.

Within each of these categories of software, capabilities of specific packages can vary widely. For example, some word processors will create columns and some won't. If you want to use word processing to create a newsletter, this may be important. Other word processors can integrate with a spreadsheet, allowing simple insertion of budget figures from the spreadsheet to the word processor. If the primary use of word processing will be in writing grant proposals, this feature may be important. No shelf software will ever do absolutely all the things you want. The bottom line is this: You must decide which capabilities are most important in your specific situation, and purchase accordingly.

Becoming Computer Literate: Hardware

The software you select will often determine the type of computer hardware you need. Hardware is the actual machinery of the computer system. Figure 16-1 illustrates each of these parts.

Many computers include a separate box that contains the memory and the disk drives, the heart of the computer system. Some computers, such as the Macintosh and the Compaq portable, have incorporated these features into the same piece of equipment as the monitor. Even though the machinery may look different for different computers, the parts function the same.

The memory of a computer is described in terms of its capacity, either as so many "k" or so many "megabytes." One "k," or kilobyte, is approximately the same as one thousand characters (numbers, letters, spaces, and other special characters). One megabyte (mb) is one million characters. So, 360k is a memory capacity of 360,000 characters and 10mb is a memory capacity of 10,000,000 characters.

The computer has both internal memory and disk storage memory. Internal memory is sometimes called random access memory (RAM) and is contained in the central processing unit (CPU). The CPU can process

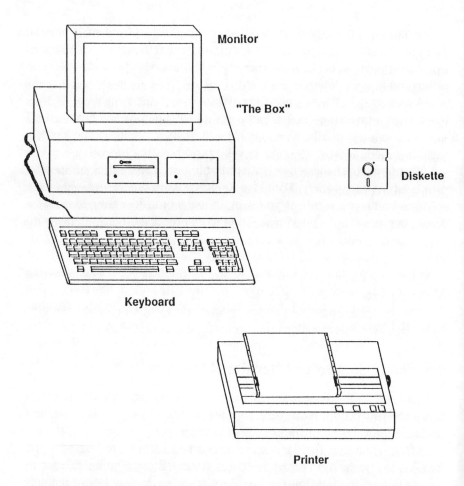

Figure 16-1 The Parts of a Computer System. Source: Artist: Jane Pickett. D.L. Webb & Associates, Kansas City, Mo. (Used with permission)

RAM information very rapidly, but is used only for temporary purposes. RAM is normally the smaller of the two types of memory. When you enter information into the computer, it usually goes into RAM, or internal memory, first. Internal memory is operated electronically, which means that when the power to the computer is turned off, the memory is erased. For this reason, data which you wish to keep must be saved in disk storage. Disk storage is magnetic, so that you can turn off the computer and still keep all of the stored information. Disk memory is usually larger than internal memory, but it is also slower. The computer will require both kinds of memory to address ADC needs.

The computer uses two types of disk drives. They are described in terms of the type of disks used on each drive: floppy and hard. Both types of disks can record information, which will remain on the disk either until the data are erased or the disk is damaged. Floppy disks (diskettes) are flexible. Some are contained in a flexible wrapper (i.e., those traditionally used with the IBM PC) and some are contained in a hard plastic case (i.e., those used with Apple computers). The wrapper or case is not designed to be removed; it allows you to handle the diskette without damaging the information contained on it. Hard disks (also called fixed disks) are installed inside the machine and cannot be removed except by a repair shop. Hard disks are faster and hold more data than floppy disks. The capacity of floppy and hard disks is measured in kilobytes and megabytes, just like the memory capacity of the machine.

The terminal, or workstation, allows you to communicate with the computer. It includes a keyboard, monitor, and sometimes a printer. You can send information to the computer via the typewriter-style keyboard. The monitor screen, also called a CRT (cathode ray tube), allows the computer to temporarily display information in numbers, letters, and pictures. The monitor and the printer are the two mechanisms that allow the computer to send information to you, the user.

Like the monitor, the printer allows the computer to communicate with you. Unlike the monitor, the printer provides a paper record (hard copy) of information from the computer. Three types of printers are commonly available for use with your computer. The letter quality printer uses an element or "daisy wheel" similar to that found in many electric typewriters. The dot matrix printer uses a series of pins that make small dots to produce letters, numbers, and graphics. The laser printer uses much smaller dots, spaced much closer together, and prints from a process much like a copier machine. The laser and letter quality printers offer the best print quality, but tend to run slowly. The dot matrix printer is the workhorse of many computer installations because, although the print quality is not as high, it can run very rapidly.

Some computer systems serve several locations such as day care centers that have satellite sites. Information may be communicated among the several computers either by physically carrying diskettes back and forth or by using a modem. The modem allows two computers to communicate directly via telephone lines.

Computers come in all sizes. Each of the hardware functions described here can be found in all sizes of computers. Microcomputers, often called personal computers (PCs), are small computers typically designed to be used by one person at a time. Minicomputers are generally larger, faster computers designed to handle more than one user simultaneously. Mainframes are very large computers, sometimes serving hundreds of users at the same time.

Multi-user computer systems have several terminals to allow two or more people to use the system at the same time. Sometimes, several micro computers are linked together in a network, to accomplish the same purpose. Each terminal in a multi-user system may be connected to its own printer or it may rely on a central printer, elsewhere in the building.

Miscellaneous pieces of hardware are often forgotten in determining the cost of a new computer. The most obvious is the electric cords, or cables. Electronic cards (also called boards) that are installed inside the box to allow special functions, such as graphics, may also be neglected in figuring costs. These cards are important, as some software will not run without them. A surge protector, to limit damage from a suddenly increasing current is also advisable. In some areas with more power problems, it may be advisable to get a line conditioner. This item works somewhat like a surge protector, but will also protect against drops in power, or brown outs.

Beginning the Search for a Computer System

The decision to purchase a computer can be a little overwhelming, unless you first realize that you already have a data processing system. Your current methods for accounting, producing documents, and maintaining participant records all form a manual system for processing data. When that manual system was first designed, someone had to define which pieces of information to record. Someone had to design report formats, and someone had to decide on frequency of reporting. Preparing for computerization is much the same.

Begin by analyzing your needs and wants relative to computerization. Will the computer function primarily in writing grants, or accounting, or other information management? Which specifications will be most important to the success of the system? Which will be of lesser importance?

Which would be nice to have, but not necessary? If the computer's functions will involve use of reporting forms, collect all forms now in use with the manual system.

Let's say you want to put accounting functions on the computer. Your accounting system currently includes general ledger (GL), accounts payable (A/P), accounts receivable (A/R), and payroll. The bookkeeper must copy numbers from one source into several records. This requires a great deal of time, and sometimes results in copying errors that are hard to find and fix. You want the computer to automatically enter the information from A/R, A/P, and payroll directly into the GL (this function is called integration). You also want to be able to enter payables into the computer system as they come due, but you may need to "hold" payment of some bills during times of poor cash flow. Further, you want to be able to enter information into the A/R and have the computer automatically print that information into bills at the end of the month. Some participants' charges will simply be billed to the family. Others, however, may have multiple payers, such as private insurance, scholarship fund, and family. Forms currently used in your center include private pay bills, insurance billing forms, and Medicaid bills, among others.

So far, you have been analyzing specifications for the software. Your primary concern in getting a new computer system should usually be with software first, and then hardware. There is a wide variety of software available, but few software packages are designed to run on multiple machines. If you buy an ABC brand computer because it looks easy to use, or because of low initial cost, you may find later that the only accounting software written for the ABC is totally inadequate to your needs. The one exception to this rule is that environmental factors may dictate the use of a specific machine. For example, you may want data from your new computer to transfer directly to the computer your parent agency already owns.

Once you have developed a list of specifications, investigate what software is already available. Generic packages for accounting and word processing are available through local computer stores, consultants, and mail order houses. You may find that some software is inadequate, or runs on a computer that is hard to find. You may discover that other packages offer features you had not previously considered. Some software may seem perfect for your setting, but it may cost more than the benefits would justify. As you discover what is available, you may want to modify your priorities on specifications.

Your research may tell you that software with integrated payroll systems cost more than you can justify with your staff of 12. You may modify your list to indicate that you want A/P, A/R, and GL integrated, and that you want to be able to manually enter payroll information into the GL. You may also find that generic accounting software will not print to Medicaid billing forms. Since billing takes a lot of time to do manually, you may feel that a computerized A/R is still desirable. You may attempt to find billing software designed for adult day care centers, or you may contract for custom-written A/R software. In either event, integration to a generic GL will be an important specification.

During the evaluation process, you should also shop around for a dealer. Some dealers offer a wider variety of software packages than others, and some can be more helpful to you in finding the information you need. Some dealers also offer better on-going support and training. Support includes cost-effective repair or replacement of dysfunctional components and advice on how to set up and use the system. Training will be advisable, in most cases, to enable your staff to make the best use of the software.

At some point, you will be ready to select a small number of software packages that appear to be closest to your needs. Investigate these packages more thoroughly by asking for a demonstration and references.

Once you have identified software, begin to shop for the machine. You do not have to get the software and the computer from the same dealer. Be absolutely certain that you can get good support for the computer, as repairs without a warranty service can be very expensive. You can often buy a service policy that will take care of all hardware malfunctions at no cost, much like insurance. In fact, where the machine is concerned, the availability of on-going support is equal in importance to the price of the system.

Buying and Installing the Computer

In making the decision to buy a computer, carefully calculate all costs for each option. Make certain that you have included all necessary parts to make the system work, such as cables and cards. If installation, set-up, training, and support are not included in the purchase price, get an estimate of costs. Finally, build in a contingency amount of at least 20% to cover unexpected expenses. In addition to out-of-pocket expenses, be prepared for a number of hidden costs. These may include the time staff spends in training, additional staff needed to load initial information into the system, and general disruption to normal routines.

Computer costs can rapidly escalate beyond what the first-time user expects. In gauging benefits versus costs, look at two factors. Financial benefits may include reduction of time to process certain information. Those benefits are fairly easy to measure in dollar terms. Management benefits are harder to convert to dollars, but they are equally valuable. These benefits include more rapid access to planning information, availability of more detailed or accurate information, and so on. Even with a substantial investment in computerization, a successful system will have benefits that far outweigh costs.

Developing a sound strategy for converting from the manual system to the computer system will greatly increase overall success. Many times, the failure of newly purchased computers has to do with a high frustration level among staff. Taking some time to predict problems and arranging for preventive action will be more than worthwhile in the long run. Do this step early in the planning process, and involve staff as much as possible. Be aware that most of the preparation for a smooth computer installation should take place before the computer arrives at the center.

Dealing with myths and fears held by staff is extremely important. Many people will become convinced that the arrival of the computer will mean the end of their jobs. Others will fear that using a computer will "turn the participants into numbers." Talk to staff early on, and inform them of the reality of the situation. If someone will lose a job, or be transferred, be honest about it. In most cases, though, the computer does not replace current staff; it merely helps them to be more productive.

Identify a staff person to be the system operator. The system operator is the person who should know more about computer functioning than other regular staff need to know. This person should have special training in troubleshooting problems with both the hardware and the software. A system operator can be a new person hired for this function, or it can be a current staff member for whom you provide extra training.

Prepare a place for the computer. While modern computers do not require separate rooms, you must make certain that there is adequate space. The computer will not "just fit on the corner of the desk." In addition to the existing desk space, you will need a workstation area for the computer. See the section on caring for your computer later in this chapter for more information.

Set priorities for which functions are to be computerized first. It is best to start using one piece (module) of software until everyone is familiar with its operation. Then bring in the next until it is routine. Continue starting up one module at a time, until all functions are computerized. You should plan that it will take some time for current data to be loaded into the system. It may even be good to hire temporary staff for this process. If you are heading into a fairly complicated computerization, you may also wish to hire a computer consultant to facilitate the change. It may take staff a while to learn how to use new computer functions. There may be temporary problems with getting accurate or timely reports. To avoid crushing problems, do not discontinue the manual system until the computerized system is functioning well. This will require a lot of staff time, but will be worth it in the end.

Develop a security system for the computer and the data. Just as you would not leave employee records sitting out for everyone to read, you will want to restrict access to some of the information in the computer. There are several ways to do this. First, arrange for some type of locking storage for diskettes. Most software offers a password option to further ensure security. You develop and enter the passwords for each person who might need to use the system. Some passwords can access the entire system, while others can only get into certain areas.

If you think all this sounds like it will take a lot of time, you are right! It may be tempting to short-cut the process, but you will only spend more time, later, in trying to fix problems. Invest the time in good planning, now, and you will be investing in a more successful computer system down the road.

Proper Care of the Computer System

Once the computer has been installed, there will be many environmental factors that will contribute directly to its proper functioning. Most of these require pre-planning and staff training. The following suggestions can be implemented before and during the installation of the computer.

Persons who use the computer for sustained periods may be at risk of developing eye strain, back pain, and/or tendonitis. To prevent this, place the monitor so as to reduce glare from the screen, use a chair designed to prevent back strain, and place the keyboard slightly lower than desk height. If users are still having difficulties, consult with a computer specialist.

Site preparation for the computer is not as complicated as it once was. It is, however, necessary to maintain some basic precautions. Adequate air circulation in the location of the computer should maintain a temperature comfortable to users. Check with your hardware vendor regarding temperature tolerances, if your building thermostat is usually set to lower levels at night. The vents on the computer should be kept free of blockage by papers or other objects. If circulation is a problem, small fans near the computer vents may help.

Static electricity can be a major problem for computers. Linoleum tile or sheet flooring is preferable to any type of carpet. Maintaining adequate humidity may help, especially in dry months. Three special methods now on the market for controlling static are the static mat, the "touch me" mat, and antistatic spray. Static mats are placed under the computer workstation and attached to an electric outlet to discharge any build-up of electrical charges. These mats are expensive and awkward to move, but effective. The "touch me" mat is a smaller version that sits on the surface of the workstation. It can be ineffective because it requires that users touch the mat before each and every contact with the computer—and people do forget. Office-quality antistatic spray is inexpensive and effective if used frequently and throughout the workstation area. It is similar to antistatic sprays developed for home laundry use, but much stronger. (Home-type sprays will not be effective in a computer setting.) In dry seasons, antistatic spray must be used daily.

The quality of the electrical power reaching the computer can significantly affect functioning. Any sudden power surges or power drains can make the computer function erratically. If at all possible, install a separate, grounded outlet for the computer. Install a surge protector or line conditioner between the outlet and the computer. Do not allow space heaters, microwaves, or other appliances to be plugged into the same surge protector. Make certain that all cords and cables are free of kinks or bends. Place electric cords so that it will be impossible for anyone to trip on them or accidentally kick the plug out of the wall.

Some buildings have central switch boxes used to turn off all power at the end of the day. If this is the case in your center, there is great danger of the computer being accidentally turned off while it is functioning. This can destroy data. If the electric line to the computer must be run through a central switch box, consider taping the switch for the computer in the "on" position.

External battery units are available to maintain electricity during a power outage. These function only long enough to allow you to shut the computer down in an orderly manner without losing data. These units cost several hundred dollars, but in some circumstances may be worth the cost.

Keep the computer as clean as possible. Ban food, drink, and smoking from the workstation area. Place the computer in a relatively dust-free area. Arrange for periodic cleaning and preventive maintenance through your hardware support agreement.

Since much of the functioning of the computer is magnetic, it is extremely important that magnets be banned from the workstation area.

Diskettes must be handled very carefully. Do not bend them or use paper clips to attach notes to them. Use only a felt-tipped pen to label diskettes. Do not cover the diskette openings with labels, tape, or anything else. Immediately upon removing a diskette from the computer, place it back in its protective sleeve. Store diskettes in protective cases. Do not expose them to temperature extremes or high humidity. Read the instructions that come with the diskette for further information.

Develop a daily process for back-up of all data in which you copy all data onto diskettes. Keep at least one week's worth of back-up diskettes available in case current data are destroyed. Before the computer arrives, make sure that at least two staff members know the processes for using back-up disks to restore data which has been damaged or destroyed.

Do not open the computer to try to fix malfunctions yourself.

These suggestions are best implemented as preventive measures. They can, however, also be used as a troubleshooting check-list once the computer is operating. Before calling a professional to assist in a disaster, go through this list of suggestions to see if you can identify what may have happened.

As adult day care grows into a new era of professional expertise, more center directors are considering computerization. The computer system can be of great benefit in providing management information and in streamlining the processing of data. It will be most effective, however, when the needs of users are considered to be primary. Analyze those needs well, include staff in planning, and make certain that everyone has good training in proper computer use.

Reference

Stewart, M.M., and A.C. Shulman. 1984. "How to get started with a small business computer." Fort Worth, TX: U.S. Small Business Administration. Management Aids Number 2.027.

CHAPTER 17

Program Evaluation

Linda Cook Webb and
Kathryn Mesler Mehlferber

Program evaluation is one of those terms that has the power to strike terror into the hearts of management and staff alike. There may be many reasons for this fear. Not many people have been fully trained in how to develop and conduct a program evaluation project; some people may feel anxiety about moving into new territory. Evaluation requires data, and that may make people heave a sigh at the thought of yet another recording requirement. To complicate matters, evaluation is frequently performed by outsiders, such as state review boards, top level agency administration, or consultants. This intensifies people's fears, as they question the goals of evaluation and suspect that the outsiders will not truly understand what the staff is doing. At base, the very term "evaluation" strikes at our fundamental human insecurities. We do not want to be judged and found lacking.

There is more to program evaluation, however. Program evaluation also functions as a powerful tool in advocacy, marketing, and fund raising campaigns. Just as the key to good programming is in preparation, so the key to good evaluation is found in thoughtful planning. The early chapters of this book stressed the importance of including preparations for program evaluation from the beginning of the program development process. This chapter will outline the many purposes of evaluation, describe the types of evaluative tools available, indicate some of the pitfalls that may make evaluation seem so fearsome, and suggest paths around these pitfalls.

Definition

Evaluation is simply a means for determining how closely the center is coming to meeting its goals. Since the goals for adult day care programs can be quite diverse, the questions to be asked during evaluation can vary widely. Some examples are the following:

- Who is the program attracting? How are they being attracted? Are these the people we thought we would attract?

- What actions do staff take in providing care? How well are they performing these actions? How well do these actions meet the needs of the people being attracted?

- Does the program make a difference in people's lives? What difference? Can this difference be measured by specific changes in behavior, or is it internal (i.e., feelings and opinions)?

- What is management doing to organize resources? How well are managers performing this function? Does the program need additional resources?

- How is the program affecting the rest of the organization?

- What is the program's image in the community?

- How much is being spent on the program?

- How much is accomplished in the program versus the effort or money expended to accomplish it?

- Does the program's functioning meet national, state, or local standards?

The list could easily be expanded by examining the goals of several adult day care centers.

The evaluation process can collect data, identify strengths and weaknesses in the program, and measure the extent to which program activities met goals. In fact, program evaluation is a specialized form of research. It is specialized in that it primarily attempts to study the variables involved in a single program. This information can, in turn, be used to develop informed management decision making. It also provides the means to compare among various methods to improve effectiveness, efficiency, and costs.

Program evaluation can also demonstrate the program's worth to the public.

For any of these purposes, the most basic question is often, "How close are we coming to meeting goals?" In attempting to answer this question, it is helpful to identify several major types of program evaluation from among the following:

- Quality assurance

- Evaluation of outcomes

- Cost containment

- Cost effectiveness

- Marketing audit

Each of these types of evaluation has specific objectives and must make use of specific types of measuring tools. It is important to ask the right questions in order to get meaningful answers.

Quality Assurance

Adult day care providers are always working toward providing quality programs. But what is quality? How can it be defined and measured? How can directors be sure that the participants in their programs receive the type of care that will meet their needs? Who sets the standards? What are valid indicators?

For many years, quality assurance mechanisms were developed and enforced at the state level by health professionals. The "medical audit" was the result, in which reviewers examined patient charts for completeness of documentation and appropriateness of the treatment recorded. The public is no longer content to abide by this arrangement. Today, the quality of health care has become a national issue. Consumers and their advocates are increasingly concerned about adequacy, accessibility, accountability, decision making processes, and other measures of quality care. Consumers are fast becoming sophisticated in knowing how to measure what they are buying.

To develop and evaluate standards of care, planners must first develop a philosophy or mission statement and establish clear criteria, objectives, and goals for the program. Planners must review and analyze the program's policies, procedures, and forms in comparison to existing standards (i.e., state regulations; professional practice standards from nursing, social work, and therapy associations; and the National Institute on Adult Daycare's *Standards for Adult Day Care*). Figure 17-1 provides a sample format for quality assurance evaluation. It indicates the policy (goal) which is to be observed in action. It makes attainment of that policy measurable by defining ten behaviors involving documentation, and indicates in exactly what location the documentation is to be found. With this type of tool, evaluators can quickly give an objective appraisal of the center's compliance with quality-of-care goals.

Once the assessment has been completed, it is extremely important that corrective measures be instituted and reevaluated periodically. In some states (Maryland and Wisconsin, among others), the adult day care associations are now performing or planning peer review procedures for quality assurance. This is an exciting new development as the field of adult day care moves into a new era of learning, insights, and growth.

Quality assurance evaluation almost exclusively uses measures that observe either staff behaviors or documentation of staff actions. The assumption underlying this approach is that good clinical practices lead to good outcomes. The question remains, however: "What if we are implementing a particular technique properly, from a clinical sense, and it still does not have the desired result?" This leads us to another technique, evaluation of outcomes.

Evaluation of Outcomes

Traditional quality assurance methods have focused on clinical practice, while other, newer methods have stressed outcomes (Health Care Quality Alliance 1988, 17). In an evaluation of outcomes, testing tools focus not on staff, but on participants or family members. For example, family members might be asked to answer a questionnaire designed to measure caregiver stress, both at the time of admission and six months later. The desired outcome would be for caregivers to feel less stress in caring for their family member, once adult day care services were in place. Figure 17-2 illustrates another way of measuring participant outcomes, through a family interview. Chapter Eighteen provides a more detailed discussion of outcome evaluation.

Essential Services - Participants are served by well qualified and trained staff while they are at the Center.

	Documentation or Data	Above	Average	Improve
1) The program has a detailed written job description for each staff position.	Written Job Description			
2) The program has a clearly defined organizational chart which specifies lines of supervision and responsibility.	Organizational Chart			
3) Job descriptions specify qualifications necessary for the position.	Written Job Description			
4) Each staff position has a specific performance evaluation which relate to the duties as defined in the job description.	Performance Evaluations			
5) Each staff member's job performance is evaluated at 3 months, 6 months, 12 months, and annually thereafter.	Performance Evaluation Personnel Records			
6) The program has a written procedure for dealing with problems in job performance.	Personnel Policies			
7) The program has a written employee grievance procedure.	Personnel Policies			
8) The program has a well developed orientation program for new employees.	Orientation Program Documentation of Attendance			
9) Staff attend mandatory in-service training as required by law annually.	Employee Documentation of Attendance			
10) Staff are able to attend optional in-service training and workshops as programatically and financially feasible.	Employee Documentation of Attendance			

Figure 17-1 Excerpt from Quality Assurance Questionnaire. Source: Madonna Centers, Lincoln, Nebraska. (Used with permission)

Date_____

Interview Questions

* Length of time attending Center_____(yrs. mos.)
* Length of day_____(hrs.) Number of days per week attends_____
* Family's perceived level of client's functioning   Good   Fair   Poor

1. Where would your_____be if (s)he was not attending day care?

2. What are you able to do now, that you were not able to do before your _____began attending day care?

3. Have_____Activity of Daily Living skills changed since (s)he began attending day care?

4. How were his/her slepp habits before day care?   Since?

5. Have you seen any changes in the way the individual is dealing with his/her impairment?

6. Has_____level of physical ability changed since attending Q.A.C. Adult Day Care Center?   In what way?

7. Has his/her interest in socializing changed?   In what way?

8. Does_____look forward to coming to the Center?

9. What are his/her typical comments at the end of a day spent at the Center?

10. What would your life be like if _____was living in a nursing home or other form of care outside of the home? Do you see this as a positive option?

11. Has your_____level of independence changed?

12. After a day at the Center, do you see any differences in his/her behavior as opposed to a day (s)he does not attend?

13. Has_____picked up any new interests since attending the Center?

14. Would your_____come to the Center if van transportation was not provided?

15. Is our van transportation service meeting your needs?

16. What other services could we offer which would make caregiving easier for you and your family?

17. If fees were different (less or more), would that effect your attendance?

Figure 17-2 Family Caregiver Evaluation. Source: Queen Anne's County Adult Day Care Center, Grasonville, MD. (Used with permission)

Cost Containment

With fewer funds available for health and social services, cost containment is of paramount importance. On the one hand, cost containment evaluation asks whether the staff is doing everything possible to contain costs without changing program goals or services. For example, when major purchases of supplies or equipment must be made, is there a bid process or cost comparison conducted? Chapter Ten outlines additional cost containment strategies that may be investigated. On the other hand, cost containment evaluation asks whether basic costs for this program or service are such that management should change or amend the program's goals. For example, as discussed in Chapter Ten, some adult day care centers are open only two or three days a week, in an effort to limit costs.

Cost Effectiveness

Cost effectiveness studies investigate the costs of a given pattern of care compared with another alternative. This has been a big issue for the field of adult day care, as it relates closely to governmental decisions to reimburse for community-based alternative services versus nursing home care. Chapter Eighteen discusses cost effectiveness studies of adult day care in more detail.

Marketing Audit

Just as it is important to evaluate our services and financial structure, so it is important to evaluate the ways in which we inform and motivate the community regarding adult day care. As with the evaluation of services, it is appropriate to assess marketing activities both from the standpoint of quality assurance and of outcomes. Quality assurance questions in the marketing audit assess the impact of place, price, product, and promotions represented in ADC centers.

Marketing outcomes can be roughly measured by keeping records of promotions and logging the referrals, admissions, and days of participation that followed the promotions and referrals. The difficulty in this simple measurement of marketing outcomes is that it is necessary to make an assumption that is actually a logical fallacy: "It happened after this, therefore it must have happened *because* of this." It is not unusual that some families may take up to six months to respond to a particular promotional event. A more accurate picture can be obtained, therefore, by questioning customers, and asking them what brought them to the program or what encouraged them to increase their days. Again, there may be difficulties because some people can't remember when or how they first heard of the center. Using both techniques together is probably the most effective approach.

Getting Started

Trocchio and O'Donoghue (1988) state that successful evaluation will require the commitment of everyone involved, including the governing body, administration, staff, participants, their family members, and others affected by the program. To this end, it is helpful to involve all of these groups from the outset in planning and implementing the evaluation project. A designated project task force or informal meetings with groups of interested persons can both be effective methods of involvement.

The evaluation process must be reasonably simple and not too time consuming, or it will not be fully completed. At the same time, it must be detailed enough to provide useful information. Its purpose is to help, not to interfere with giving care. Begin by identifying the reason for evaluation. Why are you talking about evaluation at all? What specific aspects of the program or its functioning are of most interest for evaluation? What do you hope to achieve with the evaluation?

Once goals are established, select methods that will answer your specific questions. Use one or more of the models already described, and find or develop assessment tools appropriate to that model. It is vital to realize that a combination of these approaches is needed to successfully evaluate clinical outcome, consumer satisfaction, and cost-effectiveness. Use combinations of methods, as appropriate. Just be certain that you identify a specific method with a particular evaluation goal and appropriate testing instruments.

Determine who will evaluate. Often, evaluations can be performed by in-house staff. This is especially true when objective data are involved, such as a review of participant demographics, or audit of charts to measure frequency of recording. At times, it may be preferable to contract with a consultant or other outside party to assist in planning and carrying out the evaluation. Outside evaluation can be most effective when expert opinion or an analysis of subjective data is indicated.

Develop a work plan specifically for the evaluation process. The plan should state who will do what, and by when. A time management form, such as that illustrated in Figure 4-1, can help to keep everyone "on track" with their responsibilities to the project.

Once the mechanism for measuring and assuring quality is chosen or developed, describe the process clearly to all interested parties who are not already a part of the planning group. A series of orientation meetings works well in this regard. Following the introduction of the concept, encourage open communication among group members. Common concerns should be shared, constructive approaches discussed, a timetable developed, and expectations of involvement defined. Trocchio and O'Donoghue (1988) identify five areas to stress at the first meeting:

- Establish clear objectives for the program (e.g., "We are evaluating as a first step to help in improving services." or "We are going to evaluate our program to see if it meets nationally established standards.")

- Maintain a safe learning environment. Reassure staff that the evaluation will not be used for disciplinary reasons.

- Answer all questions and consider all suggestions for improving the program.

- Praise members for their contribution to the program.

- Make clear that you realize participation in the evaluation will take some time and that when necessary, staff members will be relieved of other responsibilities.

As the evaluation project progresses, continue to hold brief meetings to keep everyone informed and to minimize any unforeseen barriers. Once the process has been explained, most staff members enjoy evaluating services and solving problems. Participants and their families can maintain involvement by helping to identify problems and suggesting ways to improve the services.

Collect and analyze data, being sure to follow the methods already developed. If evaluation planning has occurred simultaneously with program planning, much of the data needed can easily be collected as a part of normal program operations. This can only happen, however, if the daily, weekly, or monthly recording of information is established in advance as a normal procedure. If staff must retroactively pull together data from diverse sources or attempt to reconstruct from memory, data collection can be a daunting process. Since this is one of the most common errors in evaluation, planners and managers are advised to give serious consideration to this issue.

Make recommendations and, as appropriate, report suggestions for change to everyone involved in planning or participating in the evaluation. Work with staff, participants, and families to implement the changes recommended through the project. Allow time for the changes to take effect, and then start all over again.

Down the Road

Program evaluation is detailed enough that it can become a lifelong field of study. This chapter has outlined some of the major pathways through this field. It would be a good idea, however, to continue reading in this area. O'Brien and Sweem and colleagues present good, detailed overviews of additional and fascinating types of evaluation.

References

Donabedian, A. 1982. *The criteria and standards of quality*. Ann Arbor, MI: Health Administration Press.

Health Care Quality Alliance. 1988. *Quality health care: Critical issues before the nation*. Washington, DC: Health Care Quality Alliance.

O'Brien, C.L. 1982. *Adult day care: A practical guide*. Monterey, CA: Jones Bartlett Publishing Co.

Sweem, M., J.L. Brandt, and P.A. Apthorpe. 1986. *Implementing program evaluation and quality assurance programs in adult day care settings*. Lincoln, NE: Madonna Centers.

Trocchio, J. and K. O'Donoghue. 1988. *A self-appraisal guide for the residential care facility*. Washington, DC: American Health Care Association.

Further Readings

Ainsworth, T.H. 1977. *Quality assurance in long term care*. Germantown, MA: Aspen Press.

Bachman, H., M. Burba-Babbitt, D. England, and J. MacRae. 1986. *Peer review consultation program*. Grasonville, MD: Maryland Association for Adult Day Care.

Conrad, K., S. Hughes, P. Campione, and R. Goldberg. 1987. Shedding New Light on Adult Day Care. *Perspective on aging*. XVI(6):18-21.

Eliopoulous, C. 1983. *Nursing administration of long-term care*. Rockville, MD: Aspen.

Fink, A., A. Siu, R. Brook, R. Park, and D. Solomon. 1987. Assuring the Quality of Health Care for Older Persons. *JAMA*. 258(14):1095-1098.

Luke, D.J., J.C. Krueger, and R.E. Modrow. 1983. *Organization and change in health care quality assurance*. Rockville, MD: Aspen.

Meisenheimer, C.G., Ed. 1985. *Quality assurance: A complete guide to effective programs*. Rockville, MD: Aspen.

National Institute on Adult Daycare. 1984. *Standards for adult day care*. Washington, DC: National Council on the Aging.

CHAPTER 18

Research as a Planning and Management Tool

Ruth Von Behren

This chapter will provide the adult day care planner or manager with information about research: what it is, how it's done, its limitations, and its usefulness.

Research can be defined as an attempt to describe and to understand relationships between various items and to determine cause and effect sequence. To do this, a researcher establishes a research design that states the research questions, hypotheses, how data will be collected and measured, and the various statistical tests for analysis. Sometimes research is classified by the area of emphasis. For example, a study whose focus is the facility, equipment, organization, and qualifications of staff would be studying the structure.

Process research refers to a study of the sequence of events and the nature of services. As changes occur, these changes are studied to determine their impact. Although an adult day care center may conduct outcome research, some of the most useful research may be process research— documenting and analyzing changes that occur as the center expands its scope of services.

The most common use of research is a study of outcomes (effects). When the study is directed toward the outcomes of a program as compared to its goals as a means of subsequent decisions about the program and improvement in future programs, it is called program evaluation. Studies conducted by or for state or federal government (such as those done by California, Massachusetts, and New Jersey) are almost always evaluations.

Other outcomes, such as improvement in physical functioning, greater life satisfaction, and less stress on caregivers have also been studied.

Elements of Research

The Research Design

The research design is a plan to select the people to be studied, and when and how the data will be collected. Internal validity describes how well the findings apply to the situation under investigation. External validity means the degree to which findings can be generalized to other research situations. Research designs may strengthen control to achieve greater internal validity and consequently weaken external validity and vice versa. That is, experimental rigor sometimes compromises the ability to generalize.

Although the concept of research is broad and incorporates many methods of collecting information, "prestige" in today's research world goes to the test and control randomized selected groups. Applicants to the project are assessed and randomly assigned to either receive the service being studied (the test group) or receive other services (the control group). Periodic observations are made of both groups. Social sciences have borrowed the scientific experimental design from the laboratory and attempted to fit the complexities of human society into a simplistic format.

Many problems have been identified in attempts to conduct a controlled experiment in a real-life setting. Ethical questions have been raised regarding the provision of a program of intervention to one group and not to the other. Professionals are accustomed to assigning people to treatment on the basis of need as determined by their professional expertise—they do not want to leave the process to chance. Participants in both test and control groups may drop out, upsetting the equivalency of the group.

Contamination may also occur through the Hawthorne effect—that is, the extra attention paid to participants in the control project. Other agencies may actually provide the same kinds of services to the control group members. In an early research project at one center, a double blind assessment used for quasi-experimental test and comparison groups did not work because the test participants identified themselves to the state assessment team. (State team members were not told whether the person to be assessed was in the test or comparison group.)

The researcher is an active participant in the research study. The researcher comes to the research study with assumptions, goals, and values that interact with the data collected. Such assumptions, goals, and values are often hidden and may result in bias in the analysis and presentation of the data. There is no such thing as a perfect research study. Therefore, many techniques are devised to minimize the degree of error. Such techniques may strengthen the internal validity but reduce the generalizability (external validity) factor, (e.g., random selection of test or control group members). Due to the limitations inherent in the process, claims are often made in the findings with need for more research indicated.

Research design is influenced by time, access, and costs. The elaborate test and control group process is expensive, time consuming, and ethically questionable. For these reasons, quasi-experimental studies are done, utilizing a variety of techniques such as comparison groups, probably the most common design in practice. The comparison group is matched in a selected number of items, such as age, sex, functional status, etc., to the test group. Quasi-experimental design is feasible and can produce results for many practical purposes.

Other non-experimental studies can be valuable sources of information. These studies make no attempt to use a comparison or control group. Pre-test and post-test of the same group is an example of a common experimental technique and is often used to determine training effectiveness. One-shot studies such as surveys, either conducted via the telephone, personal interviews, or by mail are perhaps the most common method used to gather information. Mail questionnaires such as that utilized by the National Institute for Adult Daycare (NIAD) in its 1985 survey and Northwestern University in its recent ADC study is the most practical way to gather information from large groups. NIAD intends to repeat its survey periodically, thus developing a data base showing changes over time.

Surveys can be conducted via a sample which may be selected a variety of ways such as random selection, stratified (division of population to be tested into groups and random selection from groups), and information sought from the known universe (e.g., all ADC providers). Public opinion polls are examples of commonly accepted survey techniques.

Conducting any type of research study in an action setting such as ADC creates additional problems. Research is usually static—a snapshot in time, and applicable only to that time. Repeated data collection at various intervals is an attempt to overcome the limitations of one-shot studies. However, the program itself and the participants change over time. Each program exists in a social context. It may be part of a larger organization or free standing. It is also part of a community which is part of a state or a nation. The context has values, laws, and beliefs as do the individual participants. All of this interacts with the program.

Measurement Instruments

Validity and reliability are terms often applied to methods of measurement for research. For example, many scales are used to measure a participant's functional status in Activities of Daily Living (ADL) and Instrumental Activities of Daily Living (IADL). Validity would reflect how accurately your instrument measures functional status. The construct of the instrument, the background of the person using it, and the method of getting the answer (e.g., verbal responses from participant, professional judgment, observation, etc.) affect validity. Reliability means that the same scale used by another rater gets the same results, or the same scale produces the same results when used repeatedly over time.

However, as Kane and Kane in their *Assessing the Elderly: A Practical Guide to Measurement* (1981, 1) pointed out, an individualized comprehensive assessment provides access to the long-term care services needed and provides program accountability. However, "unfortunately, no agreement has been achieved on two of the most crucial points: the identification of the important factors (e.g., physical, mental, and social) to be measured, and the technology for making the measures (e.g., there is no widely accepted standard assessment instrument)." Lengthy assessment instruments are developed in an attempt to present accurate status of functioning that serves as a basis for service allocation. Yet these instruments lack the fine tuning necessary to identify small gains in functional independence that occur over time to ADC participants. Nor are they capable of measuring the prevention or slowing of deterioration.

Satisfactory measurement instruments have not been developed to measure intangible ADC benefits such as quality of life, effect of improved morale on physical status, and caregiver relief. Consensus today, however, is that measures of functional status that examine the person's ability to function independently despite disease, physical and mental disability and social deprivation are the most useful overall indicators for providers.

Data Collection

Techniques used for data collection are many and varied—interviews, extracts from documents, surveys, observation, and information from knowledgeable people are a few. Many of these techniques are utilized in planning and managing ADC. For example, interviews with participants and family, information from physicians' medical records and referral agencies, and professional judgment and observation are used when you assess a new participant. You may have utilized a needs assessment survey before determining your center's location. The difference between you and a researcher is the purpose for which this information is collected. You are focusing on the individual with the purpose of developing an individualized care plan. You are alert to the individual differences and recognize and applaud the uniqueness of each participant. The researcher is likely to lack your commitment to the individual and the ADC program. The researcher is likely to deal in statistics—gross measures that group people together.

Data Analysis

Today's dominant method of analysis of data is the use of statistical tests. Various tests are used to determine the sampling error, the degree of relationship between variables (correlation) and the predictability of a given variable from one or more other variables (regression). Simpler descriptive measures such as percentages, various ways of identifying the average such as the mean (the sum of all the elements divided by the number of elements), median (midpoint—half are above, half below), mode (point with greatest number of entries) and the range (lowest to highest entries) are often more useful. In program evaluation, for example, an appropriate and often used method is analysis of outcomes, or the impact of the program upon those who have received its services. The basis for measuring the outcome is the assessment data collected at admission and periodically throughout the person's involvement with the program.

Research Issues in ADC

Although research issues may have little impact on your program operation, these issues do play a part in the public debate about long-term care services. Policy decisions affecting funding are sometimes influenced by research. This section discusses major controversial questions to help you understand what the debate is about. The key issues are listed below:

- ADC as an alternative or a supplement to long-term care institutionalization

- Impact of ADC on functional status, life satisfaction, and mortality (outcomes)

- Cost effectiveness

- Benefits to caregivers

- Specialized programs

Alternative or Supplement

The issue of alternative or supplement care is important for its fiscal implications. If ADC is an alternative to nursing homes, then cost shifts, cost avoidance, or cost saving may be realized. If ADC is a supplement, that is, a new or "add-on" service, perhaps serving a different population, then "new" money is needed.

ADC developed as a result of the demand for alternatives to institutionalization that was stimulated by horror stories in the early seventies about nursing home care and the findings of many studies indicating various percentages of nursing home patients did not need to be there. The public, particularly seniors, wanted the availability of a wide range of home and community-based services and programs so they could make choices.

In the minds of many relatives of ADC participants, there is no doubt that ADC is an alternative to nursing home care. Researchers have found, and ADC providers know, that ADC does serve persons meeting their state's criteria for intermediate care or skilled nursing facility care. States have utilized the same review criteria or staff used to determine eligibility for nursing home care to determine eligibility for ADC. California, for example, asks the state Medicaid consultant to determine for each participant if adult day health care (ADHC) were not available, would the person be eligible for Intermediate Care Facility (ICF), Skilled Nursing Facility (SNF) or at risk (which is defined as a medical decision by the Medicaid consultant that without ADHC intervention, the person would be eligible within six months). A 1982 state evaluation found 37% were ICF-eligible and 26% were SNF-eligible. Persons must meet the criteria of one of these three levels of care for Medicaid reimbursement in California. In states where ADC is funded via Section 1915(c) Medicaid Community Care Waivers, by definition ADC participants must be eligible for nursing home care.

The alternatives or supplement question has been applied to all community and home long-term care (LTC) demonstration projects including the channeling project conducted by the Health Care Financing Administration. Interestingly enough, the rapid growth of special programs (including ADC) for persons with Alzheimer's disease receiving "new" government funds is occurring without this question asked or prior research demanded.

For some researchers, (often those not conducting the study but commenting on another's project), meeting nursing home eligibility is not conclusive evidence that ADC is an alternative. Their response is, "These people might be eligible for nursing home care, but would they actually use it?"

Answering this question either involves prediction based on comparison with the average nursing home patient profiles or observation of test/ control or comparison group over a limited period of time. Group statistics are used. Remember that within each group there is a wide range of patient characteristics which are constantly changing. Predictions about specific individuals' nursing home utilization based on group characteristics are very shaky (Palmer 1982, 258). There is no way to accurately predict nursing home utilization, which means that however the target population is defined, some who do not meet the criteria will be included and some who will use a nursing home are excluded.

The issue of adult day care as an alternative or supplement to nursing home care is frequently cited by policy makers and governmental officials who wish to avoid funding adult day care. It is, perhaps, the major issue in the Congressional debate regarding the inclusion of ADC in comprehensive Medicare-funded long-term care benefit package. To Congress, supplement means new money for a new program, not a trade-off in use of funds which would be the case in alternatives. ADC managers may be confronted with this issue in negotiations with government funders. Do not be drawn into an argument on this issue. This is a question with no reliable answer. To argue about whether or not a person would go to a nursing home is about as productive an argument today as how many angels can dance on the head of a pin was in the Middle Ages. It should be remembered that a discussion of alternatives to nursing home care also involves the proper use of institutionalization. Eligibility criteria is often very broad and depends heavily on a physician's certification. However, people are institutionalized for many reasons that may be social or economic, rather than medical, and sometimes simply because nothing else is available.

ADC advocates recognize that there is a need and a place for appropriate use of nursing home care. This is not necessarily reflected in nursing home placement criteria. However, they also know people are often institutionalized inappropriately. Therefore, the claim is made that ADC is an alternative to inappropriate or premature nursing home care. In most ADC programs, ADC is serving as an alternative to nursing home care for some participants. Although they meet state nursing home criteria, their needs are being met in a different way. Without ADC, they would be in a nursing home. For other participants, ADC may not be an alternative to nursing home care at that point in time. However, who can predict tomorrow when a stroke, a hip fracture, or the death of a caregiver may occur which changes circumstances entirely?

Impact of Adult Day Care

Attempts to measure the impact or outcomes of ADC usually center around changes in functional status, life satisfaction, and mortality. The following are several problems associated with this:

- Inadequate measurement tools and uncertainty about what to measure

- Difficulty in measuring the benefits of maintenance—maintenance at the same level can actually be a gain, in that deterioration that may otherwise have occurred is slowed. The difficulty is measuring what did not happen.

- Uncertainty about what in the aging process is reversible, treatable, or inevitable.

- Difficulty about measuring utilization of other services, such as hospitalization, which did not occur

Researchers reach their own conclusions based on their research design, measurement instruments and scope of study. Providers should be guided by their own experiences and remember the limitations of the current art of research.

Cost Effectiveness

The cost effective question is also important to consider since a comparison is often made between ADC and nursing home costs. ADC utilization per month costs less than a month in a nursing home because most ADC participants attend three days per week and reimbursement is often only for days attended. Therefore, money can be saved if a person can be served in ADC who would otherwise be in a nursing home. This assumes the desired outcomes of ADC and nursing home care are the same and that the input (service package) is the same. However, there are distinct differences in the service package and expected outcomes of the two programs. ADC emphasizes restorative as well as maintenance of functional status. A major objective is to keep participants in their own home and out of the nursing home. Although both ADC and nursing homes offer personal care, nursing, supervision, and meals, ADC is service-intensive, providing a wide variety of health and health-related services in approximately six hours a day, three days a week. Much of the nursing home day is essentially board and room.

A researcher once compared licensing requirements for nursing care (all levels—Registered Nurse, Licensed Vocational Nurse, and Aide) in California's ICF and SNF facilities with actual nursing time (again, at all levels) provided in existing ADC centers. Using a model of 50 Average Daily Attendance, a SNF would be required to provide 140 hours of nursing care and an ICF 45 hours in a 24-hour day, while the Adult Day Health Center provided 52.5 hours of nursing care in a 4–8 hour day. This comparison did not even include nutritional counseling; social services; recreational activities; meals; transportation; occupational, physical or speech therapy, which are mandated for ADHC in California.

ADC offers the benefits of multiple services to maintain and restore optimal functional independence. These services are provided within a limited time frame in a group setting at a centralized location. The cost per unit of service is less than if a service were provided on a one-to-one basis in the person's home. Ordinary costs of living, which form a part of nursing home costs, are not part of the ADC center expenses. More services are provided during shorter hours at the ADC center than during the longer hours in a nursing home.

Cost-effectiveness analysis, when properly used, is appropriate for ADC as both economic and noneconomic outcomes may be compared. Doherty and Hicks (1975, 412-417) recommend the use of cost-effectiveness analysis for ADC as the outcomes are often noneconomic—life satisfaction, respite for caregivers, and independence of the participants. The problem arises when researchers try to measure these outcomes. Adequate instruments are lacking and consequently most researchers limit analysis to items that can be assigned a dollar value.

There is also basic disagreement among those providing funds, however, regarding the definition of costs when applied to ADC. The funding source is usually primarily interested in costs relating to its program. Medicaid programs are concerned about Medicaid, aging programs about Older Americans Act, and social programs about the Social Services Block Grant. Medicare costs are a federal concern. Other funding sources, such as SSI and housing subsidies, are also concerned about their own funds.

The easiest cost data to obtain is the rate paid by a government agency to ADC. However, this is the cost to the government, which is *not* the cost to the ADC center for providing the service. The cost of providing ADC is often higher than the government rate paid. Costs may also include in-kind contributions at less than market value, or at no cost to the center such as space, personnel, equipment, transportation and meals.

In developing cost data it is difficult to identify the in-kind contributions and to assign an accurate dollar value to them. The cost of providing ADC is considered the first level of costs, according to Doherty and Hicks (1975). The second level of costs is the cost of all other services provided to the ADC participants. Since multiple funding sources provide these services and many are subsidized by state or federal government, determining cost is difficult. Case management programs often limit cost tracking to the services they pay and lack data on additional services. It is difficult to determine the true cost of informal support services provided by family members. This is both a problem of identification and dollar value. The third level is all costs associated with living at home, such as food and housing. Costs ideally should include out-of-pocket as well as government costs.

Achieving accurate information about all three levels of cost is seldom actually done. Providers should concentrate their efforts on identifying the true costs of the ADC program in terms of cost per participant per day, and fixed and variable costs. This information is helpful in program management and can be useful in contract or rate negotiation with government and private per rate setting. Dedicated researchers may try to track other service costs. Even if limited to government funds, this is still a formidable, time consuming task, and provides little benefit to the ADC provider.

Benefits to Caregivers

Another measure of increasing interest in recent years is the outcome of ADC for caregivers. This is an area of research where there appears to be agreement. Caregivers benefit from the support, counseling, and respite provided by ADC and are often strong, vocal advocates of ADC. A variety of recent surveys identifying needs of employed caregivers have served to highlight ADC as a needed service for caregivers.

As an increasing number of employers become concerned about the effects of caregiving on employees, the value of ADC will be recognized as an employee benefit. One insurance company has already made available group employee insurance coverage that includes ADC coverage. The state of Maryland now offers this coverage to active and retired employees and spouses who are less than 80 years of age. In addition, parents of active employees and spouses who are less than 80 years of age are eligible to enroll. Children, brothers and sisters are not eligible. Premiums vary depending on age at enrollment and the daily benefit amount of coverage selected.

Specialized ADC Programs

ADC programs serving exclusively developmentally disabled or mentally disabled persons predate ADC serving a predominantly elderly population. In recent years, specialized programs have been developed targeted to persons with Alzheimer's disease and other dementias. It should be noted that persons with dementia are served in all ADC centers. The increasing attention, availability of funds, and growing clientele have led to special programming within ADC or a separate setting. At this stage, there is no clear answer regarding the effectiveness, desirability, and feasibility of specialized programs.

One factor influencing an ADC provider's choice of offering specialized versus generalized care is supply. Many communities have difficulty supporting one ADC. It is not economically feasible to operate a variety of small programs targeting specialty groups (specialized programs are not likely to stop with dementia clients—already being planned are specialized ADC for persons with AIDS and head trauma). The ADC may also prefer working with persons with a variety of impairments or they may find it easier if there is greater homogeneity. Finally, generalizations that persons with Alzheimer's desease don't need nursing or therapy are not necessarily true. The risk with specialized programs is treating only that impairment and ignoring the rest. In the past, for example, some mental hospitals have sometimes been notorious for their neglect of the physical health of their patients.

Disease-specific programs have been criticized for the exclusion of others who need the services but do not have the required diagnosis. People often "fell through the cracks." The history of programs for the developmentally disabled provides illustration of the problems of diagnosis related eligibility. ADC was developed to serve the whole person in one setting to the extent this is feasible. The trend today is to emphasize the functional status of the person, not the medical diagnosis, as an indicator for long-term care services. Consequently, decisions regarding targeting special populations need to be made with care, never forgetting the multiple needs and infinite variety of ADC participants.

How to Read Research

Many people are intimidated by the jargon used in statistical analysis and do not question the information presented through the media and various professional publications. Statistics are commonly used to sell us products and influence our actions. Although we may be skeptical of product claims, we may be more susceptible to researchers.

In 1954 an interesting book appeared entitled, *How to Lie With Statistics*. Now in its 38th printing, this book, written by Darrell Huff and illustrated by Irving Geis, presents an amusing, informative guide to the ways statistics are used to deceive. The intent of the book is not to teach ways to use statistics to deceive. Those who do so already know how. It's the rest of us who need to learn these techniques to protect ourselves. Although the illustrative anecdotes may be dated, the points made are valuable. Chapter 10, "How to Talk Back to a Statistic," presents five simple questions that can be used to analyze the soundness and usefulness of data. These five questions are listed and explained below:

Who says so? Huff advises us to look for conscious and unconscious bias. Every researcher's biases, values and assumptions influence the research and how the data are analyzed and presented. Determining bias is not always easy, but a careful reading will often reveal examples. Some researchers will let you know "up front" what their biases are. Reading this chapter, it will be obvious to you that there is a bias here against the overemphasis placed on the test and control randomized group selection research design utilizing only quantifiable elements appropriate for statistical analysis and rigid researchers who see research only in these terms. This is too narrow a focus and cheats us of the richness available when a wide variety of research methods are utilized and appreciated.

Importantly, what is *not* said is often the key to bias. Do not be misled by academic titles or prestigious institutions. Neither necessarily means the data are unbiased.

How does s/he know? This involves the research design, method of data collection, the size of the sample, the response rate to a questionnaire and the method of analysis. Be particularly alert to generalizations made based on a small number of examples or on a one-time-only study. Does what was found at Center X at X time mean the findings apply to other programs? Information to help you decide how the information was gathered may not be given. This leads to the next question.

What's missing? Often, not enough information is provided. For example, percentages may be given but not the number, a comparison may be made to an unnamed item, or a misleading average may be used.

Did somebody change the subject? This refers to a conclusion reached that is not warranted by the data, or two items that occur at the same time may be stated as a cause and effect relationship which has not been proven. Both of these occur frequently.

Does it make sense? Apply your common sense and your experience. Does what is said seem right to you? An example of applied common sense appeared in a recent edition of a local paper. A reader observed in a letter to the editor that the paper had stated in an article about a 1932 high school class reunion that the average age of the men was 72 and the women, 63. As the reader noted, this makes the men 17 at graduation (possible) but the women age 8!

Practical Applications

As a manager, a sixth question could be added to Huff's list—does this research have practical applications for my program? Perhaps a new approach to marketing, fundraising, or programming has been tested. The results seem to show that the new idea was effective—you may want to try it. Studies showing profiles of "norms" or national averages such as the NIAD survey, Northwestern University survey, or current Weissert survey can prove an interesting comparison basis for your program. Always keep in mind, however, that averages are not standards—they reflect what is reported about a particular item in a certain time period. Such profiles are especially useful to ADC planners, policymakers, and the public as they provide a general description of the program.

In order for you to compare your program to others, you must have data. You probably have already set up data collection instruments and a report system to satisfy your board, funders, management needs, or your own curiosity. The necessity of proper documentation and recordkeeping is discussed elsewhere in this book. Keep in mind that the primary function of your program is to provide ADC services. Scrutinize your data elements to be sure each one meets a need—either in service planning and provision or an external requirement. Documentation is probably the least favorite activity of your staff—don't overburden them with data collection because you think it might be nice to know this. Collection of unused data results in frustrated staff. Provide feedback to the staff to demonstrate the importance of their documentation. Use the information you get.

Train your staff to develop measurable, attainable goals in care planning. At reassessment time, determine progress towards attaining the goals and reset new goals. Participants and families should be involved in goal setting. Small triumphs occur daily in adult day care that give pride to the participants and satisfaction to the staff, yet may not show up on assessment measurements that measure gross changes. Address your goals to these achievable tasks and celebrate your victories. Doing this over time demonstrates to you, your staff, participants and their families your accomplishments, and provides excellent information to funders.

Goal setting often is vague. Progress cannot be measured and staff may feel that nothing is accomplished. Reassure your staff that specific goal setting is not a threat to them, nor have they failed if it's not attained. Setting a specific goal is taking a risk for staff, and it needs to be nonthreatening. Evaluate in terms of progress towards the goal, analyze problems that occur, and reset goals.

Use research techniques for problem solving. Identify the problem, discuss possible solutions with staff and test one or more alternatives. Agree on criteria for determining effectiveness and what, if any, new data are to be collected. Try your solutions, document what happens, and discuss findings with staff. For example, your average daily attendance is low and growth is slow. You want more people in your program. First, identify the problem. Has the number of referrals dropped? If so, why? Has the number of persons voluntarily dropping out of your program increased? If so, why? Let's say that you are receiving an adequate number of referrals and your disenrollment level has remained the same. The problem may be in the intake process—how long does it take from referral to admission? What steps are involved? In one center, getting the information from the physician was taking an inordinate amount of time and potential participants were kept dangling for weeks and months. At every step of this process, data are needed. You need to know the number of referrals, when received, where from, when intake was done, and when information was requested and received from the physician. You can compare data from your trial solution to the former method and determine success by the increase in attendance.

Program evaluation (discussed in Chapter Four) is another form of practical research you can do. The scope of the evaluation will vary depending upon the resources you wish to devote to it. The basic point is to set your goals and determine the degree to which your program has met these goals. External evaluations may be done by consultants, funders, or regulators. However, these evaluations may have different goals than those that would be useful to you. There may be aspects not covered in other evaluations and you should focus on these. The keys are the setting of goals, and how you will measure your progress. These are developed in your research design.

You may be approached by a student or researcher wishing to use your program in a research study. However flattered you may feel, there are some precautions you should take. Ask for the researcher's credentials, such as what past studies the researcher has done. Get a copy of the complete research design being proposed and look carefully at the methodology. During discussions and while reading material, be alert to bias, value systems, or just plain ignorance. The researcher may have good technical skills but completely lack program knowledge or understanding. You may need to spend much of your time educating the researcher about your program. You need to be sure that the researcher understands what ADC is all about.

Don't be intimidated by technical jargon. Insist that plain English be used in reference to the research design, the findings and the implications. Insist on reviewing the report before issued. You can identify and correct factual errors and misunderstandings *before* others see the report. You can spend hours of your time coping with the effects of a misleading or inaccurate research study. Finally, be cautious. Your time and your data are valuable. Put in writing the terms of agreement reached by you and the researcher and get the researcher to sign it.

Current Studies

Five Congressional bills in the 100th Congress included ADC in some way. One which was enacted includes a survey. The Medicare Catastrophic Coverage Act of 1988 includes a Congressional mandate for a 12-month ADC survey conducted by the Secretary of Health and Human Services collecting information regarding services, provider characteristics, licensure, certification and other quality standards, costs, and participant characteristics. The report shall include recommendations for standards for ADC as a Medicare benefit, including how ADC should be defined, who it should serve, provider qualifications, and reimbursement mechanisms.

This report will obviously be used for national policy decisions. It is important that you be familiar with the information found in other current and past studies which may also influence policy at state or national levels. In recent years, several research studies have been conducted and the results are or will soon be distributed. Research design and issues for these studies are discussed here. See Appendix B for a selected annotated bibliography about past studies. Indications are that a comprehensive long-term care service package will be a major Congressional agenda item for the 101st Congress. Frequently, data from studies are used, regardless of research quality by both persons in opposition to the inclusion of ADC in federal financing, and persons supporting its inclusion. Familiarity with past and current studies and the issues involved provides you with a context in which to understand the debate and a basis for promoting favorable policy decisions.

Northwestern University Survey

Conrad and colleagues (1986) developed a survey questionnaire for data collection. They received responses from 949 centers. Objectives of the study were to provide a data base that could be used to model ADC programs, assess their effectiveness, and promote programs' involvement. Results of the project are the descriptive report, program profiles, and an Adult Day Care Assessment Procedure (ADCAP) Manual (a set of instruments designed to measure structure, patient population and processes).

The study report discusses norms that could be used in program evaluation or modeling without expressing the values implied in the content of the scales. As is the case in many self-rating scales appearing in popular literature, it is quite easy to identify the "desirable" attributes in the social environment scales. Averages or norms for modeling or evaluation implies that averages or norms are desirable standards to achieve. However, none of us in our personal or professional lives tries to be average or uses that as a goal. The average is a statistical artifact that often does not exist in reality, e.g., the center's average daily attendance is 18.3 persons, or the van could accommodate 3.6 wheelchairs. Standards are intended to establish goals that incorporate quality and effectiveness.

At this time, tests of reliability and validity of the ADCAP, the instrument used, have not been done. Managers may find this information useful as a basis for comparison with their program. Its usefulness as a model to emulate or as an evaluation tool is questionable.

Hawaiian Legislative Study

Hayashida and coworkers (1987) prepared a report as the result of a 1986 legislative initiative to assess ADC as an alternative to nursing home care. The research has been completed. Reports have been submitted to the legislature and two bills have been introduced.

The objectives of the study were:

- to identify historical development of ADC with emphasis on Hawaii, as well as to define the conceptual differences in terminology
- to compare the functional disability level of ADC participants with patients in intermediate care facilities
- to project ADC demand over the next 15 years
- to compare ADC costs with intermediate care facilities
- to review ADC models

Pennsylvania ADC Evaluation

Bryn Mawr College School of Social Work and Social Research was awarded an 18-month contract in 1987 by the Pennsylvania Department on Aging to perform a statewide evaluation of ADC programs funded by the State office headed by Kaye and Kirwin. The project should be completed in 1989.

Survey questionnaires will be administered by trained researchers to 75 caregivers and 75 clients who will be selected from the 11 participating counties. Questionnaires will also be sent to the ADC Director and Area Agency on Aging Program Manager in these counties. In addition, 300 randomly selected ADC client files will be used to collect assessment/ reassessment information.

Veterans' Administration Adult Day Health Care (ADHC) Research and Evaluation

Public Law 98-160 authorized the Veterans' Administration (VA) to operate ADHC centers, contract with existing adult day health centers, and provide in-kind assistance to community ADHC centers with which the VA wished to contract with corresponding rate adjustment.

Congress mandated a study of the medical efficacy and cost-effectiveness of ADHC as an alternative to nursing home care. Program evaluation is under the direction of Susan Hendrick, Principal Investigator, American Lake VA Medical Center, Tacoma, WA. Four VA ADHC programs out of eight were selected to be the sample. These four are located in Portland, OR; Minneapolis, MN; Little Rock, AR and Miami, FL. VA patients after initial assessment were randomly assigned to either the test group, who will receive ADHC, or the control group, who will receive traditional services. The study anticipates that there will be 428 patients in each group. Patient enrollment for the research phase began July 1987. As of October 1987, 141 patients were in the randomized trial. The second phase is the evaluation of ADHC provided by community ADHC programs under contract to the VA. Twenty-one VA hospitals were given contract authority. Five of these sites were chosen to attain 535 patients (107 at each site). This group will be compared with the VA ADHC centers' test group and control group. The emphasis in the research is on outcomes. The research questions are:

- What is the relative effect of ADHC compared to customary care on patient (survival, functional status, care satisfaction) and caregiver (functional status, response to caregiving, satisfaction with patient care) outcomes, health care utilization, and costs?

- Does the effect (outcome) of ADHC differ across sites (and between VA ADHC centers and community ADHC centers)?

- Does the effect (outcome) of ADHC differ for subgroups of patients, grouped by characteristics such as functional status and eligibility at intake?

Data will be collected periodically through in-person interviews, VA records, and other provider records. A set of data collection instruments and statistical tests have been selected. Each patient will be followed for one year after intake. Total study period is expected to be about 3 1/2 years, with the final report due in 1991.

ADC providers are somewhat concerned about the VA evaluation report due to Congress in 1991. Not only is the future of VA funded ADHC programs at stake, but the impact of the study may influence federal funding for all ADC programs. VA ADHC programs, with a medical orientation, are not representative of ADC programs in general or ADHC programs in particular. Cost analysis will, therefore, reflect the medical component as well as start-up costs, and costs resulting from the VA hospital affiliation. Public policy decisions made on the basis of this evaluation are likely to affect all ADC programs regardless of the difference between the VA model and other ADC programs.

NIAD Survey

Program characteristics, participant profiles, costs, and funding sources are summarized in one of two reports presenting the findings of a study by Von Behren (1986). Data were obtained by a survey questionnaire conducted in 1985-86 by the National Institute on Adult Daycare and the National Council on Aging. Responses from 847 centers in 46 states were received.

The second report, an intensive statistical analysis, addresses the questions raised by the summary report. The primary research question was to discover, if possible, a useful method of categorizing adult day care to improve our understanding of the differences among programs. The lack of federal standards and a common nomenclature for the various ADC programs meant this was not a simple task.

To determine the existence or nonexistence of categories or "models," the following questions were asked:

- Are the services offered by day centers related to the functional and demographic characteristics of participants served? For example, the summary report noted that some centers do not accept incontinent participants and some centers do not have nurses on staff. We wondered if these two factors were related.

- Licensing categories are a traditional determinant of programs. This factor is of limited application for adult day care, considering that only 15 states required licensing in 1985-86, and the terminology used may vary across states. However, as licensing does prescribe program elements, we asked: Do services vary among centers in different licensing categories, and are these centers serving different kinds of participants?

- A second possible influence on centers is funding sources. Funding sources may prescribe participant eligibility, center services, and staffing. Do centers with different funding sources serve different kinds of participants?

- Program costs vary from center to center. What influences cost? Is it services? License? Funding source? Center census? Participant functional level?

- One question raised was age of participants. Do centers that serve relatively younger participants differ from other programs?

- Relationships between participant demographic and functional characteristics were also explored. Does living situation relate to functional impairments? That is, can we identify what might be called "clusters" of participants who share similar characteristics? If so, do these clusters tend to be served by centers with a certain license or major funding source? (Von Behren, 1988, 4)

The report concluded that ADC is not several discrete models but rather is a program providing a range of services in a structured, centralized setting, designed to meet the needs of functionally impaired individuals and their families. The configuration of a particular center at a given point in time reflects external factors such as licensing or major funding source, and internal factors such as perceived need and the center's ability to meet these needs in terms of resources available.

University of North Carolina Study

Weissert and colleagues are completing a 3-year study in which information was gathered from 59 programs identified through a sampling process utilizing the 1980 ADC Directory. On-site visits, interviews and documents were the means of data collection. Expected products are a software program to be utilized by ADC managers in fiscal planning and program development, and a book describing the programs studied and information gathered. An advisory committee with four NIAD representatives has met periodically to hear research progress and process.

Preliminary data have been presented to NIAD and NCOA. It is anticipated that the software will be user tested before production and a draft of the book made available for review by the advisory committee. At issue will be the external validity of the research design, particularly the methods of sample selection, i.e., how representative the sample is, and the study's use or nonuse of generalizations, assumptions, and interpretations.

References

Conrad, K.J. et al. 1986. *Assessing the structure, population and process of adult day care programs: Report to Andrus Foundation.* Evanston: Northwestern University.

Doherty, N.J.G., and B.C. Hicks. 1975. The use of cost-effectiveness analysis in geriatric day care. *The Gerontologist.* 15(5) Part II: 412-417.

Hayashida, C. et al. 1987. *Adult day centers in Hawaii: A comprehensive assessment for strategic planning for the 1990s.* Hawaii: Department of Human Services.

Huff, D., pictures by I. Geis. 1954. *How to lie with statistics.* New York: W.W. Norton and Company.

Kane, R.A., and R.L. Kane. 1981. *Assessing the elderly: A practical guide to measurement.* Lexington, MA: DC Health and Company.

Kaye, L.W., and P.M. Kirwin, Co-project directors. 1989. *Pennsylvania evaluation of adult day care programs.*

Palmer, H.C. nd c. 1982. The alternatives question. *Long-term care: Perspectives from research and demonstration.* eds. R.J. Vogel and H.C. Palmer. Washington, DC: Health Care Financing Administration. 255-299.

Von Behren, R. 1986. *Adult daycare in America: Summary of a national survey.* Washington, DC: The National Council on Aging.

Von Behren, R. 1988. *Adult day care: A program of services for the functionally impaired.* Washington, DC: The National Council on Aging.

Weissert, W. et al. In process. The University of North Carolina national adult day care study.

Components of the Health and Social Services Network for Older Persons

Linda Cook Webb

The health and social services network is a continuum of sometimes overlapping programs designed to meet a wide range of needs. At one end of the continuum, services are designed for people who are relatively healthy physically, and who are needing minimal social supports. At the opposite end, services are designed for people who are extremely dependent, physically, mentally, and/or emotionally. Throughout the continuum, there is a blending of health care and social services. For example, a recreation center for well elders may include health care screening and health education programs. At the other extreme, a nursing home offering total physical care for very impaired persons should also include some type of socialization experiences—even if these are only one-to-one visiting. The following are some of the services in the network.

Information and referral (I&R) services are designed to give people information about existing elder care resources in their communities. I&R workers do not perform assessments or tell individuals what services they may need.

Case management programs can perform detailed assessment of a frail or disabled person's special needs and help the individual/family obtain the needed services.

Congregate meals programs offer a nutritious meal at a central community location, such as a recreation center, church or school. Many meal sites also provide transportation and recreation.

Senior transportation includes several types of services. A van or bus may provide door-to-door transportation for persons who can walk unassisted. Specially adapted vehicles may carry persons in wheelchairs. Escort, found in a few communities, serves those who need the assistance of another person to have a successful trip (usually for persons who are confused or disoriented).

Senior centers are places where well elders come together for services and activities that enhance their independence and encourage their involvement in the community. Most senior centers also offer information and referral, a congregate meals program and transportation.

Senior housing includes options as varied as publicly funded senior apartments and private retirement communities. Senior housing usually has provision for a small number of apartments which are handicapped-accessible. Health care services are not usually provided.

Homemakers go into the home of a frail person to provide light housekeeping and meal preparation. They do not offer personal care, such as bathing or dressing assistance, although they may provide reminders of when to take medicines.

Chore services provide workers to help with lawn mowing, snow shoveling, window washing, home repair, etc. in the homes of frail older persons.

Meals on Wheels (MOW) programs prepare meals centrally and transport them to homebound persons. Usually, service is limited to the noon meal only, five days a week.

Friendly visitors are volunteers who visit isolated homebound persons on a regular basis.

Reassurance programs are designed for very frail or homebound persons who fear that they may face a physical crisis without being able to obtain assistance. These programs make provision for daily contact with the client. If contact cannot be made, the family, the local police department, or other designated source is alerted to provide help.

Respite care attempts to meet family caregivers' needs for a break from constant caregiving responsibilities, by providing temporary supervision for the impaired relative. Respite may be provided in the individual's home, in an adult day care center, or in a nursing home.

Adult day care provides supervision, motivation, and therapeutic activities for frail or disabled adults in a group setting. Many day care centers provide meals and transportation. Some centers may also provide skilled nursing and professional therapy services. (See Chapter One for a fuller definition.)

Home health agencies provide brief professional in-home treatment over a limited period of time. Specific services may include nursing, physical therapy, occupational therapy, speech therapy, personal care, and others.

Private duty services provide nursing, nurse aide, and therapy services from four to 24 hours a day. Some agencies have a "bath program" that provides an aide for only that time needed to give either a bed bath or a tub bath.

Protective services provide legal and financial help to mentally impaired or handicapped persons who are unable to manage their own affairs or protect themselves from abuse or exploitation.

Nursing homes provide 24-hour a day room, board, personal care, and health supervision. Depending on the type of nursing home, there may be a greater or lesser degree of professional nursing and therapy services provided.

Hospice programs care for persons with life-threatening illnesses (usually cancer), with an individually prescribed regimen designed to relieve and control pain. Hospice also serves the families of patients, with supportive care. It may be based on in-home services or located in special health care environment.

APPENDIX B

Research in Adult Day Care

Ruth Von Behren

Contents:

The following list is a selection of ADC research reports. Much of the data available were not published in a formal sense. Reports were issued and distributed, but were not published as a journal article or monograph. Consequently, many of these reports are not widely available today. Copies may be found in some libraries or at the agency sponsoring the research.

Reports prior to 1980 are probably most valuable as historical documents—they reveal where we were then. Even today's research, however, often quotes data or conclusions from these very early reports. Familiarity with past studies increases a manager's understanding of current issues and helps the manager respond when issues are raised by policy makers and researchers.

Alzheimer's and Adult Day Care

Mace, N.L. and P.V. Rabins. 1984. *A survey of daycare for the demented adult in the United States.* Washington, DC: The National Council on Aging.

This report includes the findings of a survey of 346 adult day care centers that serve at least some clients with dementia. The majority are centers serving a mixed population of demented and nondemented, with a few specializing in dementia participants. The authors conclude that day care is a vitally important form of respite for caregivers and that some very confused people can be successfully managed in adult day care.

Sands, D., and T. Suzuki. 1983. Adult day care for Alzheimer's patients and their families. *The Gerontologist* 23(1): 21-23.

Sands, D., and T. Suzuki. 1984. The Harbor Area Adult Day Care Center: A model program. *Pride Journal of Long-Term Health Care,* Fall.

Both articles describe development, philosophy, structure, and costs of a day care program designed to serve dementia clients.

Caregivers

Crossman, L., C. London, and C. Barry. 1981. Older women caring for disabled spouses: A model of supportive services. *The Gerontologist* 21(5): 464-470.

Expanded respite services involving ADC, overnight, and in-home services.

Rathbone-McCuan, E. 1976. Geriatric day care: A family perspective. *The Gerontologist* 16(6): 517-524.

Study of 28 Levindale Adult Treatment Center participants who lived with family members, and 26 of their family members. Data were gathered from in-depth interviews. The author concludes that day care benefits families by providing a service that shares in the physical care, provides psychological support, and provides a means by which the family is able to fulfill its desire to keep the aged person at home as long as possible.

Zimmerman, S.L. 1986. Adult day care: Correlation of its coping effects for families of an elderly disabled member. *Family Relations* 35: 305-311.

Telephone survey of 94 caregivers of elderly disabled persons attending ADC in three Minnesota counties. Report concludes that ADC is a resource enabling primary caregivers to care for the older person, helping them to better attend to the person's needs, as well as their own.

Directories

Department of Health, Education and Welfare. 1978. *Directory of adult day care centers*. Washington, DC: Government Printing Office.

The second national ADC directory listing nearly 300 programs (original version issued in September 1977). Classifies programs by maintenance, restorative and social models with descriptive information provided by the centers. Compiled by Edith Robins, special assistant for Adult Day Health Services.

Department of Health and Human Services. 1980. *Directory of adult day care centers*. Washington, DC: Government Printing Office.

Also compiled by Edith Robins. This is an update of the 1978 directory with 618 programs listed.

National Council on Aging. National Institute of Adult Daycare. 1987. *Directory of adult daycare in America*. Washington, DC: National Council on Aging.

Compiled by On Lok Senior Health Services, the directory contains descriptive information about 847 ADC centers, based on information supplied by the programs in response to NIAD/NCOA 1985-1986 National Survey Questionnaire.

Sammer, J.M. 1986. *The national directory of adult day care centers.* New Jersey: Health Resources Publishing.

Mailing information is given for more than 600 centers, and a profile of 217 programs with descriptive information is included.

Models Theory

Early researchers analyzed ADC programs and attempted to classify program variations as models. Their studies were static, often describing programs in early stages of development and did not address the evolutionary growth of a new program concept, both in the case of individual centers and the programs as a whole. Consequently, most of the early Models Theory has been discarded. Today, NIAD prefers a generic term—adult day care—for all types of programs. Although funding and licensing requirements (where they exist) have shaped programs roughly around a social model that does not provide health services and a health model that does, in practice there is a continuum of ADC and the old lines of distinction are blurring. Services provided depend on the needs of the participants and the resources available.

TransCentury Corporation. 1975. *Adult day care in the U.S.: A comparative study* (final report). Washington, DC: National Center for Health Services Research, Division of Health Services Evaluations.

This report, done under contract for HCFA by the TransCentury Corporation, is a description of 10 adult day care centers. Drawing on an earlier DHEW publication (*Preliminary analysis of select geriatric day care programs*, 1974) which had identified 15 programs, the study team, headed by William Weissert, selected 10 representative programs. Data were collected during a 3-day site visit by a 3-5 member team. Two models were identified in this report: Model 1—relatively heavy emphasis on health services and health professional staff with emphasis on rehabilitation; Model 2—smaller proportion of professional staff, less emphasis on rehabilitation. Model 2 could have multi-purpose service objectives that could be physical and mental maintenance or physical and mental health maintenance and rehabilitation.

Robins, Edith. 1976. Operational research in geriatric day care in the United States. *Adult day facilities for treatment, health care and related services,* Special Committee on Aging. U.S. Senate, Washington, DC: Government Printing Office, 82-87.

Another early proponent of the models theory was Edith Robins, special assistant for Adult Day Health Services, HCFA, who described four models in a report prepared in 1976 for the Senate Special Committee on the Aging. The four models are:

Model 1—Intensive restorative in lieu of inpatient rehabilitation services (day hospital). Primary physician care included.
Model 2—Time-limited, intense restorative services to post-hospital or post-nursing home patients. Primary physician care provided in other settings.
Model 3—Health maintenance to persons either eligible or at risk for institutional care.
Model 4—Psychological activities in a protected environment. Emphasis on socialization.

In 1980 at a presentation at American Public Health Association (*Adult day care: An idea whose time has come*), Ms. Robins moved away from the models idea and stated that a valid question can be raised about whether there should be distinct program models or whether it is preferable for a single program to serve varying levels of needs as a number of authorities are indicating.

Trager, B. 1976. *Adult day facilities for treatment, health care and related services,* Special Committee on Aging. U.S. Senate, Washington, DC: Government Printing Office.

Subcommittee on Health and Long-Term Care of the Select Committee on Aging, House of Representatives. 1980. *Adult day health care programs hearing report.* Pub. 96-260. Washington, DC: Government Printing Office.

For the viewpoints of those who rejected the Models Theories, see pages 15-17 in the Senate report and pages 175-187 in the House report. B. Trager has prepared a report on a conference about adult day health care that includes discussion of this issue. The conference report is the outcome of a National Center for Health Services Research grant that sponsored a two-part conference held in Arlington, VA in 1977 and Tuscon, AZ in 1978. More than 80 people attended the Arlington meeting—representing providers, planners, policymakers, funding sources, and related government and provider service fields. Although the purported purpose was to identify research issues, discussion ranged over all aspects of the field. Two subject areas were of overriding interest: the "models" concept and the funding situation. The conclusion for the group was the principle that adult day health care is not a single service but a range of services provided in a variety of settings in the community care continuum. The group chose adult day health care as the name for a generic concept.

Section 222: A Medicare Demonstration Project

Weissert, W.G. et al. 1979. *Effects and costs of day care and homemaker services for the chronically ill.* Hyattsville, MD: National Center for Health Services Research.

Comments on the Weissert report. 1980. *Home Health Services Quarterly* 1(3): 97-121.

The Weissert report is commonly referred to as the Section 222 report. The name comes from the authorizing legislation, Section 222 of the 1972 amendments to the U.S. Social Security Act. Section 222 authorizes waivers of Medicare regulations for demonstration projects.

The report is an evaluation of the 1975-77 Medicare Waiver demonstration project utilizing four sites to test the effectiveness of adult day care for a Medicare-eligible population. Randomized test/control groups were used.

Since this report is the only study of a Medicare-funded adult day care demonstration project, and the reports and articles derived from this study are widely available, reference is often made to its findings despite criticism of its methodology. In many instances, quotes are used without knowledge of the issues surrounding the report. The unwary ready can be misled as can the policy maker who uses the data to avoid funding ADC.

Both internal and external validity of the research design have been heavily criticized by policymakers, researchers, and providers. In short, there are serious questions regarding whether this study tested what it said it did, i.e., alternatives to nursing home care, when nursing home-eligible persons were not eligible for the demonstrations project. Serious charges of bias, questionable statistical methods, unsupported value judgments and personal interpretation have been made.

Generalizability is highly questionable, as the sites chosen were not randomly selected nor representative and were individually quite different. Two were in New York, one in Kentucky and one in California. Nevertheless, due to the publication of various articles about this research, no account of ADC research is complete without reference to the 222 project.

How these data were analyzed and presented illustrates why ADC managers need to understand the elements of research design. Negative research findings, despite questionable methodology, always prove to be a useful excuse for government inaction.

Site-Specific Early Studies

Kalish, R.A., et al. 1975. *On Lok Senior Health Services: Evaluation of a success*. San Francisco, CA: On Lok Senior Health Services.

Zawadski, R.T., with C.L. Yordi. 1979. *On Lok Senior Health Services: Towards a continuum of care*. San Francisco, CA: On Lok Senior Health Services.

These two studies contain the evaluation of On Lok's early years, discussing process, participants, services, and outcomes.

Rathbone-McCuan, E., and M.G. Rose. 1973. *Cost effectiveness of an urban geriatric day care center*. Paper read at Gerontological Society 26th Annual Scientific Meeting, Nov. 5-9, at Miami Beach, FL.

Research findings are presented from the Levendale Geriatric Day Treatment Center study. Describes methodology used for cost-benefit analysis. Results are summarized in Weiler, P.G., and E. Rathbone-McCuan. 1978, *Adult day care: Community work with the elderly* 139-143. New York: Springer Publishing Company. In this study, day care was more cost-effective than institutional care: the effectiveness/cost ratio was almost five to one.

Also included in the Weiler Rathbone-McCuan book are summaries of the Lexington Kentucky Center for Creative Living research (145-146) which concluded that ADC was effective and a less costly alternative.

Both Weiler and Rathbone-McCuan have published various articles about their research based on the Lexington and Levendale programs.

State Studies

California

Demonstration Projects

Von Behren, R. 1978. *On Lok Senior Health Services: Adult day health care—from pilot project to permanent program*, final report. Sacramento: Department of Health Services.

Von Behren, R. 1978. *Adult day health services*, final report. (San Diego and Sacramento Centers), Sacramento: Department of Health Services.

Von Behren, R., and M. Duveneck. 1978. *Adult day health care— nursing home alternatives*, final report. (Garden-Sullivan and Mt. Zion Centers) San Francisco, CA: Department of Health Services.

RTZ Associates. 1977. *Day health services—Its impacts on the frail elderly and the quality and cost of long-term care*, 5 volumes. Sacramento, CA: Department of Health Services.

Evaluation

Capitman, J. 1982. *Evaluation of adult day health care programs in California pursuant to Assembly Bill 1611, Chapter 1066, Statutes of 1977.* Sacramento: Department of Health Services.

Capitman, J. 1984. *Supplemental report on the adult day health care program in California: A comparative cost analysis.* Sacramento: Department of Health Services.

California research efforts are divided into two phases: During 1975 to 1978 the State tested adult day health care at five sites, utilizing three Section 1115 Waivers. Each of the waivers had different research designs and objectives.

California tested elements of the program design and examined outcomes and costs. Final reports were written on all three waivers. During year two of the On Lok demonstration, the State contracted with RTZ Associates for the evaluation. Test and comparison groups were utilized. The study concluded that total government costs were less for the test group members than those in the On Lok program.

The successful enactment of AB 1611, Chapter 1066, Statutes of 1977 made ADHC a Medicaid benefit available statewide with a 5-year sunset clause dependent on the results of a mandated evaluation.

Capitman's findings covered a variety of ADHC areas. His conclusions may be summarized by the following excerpts relating to cost effectiveness and participant outcomes:

…when ADHC users' public costs for health and social support are compared with patterns of payments for the normative Medi-Cal population, aged 50 and over, results suggest that ADHC is a cost-effective component in the continuum of long-term care services.

The most encouraging results were found in comparisons of ADHC users who were independently judged at SNF/ICF levels with actual residents of such facilities. Functional status measures derived from the data obtained on the control groups in the MSSP evaluation and other sources supported the reasonableness of this comparison. Even when total Medi-Cal, IHSS, SSI/SSP payments were taken into account, ADHC and complementary services together represented a substantially less expensive treatment approach than SNF/ICF care.

…the study clearly shows that the ADHC population is functionally most like SNF residents and, thus, notably more impaired than the general aged Medi-Cal population. (Capitman 1984, 21)

While enrolled as participants in ADHC, 87-96% maintained or improved functioning. Clients judged at the institutional level of care were diverted from institutional placement for an average of 15 to 22 months. (Capitman 1982, viii)

In 1982, impressed with the Capitman recommendations that state support should continue, the California legislature removed the sunset clause thus enabling ADHC to continue indefinitely as a Medicaid benefit.

Massachusetts

A 1980 Massachusetts Adult Day Health Services report is found in Appendix C, Subcommittee on Health and Long-Term Care of the Select Committee on Aging, House of Representatives. *Adult Day Care Programs,* Hearing report: Washington, DC: Government Printing Office, 287-286.

This report includes cost data and the conclusions of a 1977 state evaluation study of six demonstration projects which concluded that the program seemed to have met its goals, was cost-effective and a viable and needed service in Massachusetts. The report showed a high degree of client and family satisfaction.

New Jersey

Kurland, C. 1982. The medical day care program in New Jersey. *Home Health Care Services Quarterly.* 3(2): 45-59.

Kelly, W. 1986. Development of adult day care in the state of New Jersey. *Home Health Care Services Quarterly.* 7(2): 55-70.

Kurland discusses two studies of participants attending medical day care centers. One study presents a profile of 406 persons; the other compares the cost of 52 participants over a year and a half and finds medical day care is less expensive than institutional care. The study concludes that medical day care is a true alternative service.

Kelly's article is based on a survey of 34 centers in New Jersey. Historical development, program characteristics, costs, and participant profiles are discussed.

North Carolina

Paris, J. 1987. *Adult day care services cost study.* Raleigh, North Carolina: Department of Human Resources.

This report presents participant program and cost information drawn from survey responses from 26 programs. Comparisons were made where appropriate with NIAD survey findings.

Virginia

Arling, G., Z.B. Harkins, and M. Romanuik, 1988. *Adult daycare in perspective: A comparison of the adult daycare study and the study of the Virginia nursing home pre-admission screening program.* Richmond, VA: Virginia Center on Aging, Virginia Commonwealth University.

Arling, G., and M. Romanuik. 1982. *The final report from the study of adult daycare programs in Virginia.* Richmond, VA: Virginia Center on Aging, Virginia Commonwealth University.

The first report is a comparison of the findings of two studies: Study of Adult Daycare (ADC) and Study of the Virginia Nursing Home Pre-admission Screening Program (PASS). The studies used common working definitions of physical and mental status, types of care, uses of health services, and social and economic characteristics. A randomized sample was drawn in both studies. Interviews were conducted with the impaired individual, the caregiver, and supporting information gathered from informants and case records. A total of 116 clients were interviewed from a randomly selected sample of 154 clients, representing about 40% of the ADC clients. Ninety caregivers were interviewed.

Two subgroups were selected from PASS: those who were recommended for nursing home placement (N=110) and those denied nursing home placement and recommended for community services (N=110). Caregivers selected were 108 of the nursing home recommendations subgroup and 105 of the community service recommendation subgroup. Not included were those coming to PASS from a hospital or those whose resources meant they could pay for nursing home care for more than three months without spending down to Medicaid eligibility.

The report concluded that clients in the ADC study are quite similar in functional impairment and mental status to people who apply for nursing home care. An estimated 59% of the adult day care clients would qualify for Virginia's intermediate care facility criteria. ADC represents a complement to family caregiving, reducing major stress, which may be a contributing factor to PASS clients' nursing home placement.

The second report is the study from which the sample was drawn for the ADC comparison study with PASS clients. This study examined functional status, status of caregiver, kinds of care provided, impact on the lifestyle and well-being of care provider, the decision to seek ADC services, and the nature of ADC programs and services.

Some of the conclusions found were that ADC is a generally effective and expandable option for community long-term care. ADC was found to reduce the stress on the caregiver, while maintaining the physical and mental functioning of the client in a safe, secure setting.

APPENDIX C

Special Resources for Adult Day Care

Linda Cook Webb

Contents:

Films and Videotapes
Adult Day Care Organizations
The Foundation Center Network

Films and Videotapes

Coming Alive at 79: Marin Senior Day Services

Marin Video Center	18 minutes
251 N. San Pedro Rd.	1980
San Rafael, CA 94903	1/2" and 3/4" VHS and Beta

Depicts a 79-year old woman who has moved out of a nursing home. The film shows her being able to live with her family with the assistance of adult day care.

Daybreak

Lionshead Productions	28 minutes
5341 Prosperity Lane	
San Diego, CA 92115	16 mm film

Depicts a medically oriented adult day care center in San Diego, CA. One of the earliest films about adult day care, *Daybreak* shows only one type of service, but it is a classic.

Rescue from Isolation

Transit Media	22 minutes
P.O. Box 315	1972
Franklin Lakes, NJ 07407	16 mm film

The day care program at Maimonides Hospital and Home for the Aged in Canada is depicted. This center is designed for older persons who are extremely isolated, and it includes a strong psychiatric component.

Women Who Care: Living with Disabled Husbands

Marin Video Center	19 minutes
251 N. San Pedro Rd.	1980
San Rafael, CA 94903	1/2" and 3/4" VHS and Beta

Shows the story of a woman caring for her disabled husband, sometimes at risk to her own health. She is able to continue caregiving with the assistance of a wives support group, adult day care, home care, and overnight respite.

Adult Day Care Organizations

National Institute on Adult Daycare (NIAD)
National Council on the Aging (NCOA)
600 Maryland Avenue, SW
West Wing 100
Washington, DC 20024   (202) 479-1200

A Membership Unit of the National Council on the Aging, NIAD is the only national voice for adult day care. Membership may be obtained only through joining NCOA. Activities include research, development of standards for the field, legislative advocacy, coordination of National Adult Day Care Center Week events in the fall and presentations at the annual NCOA conference in the spring. Publications include *Adult Day Care: Annotated Bibliography, Developing Adult Day Care, Standards for Adult Day Care, Adult Day Care in America, and A Survey of Day Care for the Demented Adult in the United States*. NIAD also publishes a quarterly newsletter for affiliate members.

NIAD Regional Organizations

These are informal groups formed by the Regional Representatives to the National Institute on Adult Daycare. Activities are not limited to members. Activities may include an annual workshop on adult day care and/ or regional newsletters. Contact the NIAD office in Washington, DC for more information.

State Adult Day Care Associations

Many state associations have been formed by the directors of adult day care centers in the state. Activities range from peer support to workshops to publications to advocacy, and many others. These associations are an especially good source for networking with existing adult day care centers in your area. Contact the NIAD office in Washington, DC for more information.

The Foundation Center Network

The Foundation Center was established by foundations to provide a central point for collection and dissemination of information about grantswriting and philanthropic giving. The center sponsors training sessions and maintains a library of publications related to foundations. They also make some publications available for sale. The Foundation Center's four major locations are listed below:

The Foundation Center
79 Fifth Avenue
New York, NY 10003   (212) 620-4230

The Foundation Center
1001 Connecticut Avenue, NW
Washington, DC 20036   (202) 331-1400

The Foundation Center
Kent H. Smith Library
1422 Euclid Avenue
Cleveland, OH 44115   (216) 861-1933

The Foundation Center
312 Sutter Street
San Francisco, CA 94108   (415) 397-0902

Cooperating collections, which form the remainder of the Foundation Center Network, can be found in more than 100 cities across the United States. The cooperating collections maintain a core collection of Foundation Center publications and many other materials helpful in grantswriting. For more information about the cooperating collections near you, call 1-800-424-9836.

APPENDIX D

Governmental Agencies Related to Adult Day Care

Linda Cook Webb

Contents:

Regional Offices of the Administration on Aging
State Units on Aging
State Medicaid Agencies

Regional Offices of the Administration on Aging

The Administration on Aging (AoA) is the federal agency that deals with aging concerns and services. The regional offices of AoA may be able to provide technical assistance or information about adult day care development and/or financing. The regional offices are:

Region I: Connecticut, Maine, Massachusetts, New Hampshire, Rhode Island, and Vermont

Frank Ollivierre, RPD
Administration on Aging OHD/HHS
John F. Kennedy Bldg. Room 2007
Boston, Massachusetts 02203
(617) 565-1158

Region II: New York, New Jersey, Puerto Rico, and Virgin Islands

Judith Rackmill, RPD
Administration on Aging OHD/HHS
Broadway & Worth Street
New York, New York 10278
(212) 264-4592

Region III: Delaware, Maryland, Pennsylvania, Virginia, W. Virginia, and Washington, DC

Paul E. Ertel, Jr., RPD
Administration on Aging OHD/HHS
3535 Market Street
P.O. Box 13716
Philadelphia, Pennsylvania 19101
(215) 596-6900

Region IV: Alabama, Florida, Georgia, Kentucky, Mississippi, N. Carolina, S. Carolina, and Tennessee

Frank Nicholson, RPD
Administration on Aging OHD/HDS
101 Marietta Tower, Suite 901
Atlanta, Georgia 30323
(404) 331-5901

Region V: Illinois, Indiana, Michigan, Minnesota, Ohio, and Wisconsin

Eli Lipschultz, RPD
Administration on Aging OHD/HHS
300 South Walker Drive
Fifteenth Floor
Chicago, Illinois 60606
(312) 353-3141

Region VI: Arkansas, Louisiana, New Mexico, Oklahoma, and Texas

John Diaz, RPD
Administration on Aging OHD/HHS
1200 Main Tower Building
Room 2060
Dallas, Texas 75201
(214) 767-2623

Region VII: Iowa, Kansas, Missouri, and Nebraska

Richard E. Burnett, RPD
Administration on Aging OHD/HDS
601 East 12th, Room 384
Kansas City, Missouri 64106
(816) 374-2955

Region VIII: Colorado, Montana, N. Dakota, S. Dakota, Utah and Wyoming

Clint Hess, RPD
Administration on Aging OHD/HHS
1961 Stout Street
Federal Office Bldg. Room 1185
Denver, Colorado 80294
(303) 844-2951

Region IX: Arizona, California, Hawaii, Nevada, Guam, American Samoa, Commonwealth of N. Mariana Island, Republic of Palau, Federal States of Micronesia, and Republic of Marshal Islands

Jack McCarthy, RPD
Administration on Aging OHD/HHS
50 United Nations Plaza, Room 443
San Francisco, California 94102
(415) 556-6003

Region X: Alaska, Idaho, Oregon, and Washington

Chisato "Chazz" Kawabori, RPD
Administration on Aging OHD/HHS
2901 Third Avenue
Third & Broad Building MS4R
Seattle, Washington 94121
(206) 442-5341

State Units on Aging

Every state government has a department or division to oversee services to older people. Some of the following have standards for ADC in the state and some may have funding available.

Alabama Commission on Aging
136 Catoma Street
Montgomery, Alabama 36130
(205) 261-5743

Older Alaskans Commission
Pouch C. MS 0209
Juneau, Alaska 99811
(902) 465-3250

Arizona Department of Economic
  Security
Aging and Adult Administration
1400 Washington Street
Phoenix, Arizona 85007
(602) 255-4446

Arkansas Department of Human
  Services
Main and 7th Streets
Donaghey Building, Suite 1428
Little Rock, Arkansas 72201
(501) 371-2441

California Department on Aging
1600 K Street
Sacramento, California 95814
(916) 322-5290

Colorado Aging & Adult Services
Department of Social Services
1575 Sherman Street, Room 504
Denver, Colorado 80203
(303) 866-5122

Department on Aging
175 Main Street
Hartford, Connecticut 06106
(203) 566-4810

Delaware Division of Aging
Department of Health & Social Services
1901 North Dupont Highway, 2nd Floor
New Castle, Delaware 19720
(302) 421-6791

Mayor's Executive Office on Aging
1424 K Street, NW, 2nd Floor
Washington, DC 20005
(202) 724-5622

Aging and Adult Services
Department of Health and Rehabilitative Services
Building 2, Room 328
1323 Winewood Boulevard
Tallahassee, Florida 32301
(904) 488-8922

Office of Aging
Department of Human Resources
6th Floor
878 Peachtree Street, NE
Atlanta, Georgia 30309
(404) 894-5333

Hawaii Executive Office on Aging
335 Merchant Street, Room 241
Honolulu, Hawaii 96813
(808) 548-2593

Idaho Office on Aging
State House, Room 114
Boise, Idaho 83720
(208) 334-3833

Illinois Department on Aging
421 East Capitol Avenue
Springfield, Illinois 62706
(217) 785-2870

Indiana Department on Aging and
    Community Services
251 North Illinois - P.O. Box 783
Indianapolis, Indiana 46207-7083
(317) 232-1139

Department of Elder Affairs
Jewett Building
914 Grand, Suite 236
Des Moines, Iowa 50319
(515) 281-5187

Kansas Department on Aging
610 West 10th Street
Topeka, Kansas 66612
(913) 296-4986

Division for Aging Service
Department for Social Services
Cabinet for Human Resources
275 East Main Street
Frankfort, Kentucky 40621
(502) 564-6930

Governor's Office of Elderly Affairs
P.O. Box 8037 A
Baton Rouge, Louisiana 70898-0374
(504) 925-1700

Bureau of Maine Elderly
Department of Human Services
State House, Station 11
Augusta, Maine 04333
(207) 289-2561

Division of Planning & Evaluation
Maryland Office on Aging
301 West Preston Street
Baltimore, Maryland 21201
(301) 225-1270

Massachusetts Executive Office
of Elderly Affairs
38 Chauncy Street
Boston, Massachusetts 02111
(617) 727-7750

Office of Services to the Aging
P.O. Box 30026
Lansing, Michigan 48909
(517) 373-8230

Minnesota Board on Aging
Suite 204–Metro Square Building
7th and Robert Streets
St. Paul, Minnesota 55101
(612) 296-2770

Mississippi Council on Aging
301 West Pearl Street
Jackson, Mississippi 39203-3092
(601) 949-2013

Missouri Division of Aging
Department of Social Services
Broadway State Office Building
505 Missouri Boulevard
P.O. Box 1337
Jefferson City, Missouri 65102
(314) 751-3082

Community Services Division
Department of Social & Rehabilitation
    Services
P.O. Box 4210
Helena, Montana 59601
(406) 444-3865

Nebraska Department on Aging
301 Centennial Mall South
P.O. Box 95044
Lincoln, Nebraska 68509
(402) 471-2307

Nevada Division for Aging Services
Department of Human Resources
505 East King Street, Room 101
Carson City, Nevada 89710
(702) 885-4210

Division of Elder and Adult Services
New Hampshire Department of Human
    Services
105 Loudon Road
Prescott Park Building #3
Concord, New Hampshire 03301
(603) 271-2751

New Jersey Division on Aging
Department of Community Affairs
363 West State Street
P.O. Box 2768
Trenton, New Jersey 08625
(609) 292-4833

New Mexico State Agency on Aging
LaVilla Rivera Building, 4th Floor
Santa Fe, New Mexico 87501
(505) 827-7640

New York State Office for the Aging
Agency Building #2
Empire State Plaza
Albany, New York 12223
(518) 474-4425

Division of Aging
Department of Human Resources
1985 Umstead Drive
Kirby Building
Raleigh, North Carolina 27603
(919) 733-3983-24

Aging Services
North Dakota Department of Human
    Services
State Capitol Building
Bismarck, North Dakota 58505
(701) 224-2577

Ohio Department on Aging
50 West Broad Street
Columbus, Ohio 43215
(614) 466-5500

Oklahoma Services for the Aging
Department of Human Services
P.O. Box 25352
Oklahoma City, Oklahoma 73125
(405) 521-2281

Oregon Senior Services Division
Human Resources Department
313 Public Service Building
Salem, Oregon 97310
(503) 378-4728

Division of Program Development
Barte Building
231 State Street
Harrisburg, Pennsylvania 17101
(717) 783-6007

Department of Elderly Affairs
79 Washington Street
Providence, Rhode Island 02903
(401) 277-2858

South Carolina Commission on Aging
915 Main Street
Columbia, South Carolina 29201
(803) 758-2576

Office of Adult Services & Aging
Richard F. Kneip Building
700 North Illinois Street
Pierre, South Dakota 57501-2291
(605) 773-3656

Tennessee Commission on Aging
715 Tennessee Building
535 Church Street
Nashville, Tennessee 37219
(615) 741-2056

Texas Department on Aging
P.O. Box 12786
Capitol Station
Austin,Texas 75704
(512) 475-2717

Utah Division of Aging and Adult
    Services
150 W. North Temple, Room 326
P.O. Box 45500
Salt Lake City, Utah 84145-0500
(801) 533-6422

Vermont Office on Aging
Waterbury Complex
103 South Main Street
Waterbury, Vermont 05676
(802) 241-2400

Virginia Department for the Aging
James Monroe Building
101 North 14th Street, 18th Floor
Richmond, Virginia 23219
(804) 225-2271

Aging and Adult Services
Department of Social Health Services
Mail Stop OB 44-A
Olympia, Washington 98504
(205) 753-2502

West Virginia Commission on Aging
State Capitol Complex (Holly Grove)
Charleston, West Virginia 25305
(304) 348-2241

Bureau of Aging
Department of Health and Social
    Services, Room 480
1 West Wilson Street–P.O. Box 7851
Madison, Wisconsin 53707
(608) 266-2536

Wyoming Commission on Aging
Hathaway Building, First Floor
Cheyenne, Wyoming 82002
(307) 777-6111

State Medicaid Agencies

The following agencies may provide Medicaid reimbursement for low-income persons attending state-certified ADC centers.

Commissioner of Medicaid
Alabama Medicaid Agency
2500 Fairlane Drive
Montgomery, Alabama 36130
(205) 277-2710

Commissioner
Alaska Department of Health and Social
    Services
P.O. Box H-01
Juneau, Alaska 99811-0601
(907) 465-3030

Director
Arizona Health Care Cost
Containment System (AHCCCS)
801 East Jefferson Street
Phoenix, Arizona 85034
(602) 234-3655

Director
Arkansas Department of Human
    Services
Division of Economic and Medical
    Services
7th and Main Streets
P.O. Box 1437
Little Rock, Arkansas 72203
(501) 371-1001

Director
California State Department of Health
    Services
714 P Street, Room 1253
Sacramento, California 95814
(916) 445-1248

Executive Director
Colorado Department of Social
    Services
P.O. Box 181000
Denver, Colorado 80218-0899
(303) 294-5800

Commissioner
Connecticut Department of Income
    Maintenance
110 Bartholomew Avenue
Hartford, Connecticut 06106
(203) 566-2008

Secretary
Delaware Department of Health and
    Social Services
Administration Building
Delaware State Hospital
P.O. Box 906
New Castle, Delaware 19720
(302) 421-6705

Director
Department of Human Services
801 North Capital Street, Room 700
Washington, DC 20002
(202) 727-0450

Secretary
Florida Department of Health and
    Rehabilitative Services
1317 Winewood Boulevard
Building 2, Room 432
Tallahassee, Florida 32301
(904) 488-7721

Commissioner
Georgia Department of Medical
　Assistance
2 Martin Luther King Drive, SE
1220 West Tower
Atlanta, Georgia 30334
(404) 656-4479

Director
Hawaii Department of Social Services
　and Housing
P.O. Box 339
Honolulu, Hawaii 96809
(808) 548-6260

Director
Idaho Department of Health and
　Welfare
Statehouse
Boise, Idaho 83720
(208) 334-5500

Director
Illinois Department of Public Aid
Jesse B. Harris Building II
2nd Floor
100 S. Grand Avenue East
Springfield, Illinois 62762
(217) 782-6716

Administrator
Indiana Department of Public Welfare
State Office Building
100 North Senate Avenue, Room 701
Indianapolis, Indiana 46204
(317) 232-4705

Commissioner
Iowa Department of Human Services
Hoover State Office Building, 5th Floor
Des Moines, Iowa 50319
(515) 281-5452

Secretary
Kansas Department of Social and
　Rehabilitation Services
State Office Building, 6th Floor
Topeka, Kansas 66612
(913) 296-3271

Commissioner
Kentucky Department for Medicaid
　Services
CHR Building
275 East Main Street
Frankfort, Kentucky 40621
(502) 564-4321

Secretary and State Health Officer
Louisiana Department of Health and
　Human Resources
P.O. Box 3776
Baton Rouge, Louisiana 70821
(504) 342-6711

Commissioner
Maine Department of Human Services
221 State Street
Statehouse, Station 11
Augusta, Maine 04333
(207) 289-2736

Secretary
Maryland Department of Health and
    Mental Hygiene
Herbert R. O'Conner Building
201 West Preston Street
Baltimore, Maryland 21201
(301) 225-6500

Commissioner
Massachusetts Department of Public
    Welfare
180 Tremont Street
Boston, Massachusetts 02111
(617) 574-0200

Commssioner
Massachusetts Commission for the Blind
110 Tremont Street
Boston, Massachusetts 02108
(617) 727-5550

Director
Michigan Department of Social
    Services
P.O. Box 30037
300 South Capitol Avenue
Lansing, Michigan 48909
(517) 373-2000

Commissioner
Minnesota Department of Human
    Services
Centennial Office Building, 4th Floor
658 Cedar Street
St. Paul, Minnesota 55155
(612) 296-2701

Director
Office of the Governor
Division of Medicaid
4785 I-55 North
P.O. Box 16786
Jackson, Mississippi 39236-0786
(601) 981-4507

Acting Director
Missouri Department of Social Services
Broadway State Office Building
P.O. Box 1527
Jefferson City, Missouri 65102
(314) 751-4815

Director
Montana Department of Social
Rehabilitative Services
P.O. Box 4210
Helena, Montana 59604
(406) 444-5622

Director
Nebraska Department of Social
    Services
301 Centennial Mall South, 5th Floor
Lincoln, Nebraska 68509
(402) 471-3121

Director
Nevada Department of Human
    Resources
Kinkead Building–Capitol Complex
505 East King Street
Carson City, Nevada 89710
(702) 885-4730

Commissioner
New Hampshire Department of Health
and Human Services
6 Hazen Drive
Concord, New Hampshire 03301-6521
(603) 271-4331

Commissioner
New Jersey Department of Human
    Services
Capitol Place One
222 South Warren Street
Trenton, New Jersey 08625
(609) 292-3717

Secretary
New Mexico Department of Human
    Services
P.O. Box 2348
Santa Fe, New Mexico 87504-2348
(505) 827-4072

Commissioner
New York State Department of Social
    Services
Ten Eyck Office Building
40 North Pearl Street
Albany, New York 12243
(518) 474-9475

Secretary
North Carolina Department of Human
    Resources
325 North Salisbury Street
Raleigh, North Carolina 27611
(919) 733-4534

Executive Director
North Dakota Department of Human
    Services
State Capitol Building
Bismarck, North Dakota 58505
(701) 224-2310

Director
Ohio Department of Human Services
30 East Broad Street, 32nd Floor
Columbus, Ohio 43266-0423
(614) 466-6282

Director
Oklahoma Department of Human
    Services
P.O. Box 25352
Oklahoma City, Oklahoma 73125
(405) 521-3646

Director
Oregon Department of Human
    Resources
318 Public Service Building
Salem, Oregon 97310
(503) 378-3034

Secretary
Pennsylvania State Department of
    Public Welfare
Health and Welfare Building, Room 333
Harrisburg, Pennsylvania 17120
(717) 787-2600

Director
Rhode Island Department of Human
    Services
Aime J. Forand Building
600 New London Avenue
Cranston, Rhode Island 02920
(401) 464-2121

Executive Director
South Carolina State Health and
Human Services Finance Commission
P.O. Box 8206
Columbia, South Carolina 29202-8206
(803) 253-6100

Secretary
South Dakota Department of Social
    Services
Richard F. Kneip Building
700 North Illinois Street
Pierre, South Dakota 57501
(605) 773-3165

Commissioner
Tennessee Department of Health and
    Environment
344 Cordell Hull Building
Nashville, Tennessee 37219
(615) 741-3111

Commissioner
Texas Department of Human Services
P.O. Box 2960
Austin, Texas 78769
(512) 450-3030

Executive Director
Utah Department of Health
P.O. Box 45500
Salt Lake City, Utah 84145-0500
(801) 538-6111

Secretary
Vermont Agency of Human Services
103 South Main Street
Waterbury, Vermont 05676
(802) 241-2220

Director
Virginia Department of Medical
    Assistance Services
600 East Broad Street, Suite 1300
Richmond, Virginia 23219
(804) 786-7933

Director
Division of Medical Assistance
Washington Department of Social and
    Health Services
Mail Stop HB-41
Olympia, Washington 98504
(206) 753-1777

Interim Administrator, Medical
    Services
West Virginia Department of Human
    Services
1900 Washington Street East
Charleston, West Virginia 25305
(304) 348-8990

Secretary
Wisconsin Department of Health and
    Social Services
1 West Wilson Street, Room 650
P.O. Box 7850
Madison, Wisconsin 53702
(608) 266-3681

Director
Wyoming Department of Health and
    Social Services
Hathaway Building
Cheyenne, Wyoming 82002
(307) 777-7121

Sample Table of Contents for a Policies and Procedures Manual

Linda Cook Webb

**Policies and Procedures Manual
Sample Table of Contents**

B. Budget plan
1. Outlines who prepares the budget, and how frequently
2. Outlines processes necessary for final approval
3. Outlines responsibility for bookkeeping and accounting functions
C. Program plan
1. List of services provided
2. Hours and days of operation
D. Job descriptions
1. Staff

III. Client Care Policies and Procedures
A. Services
1. Policies
2. Procedures
B. Admission, continuing care, and discharge
1. Policies
2. Procedures
C. Coordination of care with other community agencies
1. Policies
2. Procedures
D. Client records
1. Policies
2. Procedures
E. Medical emergencies
1. Policies
2. Procedures
F. Storage, handling, and administration of medications
1. Policies
2. Procedures

IV. Physical Environment
  A. Safety and comfort of participants
    1. Policies
    2. Procedures (include preventative maintenance checklist for equipment here)
  B. Sanitation and building maintenance
    1. Policies
    2. Procedures
V. Disaster Plan
  A. Fire safety plan
    1. Policies
    2. Procedures (include documentation of fire drills here; also include annual inspection records from fire marshall)
  B. Other disasters
    1. Policies for flood, tornado, etc.
    2. Procedures (include documentation of tornado drills here)
VI. Quality Control
  A. Utilization review policies and procedures (only applicable for centers providing therapies)
  B. Client records audit policies and procedures
  C. Program evaluation policies and procedures
  D. Other
VII. Administrative Records
  Policies and procedures regarding who will maintain the following records and where they will be kept:
  A. Personnel and payroll records
  B. Correspondence
  C. Equipment inventory
  D. Fiscal books
  E. Minutes of board of directors/advisory committee meetings
  F. Other

VIII. Appendices
    A. Forms used in the program, including complete participant chart
    B. Schedule of all services provided, including a sample month's activities plan
    C. Staff schedules
    D. Personnel Policies
        1. Conditions of employment
        2. Procedures for employment
        3. Employee benefits
        4. Employee regulations (i.e., working hours, absenteeism, etc.)
        5. Grievance procedures
        6. Termination procedures
        7. Equal opportunity policies

Sample Organizational Chart and Job Descriptions

Linda Cook Webb

Contents:

Adult Day Health Care Center Organizational Chart

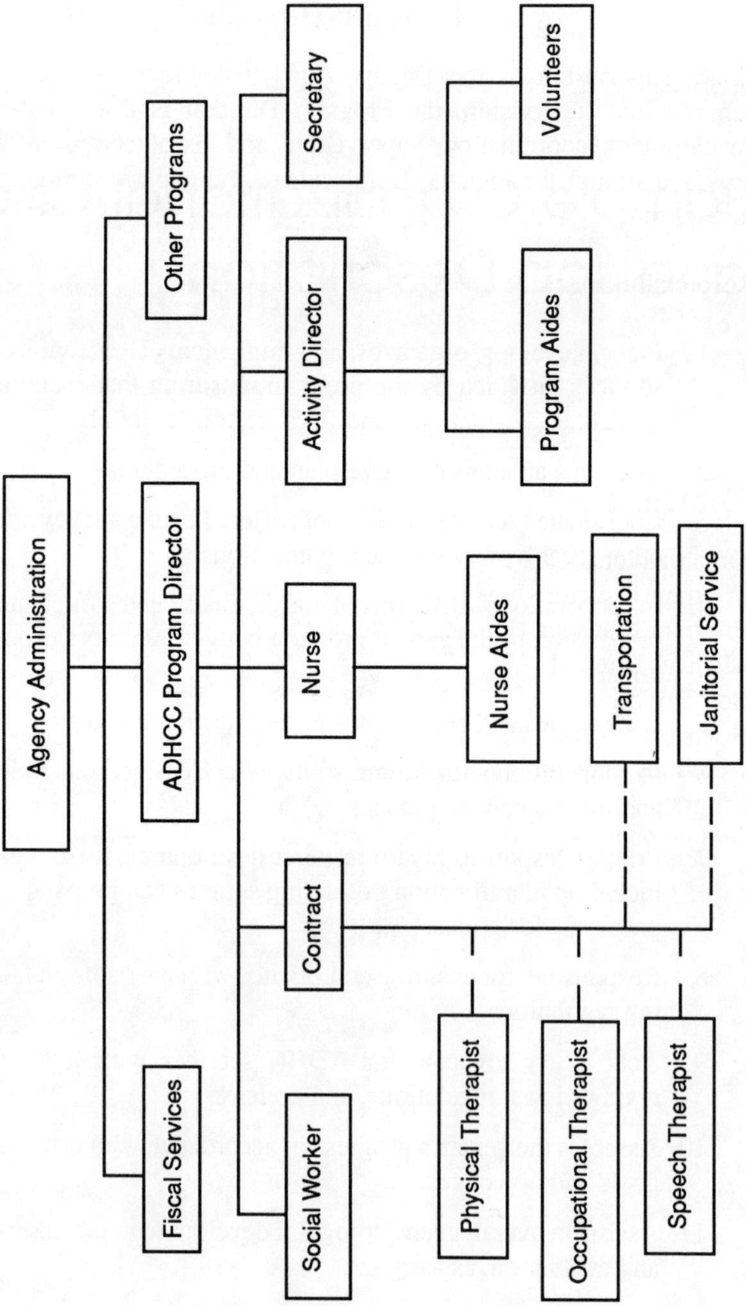

Program Director

Under supervision of the Deputy Agency Administrator and through subordinated supervision, the Program Director is responsible for the development, coordination, supervision, and fiscal control of services provided through the adult day health care program; performs related duties as required.

Responsibilities:

1. Plans, develops, organizes, and implements all activities and services provided by the program, ensuring that established guidelines, regulations, and fiscal restraints are observed.

2. Develops an administrative plan and procedures.

3. Coordinates services with others offered by the agency and by other local human service organizations.

4. In cooperation with Grants Manager, directs and participates in preparation of the annual program budget; monitors expenditures.

5. Coordinates and participates in fundraising activities.

6. In cooperation with Administrative Services, recruits, selects, and orients new employees.

7. Primary responsibility for resource development for the center, including identification of funding sources and preparation of proposals for grants.

8. Responsible for ensuring compliance with licensing and funding regulations.

9. Acts as an advocate for ADHC services with legislators; reviews laws, regulations, and policies.

10. Assesses the center's progress in accordance with established goals and objectives.

11. Assists in overall agency program development, management, and evaluation, as assigned.

12. Drives a motor vehicle incidental to the performance of work.

Minimum Qualifications

1. Knowledge in directing long-range planning, daily operations, and budget of the adult day health program.

2. Ability to read, interpret, and implement complex regulations.

3. Skill dealing with people from different backgrounds/ lifestyles.

4. Possession of a valid California driver's license.

5. Master's degree and one year supervisory experience or bachelor's degree and three years supervisory experience in a social or health service program or agency.

(Adapted from job descriptions at Elderday Adult Health Care, Santa Cruz, California. Used with permission.)

Program Manager

Under the direction of the Program Director, the Program Manager organizes, implements, and coordinates the daily operation of the adult day health care program in accordance with participants' needs and state requirements. Performs related duties as required.

Responsibilities:

1. Assists in planning and development to ensure that basic services are provided in accordance with the needs of participants, and that services meet licensing/reimbursement requirements.

2. Oversees, reviews, and monitors participants' treatment plans.

3. Evaluates participants' changing needs and makes necessary program adjustments; ensures that program does not accept or retain participants for whom proper care cannot be provided.

4. Directs and evaluates the work of all staff, volunteers, and contractors.

5. Directs proper and timely completion of forms required by MediCal.

6. Plans and implements in-service training for staff and volunteers.

7. Establishes, maintains, and monitors internal management systems to facilitate scheduling and coordination of services, and for the collection of pertinent participant data.

8. Assists in developing and maintaining fiscal control systems.

9. Prepares and submits statistical reports required by funding and regulatory agencies.

10. Prepares and conducts information, outreach, education, and advocacy programs related to services offered.

11. Conducts weekly meetings of multi-disciplinary team.

12. As needed, participates in daily program activities.

13. Drives a motor vehicle incidental to the performance of work.

Minimum Qualifications

1. Skill in organizing, directing, and implementing day-to-day operations of a complex human services program.

2. Skill in planning, organizing, and reviewing the work of line staff, professionals, volunteers, and contractors.

3. Knowledge of budget monitoring, recording, and fiscal reporting.

4. Must possess a valid California driver's license.

5. Must possess a professional degree, as outlined by state regulations and have two years' management experience in a similar program.

(Adapted from job descriptions at Elderday Adult Health Care, Santa Cruz, California. Used with permission.)

Medical Director

Duties:

1. Provides medical direction to the program, in the form of consultation regarding program development, nursing protocols, physician relations, etc.

2. Accepts referrals to provide medical services and consultation as requested by the referring physician, or when the participant does not have a personal physician.

3. Assists in establishing the program's participant care policies and procedures.

4. Participates in plan of treatment reviews, case review conferences, discharge planning and utilization review.

5. Provides physician back-up when participant's own physician cannot be reached (i.e., in crisis situations; actual emergency care will be provided through_____ Ambulance Service and the_____ Hospital Emergency Room).

Qualifications:

1. Licensed to practice in this state.

2. Specialization (with applicable professional training) in one of the following areas:

   • Physiatry or physical rehabilitation

   • Psychiatry

   • Geriatrics

3. Knowledge of the aging process required. Geriatrics experience preferred.

Responsible to: Program Director

Hours: Part-time, consult basis only.

(Copyright 1987, D. L. Webb & Associates, Kansas City, MO. Used with permission.)

Social Worker

Under the direction of the Program Manager, the Social Worker is responsible for direct social casework services to participants. Performs related duties as required.

Responsibilities:

1. Screens potential program participants, meeting with family members and referring agency representatives, and completing required forms for assessment purposes.

2. Maintains current case management records, including periodic reassessments of participants.

3. Provides individual, group, and family counseling, as requested.

4. Refers participants and families to appropriate community agencies.

5. Coordinates transportation for participants.

6. Follows up on participant absenteeism.

7. Communicates effectively and respectfully with people of different racial, ethnic, and cultural groups and from different backgrounds and lifestyles.

8. Complies with all administrative requirements, including recording procedures, staff meetings, etc.

Minimum Qualifications

1. Knowledge of social service principles and practices, including case management and counseling techniques.

2. Knowledge of community services available to seniors and families.

3. Skill in assessing and effectively meeting needs of seniors and their families; skill in preparing writtten records.

4. Graduation from an accredited college with a MSW degree.

5. Bi-lingual (English-Spanish) preferred, but not required.

(Adapted from job descriptions at Elderday Adult Health Care, Santa Cruz, California. Used with permission.)

Registered Nurse

Duties:

1. Staff supervision of nursing personnel, including employees, students, and volunteers. Supervision shall include hiring, managing, training, evaluation, and termination.

2. Consults, as needed, in initial evaluation, admission, and discharge decisions. Maintains communication with physicians regarding changes in participant status.

3. Performs or supervises all participants' nursing assessments.

4. Carries out nursing procedures, as ordered by the participant's physician, and as outlined in the *Policies and Procedures Manual.*

5. Schedules routine observations of vital signs, weight, foot condition, hearing, and vision, and follows up on any problems.

6. Responds to emergencies in patient care identified by other staff.

7. Develops, implements, and evaluates health promotion activities on both a group and individual level.

8. Acts as Primary Care Person for selected participants with more severe medical or nursing needs; coordinates their care; communicates with their families regarding progress, problems, and need for home follow-up; prepares and maintains necessary documentation, and reviews the case for team meeting discussion.

9. Reviews all charts for indication of nursing needs.

10. Coordinates the Infection Control Committee.

11. Represents the agency in the community in selected activities which are related to job function.

12. Develops nursing procedures and protocols, with the approval of the Medical Director.

13.   Serves on the Utilization Control Committee.

14.   Assists with personal care, meal service, and other services as needed, when other staff are unavailable.

Qualifications:

1.   BSN, with licensure in this state.

2.   Three to five years nursing experience, preferably in a position which involved supervision of LPNs or nurse aides.

3.   Demonstrated competence in working with the impaired elderly, and knowledgeable of their physical, social, and mental health needs.

Responsible to: Program Director

(Copyright 1987, D. L. Webb & Associates, Kansas City, MO. Used with permission.)

Activities Director

Under supervision of the Program Manager and in close cooperation with the multi-disciplinary team, the Activities Director plans, organizes, supervises, and coordinates a broad program of activities. Performs related duties as required.

Responsibilities:

1. Plans a comprehensive program of therapeutic activities, tailored to the needs and limitations of frail elderly and mentally and physically disabled persons.

2. Interfaces with other professional staff to evaluate each participant, develop an individual care plan, and meet weekly for regular participant assessments.

3. Implements planned activities by contacting agencies or individuals to provide programs or classes of interest; organizes group projects, discussions, games, graded crafts, etc.; conducts limited exercise or other physical activities; obtains music, slides, movies, tapes, books, games, and equipment as necessary; personally leads small therapeutic groups and activities; and interacts with participants on an individual basis.

4. Supervises ordering of meals after consulting with nursing staff and dietitian.

5. Organizes, trains, and supervises the work of a variety of volunteers, paid activities staff, student interns, etc.

6. Supervises the development of daily/monthly activities calendars.

7. Notes physical or emotional health changes in participants; maintains records of each participant's activities; and records quarterly progress notes on each participant.

8. Assists participants with activities of daily living (ADLs).

Minimum Qualifications: Must meet *only one* of items 1-3 *and* item 4

1. Be an occupational, art, music, dance, or recreation therapist, occupational therapy assistant, or qualified social worker.

2. Two years experience in social/recreational programs, with one being full-time in a health care or handicapped program setting.

3. Completion of 36 hours of training in a course designed specifically for this position and approved by the California Department of Health.

4. Demonstrated experience in dealing with and relating to frail elderly and/or mentally and physically handicapped persons on an on-going basis.

(Adapted from job descriptions at Elderday Adult Health Care, Santa Cruz, California. Used with permission.)

Program Aide

Under general supervision of the activities staff, the Program Aide provides assistance in a broad program of activities provided at the center for the frail elderly. Performs related duties as required.

Responsibilities:

1. Assists in providing a comprehensive program of activities, tailored to meet the needs of frail elderly persons, to promote optimum health, independence, and self-care.

2. Assists in developing specific activities for the program.

3. Sets up and operates equipment; leads games, singing, and discussions; conducts exercise activities; and interacts with participants on an individual basis.

4. Works with volunteers assigned to assist with specific projects.

5. Assists in serving and cleaning up after meals. Assists in keeping the center in a clean and orderly condition.

6. Notes changes in participants' physical or emotional health and communicates this information to the appropriate staff person.

7. Assists participants with activities of daily living (ADLs).

8. Maintains standard records of work performed. May make brief oral or written reports, as requested.

Minimum Qualifications

1. Knowledge of principles and techniques involved in dealing with the physical, mental, and emotional health of the frail elderly.

2. Skill in assisting activities staff to implement activities.

3. Skill in assisting and coordinating the work of volunteers.

4. Skill in personally leading activity groups and in using equipment, such as movie and slide projectors and record players.

5. Skill in developing positive rapport with participants.

6. Demonstrated experience in dealing with frail elderly persons.

7. Bi-lingual (English-Spanish) preferred, but not required.

(Adapted from job descriptions at Elderday Adult Health Care, Santa Cruz, California. Used with permission.)

Van Driver

Duties:

1. Transport participants to and from the center daily. Drive for special events as requested. Obtain routing information from the secretary, and report any routine problems back to the secretary.

2. Assist riders in/out of the van. Always make sure that participants get inside the house when you take them home.

3. Maintain security for passengers at all times, by using the wheelchair locks, safety belts, and other measures defined in the program's *Policies and Procedures Manual.*

4. Maintain security for the van at all times, following measures defined in the program's *Policies and Procedures Manual.*

5. Maintain the mechanical operating condition of the van. Check tires, tire pressure, oil, water, and windshield fluid, and replace as necessary. Check gas before starting on a run. Report in writing any suspected mechanical problems.

Qualifications:

1. Valid driver's license, with no tickets in the past three years. Chauffeur's license preferred.

2. Experience driving a van or other large vehicle.

3. Ability to work independently. Responsible and dependable.

4. Willingness to be patient and flexible with people and work schedules.

5. Experience with aged or handicapped persons preferred.

6. Must be trained in CPR and First Aid before driving alone.

Responsible to: Program Director

Hours: Split shift (morning and afternoon runs)

(Copyright 1987, D. L. Webb & Associates, Kansas City, MO. Used with permission.)

APPENDIX G

Sample Forms

Contents:

Program Name Face Sheet

Case #_____

CLIENT

Name_____
Address_____
_____

Phone_____
S.S.N._____
Diagnosis_____
Allergies_____
Marital Status S M W D   Sex M F

Race or   Native
Ethnicity_____ Language_____

Type of   # in
Dwelling_____ Household_____

Major_____
Occupation_____
Religion_____
Financing_____

PRIMARY PHYSICIAN

Name_____
Address_____
_____

Phone_____
Office Contact Person_____
Specialty_____

OTHER PHYSICIAN

Name_____
Address_____
_____

Phone_____
Office Contact Person_____
Specialty_____

RESPONSIBLE PERSON

Name_____
Address_____
_____

Phone   (H)_____
        (O)_____
Rel. to Client_____

OTHER EMERGENCY CONTACT

Name_____
Address_____
_____

Phone   (H)_____
        (O)_____
Rel. to Client_____

REFERRAL SOURCE

Name_____
Address_____
_____

Agency_____
Department_____
Phone_____

Source: D. L. Webb & Associates, 1987, Kansas City, MO.

Telephone Referral Form

Referral Date: _____ Visitation Date: _____ Intake Appt:_____

Name:_____ Address: _____

Zip: _____Phone:_____Date of Birth: _____

Emergency Contact: Name:_____ Relationship: _____

Address: _____Phone: _____

NDSS Worker: _____ Phone: _____

Ambulation/Appliances: _____

Transportation: _____

Medicare: _____A B   Medicaid: _____ SSN: _____

Insurance Information: _____ Religion: _____

Payment Method:_____ Annual Income: _____

Referral Source: _____ Phone: _____

Reason for Referral: _____

Information Given at Time of Referral:

Telephone Referral Form, continued.

Administrative Use Only:

Information Mailed   ___ Letter Mailed to Referral Source

(Date: _____)   (Date: _____)

Visitation Date Set   ___ Follow-Up Letter to Participant/Family

(Date: _____)   (Date: _____)

Follow-up Telephone Contact
Requested (Date: _____)

Date	Activity

Source: McAuley Bergan Center, Omaha, Nebraska. Used with permission.

Day Services Participant Data Base

Primary Care Person:_____ Participant Number: _____

Name: _____ Referral Date:_____ 1st Day of Attendance:_____

Address: _____ Zip: _____ Phone:_____

Referral Source: _____ Relationship: _____ Phone:_____

Reason for Referral:_____

D.O.B. : _____ Race:____ Sex: ___ Religion:_____ Marital Status: ____

SS#: _____ Medicare #: _____ A B Medicaid: _____

Private Insurance Information: _____

Payment Method: _____ Contact Person:_____ Phone:_____

Billing Info: _____ Billing Address: _____Zip: _____

Able to Release Info:___ Yes___No Guardian/Conservator: _____

Address: _____ Zip: _____ Phone: _____

Community Transportation Method: _____

NDSS Case Manager: _____ Phone: _____

IMT: _____ Phone: _____

Contacts: **Relationship**

Name:_____ Phone: _____

Name:_____ Phone: _____

Name:_____ Phone: _____

Name:_____ Phone: _____

Orientation:_____

Ambulation: _____

A.D.L.'s: _____

Medications to
Be given at the Center: _____

Special Diet/Allergies: _____

Significant Medical Conditions: _____

Transportation: _____ Special Instructions: _____

Weekly Schedule, Days & Approximate Hours: _____

Discharge Date: _____ Reason: _____

Attendance Period: _____ Follow-up Date: _____

Action: _____

Source: McAuley Bergan Center, Omaha, Nebraska. Used with permission.

Primary Care Assessment

A) **Attendance - Report Problems to Director**
   1) Regular attendance:_____
   2) Attends regularly but complains of being here_____
   3) Absent occasionally without cause: _____
   4) Rarely attends:_____
   5) Refuses/never attends (reasons given for non-attendance):_____

   _____

   Comments: _____

B) **Appearance**
   1) Appropriate dress and hygiene:_____
   2) Wrinkled/soiled clothing: _____
   3) Poor hygiene:_____
   Comments: _____

C) **Participation**
   1) Acts on own initiative: _____
   2) Participates after activities started: _____
   3) Participates after encouragement: _____
   4) Starts and stops; have to encourage often: _____
   5) No interest and/or refuses structural activity:_____
   Comments: _____

D) **Ambulation**
   1) Adequate: _____
   2) Unsteady—in need of supervision: _____
   3) Unsteady—in need of assistance: _____
   Comments: _____

E) **Ability to Form Individual Relationships**
   1) Relates with peers readily (note with whom person seems to be
       especially involved):
   2) Interacts with encouragement and facilitation:_____
   3) Interacting is superficial: _____
   4) Keeps to self: _____
   5) Reject/hostile to others: _____
   Comments: _____

   (note any communication problems)

Primary Care Assessment, continued.

F) **Attention Span**
   1) Able to follow:_____
   2) Frequently becomes distracted:_____
   3) Rarely follows an activity: _____
   4) Does not attend activities: _____
   Comments: _____

G) **Affect**
   1) Cheerful and appropriate: _____
   2) Manic: _____
   3) Lethargic (flat/bland): _____
   4) Sad: _____
   5) Depressed (severe): _____
   Comments: _____

H) **Eating**
   1) Independent and appropriate: _____
   2) Independent but problematic (describe—e.g., does not eat well, poor
      table manners, takes others' food): _____
      _____
   3) Needs assistance (describe):_____
   Comments: _____

I) **Toileting**
   1) Independent: _____
   2) Needs supervision: _____
   3) Needs physical assistance (describe):_____
   4) Incontinent: _____
   Comments: _____

J) What types of interaction work/don't work with person (e.g., humor, firm
   approach, mentioning family, touch): _____
   _____

K) Any comments re: family involvement (positive or negative): _____
   _____

L) Activities involved in at the Center (also note any other interests):_____
   _____

M) Other comments/problems/ideas for helping participant in the program: _____
   _____
   _____

Source: McAuley Bergan Center, Omaha, Nebraska. Used with permission.

Request for Medical Information

(Use your organization's letterhead)
Date:_____

To:_____
_____
_____
_____

Regarding your patient:

Your patient, named above, has applied for admission to the

Adult Day Care Center. As part of the admission process, we require physician's orders and a summary of medical history and physical status.

The Adult Day Care Center provides day-time care and supervision in a group setting for handicapped adults and frail elders. Physical Therapy, Occupational Therapy, Speech Therapy, and Skilled Nursing are available as needed, as well as our regular services of therapeutic activities, assistance with ADL's, noon meal, and transportation.

For further information, we have enclosed a brochure about the Center. If you have additional questions, please call me at _____.

Please complete and/or sign the enclosed "Physician's Orders" and "History and Physical", and return in the self-addressed stamped envelope provided.

Thank you for your assistance.

Sincerely,

(May be signed by Medical Director or Program Director)

Enclosures:
Brochure
Orders
H & P
Envelope
Release of Information form

Source: D. L. Webb & Associates. 1987. Kansas City, MO.

Physician's Orders

Participant Name _____   Referral From _____

Address _____   Address _____

_____   _____

Phone _____   Phone _____

D.O.B._____ S W M D Sex __   Referring Physician _____

Contact Person _____   Phone _____

Address _____   Other Physician _____

_____   Phone _____

Phone _____

Rel. To Participant _____

Services Needed	Estimated Duration	Frequency
SN		
PT		
OT		
ST		
SW		

Participant's

Hospital _____

Date Adm._____ Date D/Cd ___

Diagnoses

   Primary _____

   Secondary _____

   Functional limitations _____

   Rehabilitation potential _____

   Mental status _____   Prognosis _____

   Has diagnosis and prognosis been told to participant? __ To family? _____

   Allergies _____

Plan for treatment _____

_____

Medications

   Please indicate which of the following may be given with supervision and following label instructions: ___Tylenol ___Aspirin ___M.O.M. ___Mylanta Dosage, method, and frequency of all prescription medications: _____

_____

Dietary restrictions _____

I certify/recertify the above named patient for Adult Day Health Care.

Physician's Signature _____ Date_____

Source: D. L. Webb & Associates. 1987. Kansas City, MO.

History and Physical

Patient _____ D.O.B. _____ M F

Address _____

_____

Chief Complaint _____

Present Illness _____

Medications (Name, Dosage, Frequency, and Route)

_____

_____

_____

_____

Past History _____

_____

Operations _____

_____

Family History_____

_____

Social History _____

_____

Height_____ Weight _____ Usual Weight _____ Duration of Loss or Gain _____

Temp _____ Pulse _____ B.P._____ Resp. _____

(Please Complete Review of Systems on Reverse)

Date _____ Physician's Signature _____

Source: D. L. Webb & Associates. 1987. Kansas City, MO.

History and Physical, continued.

Review of Systems

Vision

Hearing

Speech

Respiratory

Circulatory

Gastrointestinal

Urinary

Neurological

Musculoskeletal

Reproductive

Skin

Endocrine

Other

Allergies

Emotional or Environmental Factors

Source: D. L. Webb & Associates. 1987. Kansas City, MO.

Problem Summary and Treatment Plan

Name_____   Case # _____

Diagnoses_____

#	Approximate Date of Onset	Situation	Date Recorded	Monthly Progress Code						Date Resolved
				1	2	3	4	5	6	

Mo. #	Date	Signature	Discipline

Monthly Progress Codes

1—Progressing toward goal

2—Stable, or maintaining prior level of function

3—Worsening

Source: D. L. Webb & Associates. 1987. Kansas City, MO.

Service Provision and Client Participation

Name _____

Month and Year _____

Services	1	2	3	4	5	6	7	8	9	10	11	12	13	14	15	16	17	18	19	20	21	22	23	24	25	26	27	28	29	30	31
Total Hours Scheduled																															
Total Hours Attended																															
Nursing																															
Physical Therapy																															
Occupational Therapy																															
Speech Therapy																															
Social Work Services																															
Personal Care																															
Group Activities																															
Individual Activities																															
Noon Meal																															
Transportation																															

Date _____ Signatures _____

Source: D. L. Webb & Associates, 1987. Kansas City, MO.

Participant Agreement of Participation

It is my understanding that enrollment as a participant in the McAuley Bergan Day Services program includes the following activities, responsibilities or policies.

1. Selection of regular day(s) of attendance. Planned absenses are to be called in by 12 noon the preceding day. Arrangements for changes in attendance pattern will be made through the Day Services Manager. Failure to notify the Center will result in a charge for the meal.

2. Completion of a multi-disciplinary assessment to develop an individual plan of care is required. This will generally be carried out within the first 6 weeks in the program. Information may be obtained from the participant, family, referral source, health providers, social services providers or others directly involved in the care/support of the participant.

   McAuley Bergan Center is required to obtain participant consent to request written information from other agencies.

   The assessment includes the following areas:

   —physical examination

   —functional evaluation

   —psycho-social evaluation and history

   —health history

   —health seeking practices

   —health screening (cardiovascular, diabetes, osteoporosis, nutrition, musculoskeletal, vision, hearing, dental, podiatry, and communication skills)

   —mental status

   (There is no additional cost for these initial assessments).

   The entire assessment takes a total of approximately 2-4 hours, and may be completed over several days—usually on regular days of attendance.

3. Verbal or written feedback will be given to the participant, family or other involved caretakers following the development of the individual plan of care.

4. Additional rehabilitative evaluations (occupational therapy, physical therapy and speech/audiology therapy) are available through Bergan Mercy by a contractual arrangement when deemed necessary by the assessment team members, with the approval of the participant and/or family and physician orders. The costs of these rehabilitative evaluations are in addition to day care costs and may be billed to third party payers (Medicare, Medicaid, private insurance) or directly to the participant. Financial arrangements will be discussed before completing these evaluations.

   —Information from these evaluations will be used to develop an individual exercise or activity program, or may be the basis for formal rehabilitative services.

Participant Agreement of Participation, continued.

5. The plan of care will be reviewed at 6 month intervals or at the time of any significant change in functional status or support services.

6. Voluntary participation in activities listed on the calendar as well as 1:1 staff or other client interaction is encouraged and/or facilitated by staff or volunteer workers.

7. Client safety is of paramount concern to this agency. We also recognize the importance of freedom to move about the building without undue restrictions. An alarm security system and constant staff supervision are measures to prevent wandering by participants who are disoriented or confused. If the participant's safety cannot be assured by these measures, the family will be contacted to discuss the problems and encouraged to provide personal identification - i.e., Medic-Alert bracelet.

8. Participants are encouraged to participate in a daily group exercise program. Input from the physician is sought to determine recommended activity limitations.

9. For private pay participants, charges for day care are based on the anticipated staff time to implement the plan of care requied for each participant. A classification will be assigned at the time of the initial assessment, and re-evaluated at each 6-month period, or at the time of a major change in needs.

10. If the participant's needs with regard to safety and basic human needs cannot be met with day care and additional in-home and other community services, the Center staff will work with the participant and/or family or caretaker in developing an alternative plan for care.

11. Participants are advised not to bring valuable or unnecessary articles to the Center. If a personal item is lost, staff will make every effort to find and return it to the owner. However, we cannot assume responsibility for lost belongings. Identification should be placed on articles that are brought to the Center - including eyeglasses.

   My signature below indicates I understand and agree to comply with the above activities, policies, or responsibilities as a participant at the McAuley Bergan Center. I further understand that I am free to withdraw at any time.

Participant	Date	Witness	Date

Family or Guardian	Date

Source: McAuley Bergan Center, Omaha, Nebraska. Used with permission.

Index